Son Of A Bandit

Jesse James & The Leeds Gang

ISSUED BY: RALPH A. MONACO II

Son of A Bandit
Jesse James & The Leeds Gang
All Rights Reserved.
Copyright © 2012 Ralph A. Monaco II
v3.0

Monaco Publishing, LLC

ISBN: 978-0-578-10426-3

To my mom

Who Always Encouraged Us To Read

To my friends
Don + Robin —
It's hard to believe
It's Been more than just
A couple of years since RHS

Best Wishes
Your friend

7/5/12

TABLE OF CONTENTS

	Introduction	1
Preface	A Boy Without An Identity	3
Chapter I	Identities unveiled	11
Chapter II	The Father's Funeral & A Family Auction	26
Chapter III	Growing-Up In An Adopted City	38
Chapter IV	K.C. At The Twilight of the 19Th Century	42
Chapter V	The Entrepenurer Knows the Good & Bad	57
Chapter VI	The Leeds Gang At Work	65
Chapter VII	The Investigation Begins	72
Chapter VIII	Chip Off The Ole' Block?	82
Chapter IX	Sweating Out Suspects	87
Chapter X	Charged & Arraigned	91
Chapter XI	An Indictment Or Not	102
Chapter XII	Will The Trial Begin?	109
Chapter XIII	Election Day Results	118
Chapter XIV	Reed Takes Charge	123
Chapter XV	The Trial Commences	132
Chapter XVI	Naming the Jurors	139
Chapter XVII	Let The Evidence Begin	145
Chapter XVIII	More From The State	156

Chapter XIX	Why Take Saturday Off?	165
Chapter XX	The Defense	173
Chapter XXI	The Closings & Verdict	190
Chapter XXII	Hearing From The Press	201
Epilogue	What Happened Next?	205
	Bibliography	230
	Index	240
	Illustrations	261
	Acknowledgements	263
	Cast of Characters	266
	About the Author	267

INTRODUCTION

Author David Traxel has described 1898 as a year without rival in United States history for its extravagant adventure and far-reaching significance (even for the son of a bandit). Education in America had become more widespread producing a literate and affluent public never seen before in the country's past. Advances in communication and technology enabled local, national, and international stories to reach audiences almost instantaneously. It was a period in which journalism was the principal and sometimes only source for news, sports, entertainment, editorials and advertisement. The print media monopolized information during a time period in which radios and motion pictures (forget even imagining the internet or iPads) had not become part of the nation's fabric. There were some 14,000 weeklies and 1,900 dailies with an estimated 25 per cent of adults in the U.S. subscribing to at least one paper per week. New York City with a population in excess of three million residents boasted fifteen daily papers (eight morning and seven evening).[1] In rural America, publishing papers developed into "one of the biggest industries of every little town."[2] It was a period of "yellow journalism" where New York publishers, Joseph Pulitzer (*New York World*) and William Randolph Hearst (*New York Journal*) were the most pronounced and vocal. Writers were not passively reporting stories, but they assumed active roles in generating (or fabricating)

---

1   Giessel, Jess, *Black, White and Yellow*, The Spanish American War Centennial, http://www.spanam-war.com/press/htm.

2   Traxel, David, <u>1898 The Birth of the American Century</u>, Alfred A. Knopf, New York, 1998, at p. 23.

them. They were often partisan, very partisan at times. Papers served as the Fox, CNN, C-Span, CNBC, MSNBC and other similar networks for the contemporary reader. Accounts of mayhem, sex, murder, public corruption, scandal, robberies and rogues were anxiously followed and devoured by an admiring public who were glued to every word and page as if reading a novel. Everyone was affixed to the ongoing saga of criminals, especially the exploits of the James-Younger gang and their progenies. Headlines were sensational, sultry, scandolous and sentilating (and yes, suspect)—the more so the better in attracting subscriptions and readers.

This is a work of non-fiction principally drawn from extant news accounts as told by reporters, publishers and editors to their captivated audience dating from the height of the Victorian Age to the dawn of the 20th Century. Each "dateline" presented in the chapters below includes "headlines" from newspapers across the continental United States (and even Hawaii) of related and unrelated stories. I have chosen this format in an attempt to provide today's reader with an opportunity to more fully and historically experience not only the subject of the book but also to better appreciate what Americans would have been anxiously pouring over while turning through the printed news of the day.

PREFACE
A BOY WITHOUT AN IDENTITY

In the eastern part of the city stood a one-story, white painted framed cottage with green shutters. The house held a commanding view of the river, rail-lines and city nestled below in the valley. Blood spattered the wall. A bearded-man was lying in the supine position on the living room floor. A bullet had apparently penetrated the back of his head, as blood coursed the victim's face. The assassins looking down at their prey stood stationary until they heard screams and quickly darted out the front door.

The reverberation from the fatal gunshot rattled throughout the home. Its report instantly caused a young woman to dash from the summer kitchen, located in an adjacent outbuilding, to the room of her fallen spouse. Upon entering, she clutched the side of her thirty-four year old husband, crying bitterly and making attempts to wipe the blood from his face. Her efforts were futile and though he seemed to be uttering words, he could not and would not—not ever!

Staring through the doorway, the horrified wife spotted two men scaling the fence. Gasping in shock, she howled at one of the men, "Robert you have done this, come back." Robert did not comply but ejaculated, "I swear to God I didn't shoot him!"[3] A boy about six, and his younger sister, nearly three, having heard the same echoing noise also bolted through the threshold. The lad observing his weeping mother and mortally wounded father instantly felt revenge in his heart

---

3   Good Bye, Jesse James, Six Major News Stories Concerning the Life, Death, and Funeral of America's Greatest Outlaw, First printed in 1882, The Jesse James Bank Museum, Liberty, Missouri 1967.

and soul. With intense anger and extreme effort, he lugged from the closet a "shotgun to aim at the people outside." His mother intervened by wresting the weapon from him. It would be the boy's final memory of his father.[4]

When word of the shooting reached the town below, questions quickly mounted. Who was the dead man? Did anyone know his widow? Why was he murdered? Where is his little boy? Does anyone know the victim's fatherless children? What motivated the killing? When would the coroner's inquest begin? The only known facts at that time were very sparse. Around 8:30 on the morning of April 3, 1882, one or two men had shot and killed a man inside his house located at 1318 Lafayette Street, near St. Joseph, Missouri. The true identity of the dead man and his family remained unknown.

For a six-year-old, he had experienced an unusually bizarre adolescence. His life was distinguished from any one else his age—or from anyone else at any age. Neither he nor his baby sister was aware of the falsity of their name or identity.[5] His late pa affectionately referred to him as "Timmy" or "Little Tim." So, Tim had to be his first name. His actual birth date and birthplace was as evasive: he thought he had been born in 1875, but he was not for certain of the city. Was it Nashville? He just wasn't sure.

Mysteriously, Timmy's family had more names than "Carter had pills." His father would identify himself as Jackson, J. T. Jackman, William Campbell, Charles Lawson, Williams, and Howard, J.D. or Thomas. His folks often referred to themselves as Mr. and Mrs. Howard, Mr. and Mrs. Jackman or multiple combinations of each. His paternal grandmother called his late pa Dave. Even his father's brother had different names. Sometimes, but not always, he went by the surname, Woodson. There were those who called his uncle Frank, but Timmy knew him as "Uncle Ben." Little Tim often overheard his father and uncle refer to themselves as the Williams' Brothers. His

4   James, Jesse, Jr., Jesse James My Father, The First And Only True Story Of His Adventure Ever Written, Sentinel Printing Co., 1899 (hereinafter Jesse James My Father).

5   The Yakima Herald, November 17, 1898; and Yeatman Ted, P., Frank and Jesse James, The Story Behind the Legend, Cumberland House, 2000, at p. 31.

"Uncle Ben" had a son, named Robert, or was it a daughter named Mary? The little boy was unsure either way. Certainly, his mother's name, Josie, had to be her real name, wasn't it? He simply had no clue why his entire family had chosen so many different ways in which to be identified. It was all a conundrum to the boy.

The small child faced other obstacles beyond the uncertainty of his name or the ambiguity surrounding the identity of his parents and extended family members. He was bound by certain steadfast rules: prohibited from owning a dog; precluded from playing outside; barred from having friends; sanctioned from visiting neighbors; and discouraged from playing with other kids. His parents explained that it was not in his best interest to become too attached to other boys and girls since the family would soon be moving. And so they did, again and again and again and again.

Timmy relocated so often that it was like his family lived out of luggage. Was his father a traveling salesman, a roaming cattleman or railroad superintendent? There was no way his father was a fugitive. Their travels took them from state to state, city to city and house to house. He vaguely recalled living in Tennessee. He remembered residing or staying in various residences, including at least three, maybe four, different places in Kansas City. When they arrived in St. Joseph in 1881, they lived in two homes with their final move being on Christmas Eve to that white cottage frame structure on the hill. Toward the end of March 1882, his father had been discussing the possibility of moving to yet another state—this time to Nebraska. The boy had certainly seen the Midwest!

Little Timmy's lifestyle in St. Joseph did not differ from that in which he had experienced in all the various and diverse locales in which he and his family had previously lived. His father was a cattleman (at least that's what he had been told) and was gone for extended periods of time on "business" trips. While in town, his pa often ventured into the city nestled in the valley below to purchase newspapers or visit with town folks. The young boy remained under the traditional injunctions and prohibitions that his parents continued to mandate. Sometimes the family attended the Second Presbyterian Church at 12th and Penn where the two children attended Sunday school. Ironically, the day before the shooting, the little boy had sat next to his parents and sister during the Palm Sunday church service. Reverend George Miller warned the members of the congregation of the urgency to follow the path of righteousness, and he admonished his flock to avoid the temptations of sin so as not to fall prey to the demon as had Jesse James, the notorious bandit whom the preacher solemnly denounced.[6] The elder James did not flinch, gave no response but merely smiled. Timmy knew his pa had followed the road to glory, unlike that wretched Jesse James. There was one bright and grateful change of custom for Tim during those final days before the murder. His father, Charles, J. T., J.D., Thomas, William, Dave or whatever, had given him a little puppy. The dog had been a special surprise and unique gift—the last one he would ever receive from his father.

Rumors of the shooting and identity of the murdered man began to spread like wildfire. There was a great rush to view the body. Back east in Newark, Ohio, the *Daily Advocate* reported that the "news spread with great rapidity, but most people received it with doubt and crowds of people rushed to that quarter of the city where the shooting took place, anxious to view the body and learn the particulars." Some early stories sensationally speculated, and scandalously suggested that the slain man was none other than the scoundrel, Jesse James. It was incredulous. Jesse James could not have been the man shot in the back of the head. The outlaw Jesse James could not have been Little Timmy's father. He could not have been the son of a bandit. He unquestionably

6   *Kansas City Journal-Post*, April 3, 1938. Reverend George Miller was known as a strong abolitionist before the Civil War. He was the author of Missouri's Memorable Decade. Ms. Nancy Ehrlich of Independence, Missouri, confirmed the story of Rev. Miller's Palm Sunday sermon during a telephone conversation with the author on December 7, 2011. Nancy is a member of the Hill family, and a cousin of Ann Ralston the wife of Frank James. Nancy is the great granddaughter of William Hill who was a brother of Mary Catherine Hill, and Mary was the second wife of Sam Ralston. Sam's first wife was Sarah Jordan, who was from South Carolina, and they had two children, John and Rowena. Following Sarah's death, Sam Ralston then married Mary Catherine Hill. Sam and Mary had eight children, including Ann Ralston. Frank and Ann James had only one child, Robert James. Nancy Ehrlich was a young girl when Ann Ralston James died, but she did get to know her Cousin Robert James. She reported that the story about Rev. Miller's Palm Sunday sermon has been a part of the Hill and James family's oral history, and had been passed down to her by her grandfather Adam Hill, who was a son of William Hill.

had never heard that name being used by the family.

No one believed or perhaps wanted to accept as true that the long-hunted desperado was dead. Citizens of St. Joseph merely scoffed and "laughed at the idea that Jesse James was really the slain man."[7] Many insisted he had not been killed or adamently required "a good deal of confirmation before it was accepted."[8] Those intimate with Jesse James declared "the dead man at St. Joseph" was not "Jesse at all and that the killing" had been a scheme by the James family "to secure the reward" or that someone else had been murdered who had been induced on "some false pretext to impersonate Jesse James."[9] The *Los Angeles Times* on April 4, 1882 editorialized its doubt by proclaiming that "Jesse James is like a cat; he has been killed a great many times, only to as often enjoy a resurrection."[10] Hadn't the *Kansas City Times* reported on November 4, 1879, that George Shepard had killed the "cat" near Joplin, Missouri? Like all those other stories the Shepard tale had been unfounded.

On April 1, 1882, merely two days before the shooting, Richard K. Fox, the editor and owner of the New York national gossip tabloid, *National Police Gazette* (a contemporary blend of *People Magazine*, *True Crime* and the *National Inquirer*) continued this long-standing tradition with a headline and byline story about yet another putative death story.

The Much-Killed Jesse James Writes To the Police Gazette

We have received a communication from the grave. From a veritable corpse. Yes, a dead man. Not only a dead man but a dead man who has been riddled to hash by bullets and slashed to ribbons with bowie knives. That is, if we can believe the newspapers. The alleged corpse that has written us is none other than the remains or the ghost or what is left of the much-killed

7   *The Daily Gazette*, April 5, 1882, St. Joseph, Missouri.

8   <u>Lives, Adventures, Exploits, Frank and Jesse James with an Account of the Tragic Death of Jesse James</u>, reprinted by Nifty Nut Novelty Co., Excelsior Springs, Missouri, 1947.

9   *Kansas City Evening Star*, April 4, 1882, and *Liberty Tribune*, April 14, 1882.

10   Yeatman, Ted, P., *Jesse James' Assassination and the Ford Boys*, Wildwest, December, 2006, at p. 46.

Jesse James, the terror of Missouri.

This famous bandit, train robber and desperado has been killed so often, however, in newspaper reports and has turned up safe and sound thereafter, that the people of Kansas have lost faith in death. Every time he was reported positively defunct he would resurrect himself, board another train at an unexpected point, clean out the express packages and the passengers and then hie him away to the setting sun with many merry cuss words on his lips and his thumb pivoted on his nose and his fingers agitated in insulting suggestions to the minions of the law.

Fox then boasted to the readers of the *Police Gazette* that the "brigand of Missouri" subscribed to his paper and often contributed letters to him for publication. The April 1st article also contained what Fox described as "a photographic facsimile" of a letter from the "corpse of Missouri" in which the "dead man" insisted "it was no use" for "sheriffs, detectives and senators" to try to bring him to justice as he would retire from his chosen career only upon his own "time schedule."[11] If the dead man in St. Joseph had been in fact the scrivener of the letter to the *Police Gazette* his retirement would not have been under his own "time schedule." The April 3rd stories of the murder of Jesse James had been unquestionably as fabricated as the story of his demise reported in the April 1st *Police Gazette*.

If on the other hand reports were true that *the* Jesse James had been murdered, the press had many questions. Was the murder motivated out of fear or revenge? Who was behind the plot? Had the killers been hired by the railroads? Were Pinkerton Agents once again involved? Did the governor's reward lead to the shooting? Was it a conspiracy? If so, had public officials, including the governor, participated? It could not have been Governor Crittenden. His posted proclamation and circular only announced rewards "For the Arrest & Conviction Of" Frank and Jesse James, not their murder. It was unbelievable to imagine

---

11   *National Police Gazette*, April 1, 1882, New York; See, http://policegazette.us/FromTheMorgue.

state officials being in duplicity with known criminals for homicidal purposes. Would they?

My Name is Tim!

They said my name was Tim,
Six years that's how it been!
My pa left us a lot,
To what place I knew not!
He always returned to home,
Fearing us being alone!
Cattle or things he sold,
That's what they'd always told!
We moved quite frequently,
Had been for our safety!
Bad men wanted him dead
That's what ma and pa said,
We last moved to St. Joe,
They'd said I'd like it so.
Pa had many a name,
It'd been his little game.
He'd joke about each one,
No, we weren't on the run.
Pa loved us one and all,
And told me to stand tall.
The last gift he gave me,
It was my first puppy.
The preacher gave out palms
And then read from the psalms.
He told us not to sin,
Like Jesse James' had been.

Pa just nod his head,
He had nothing to dread!
After church we went home,
But we were not alone.
Charlie and Bob were there,
Pa had friends everywhere.
Next morning it was hot,
Cousin Bob fired a shot.
The house rattled with noise,
I discarded my toys.
Mother began to cry,
"Oh husband, please don't die."
Rushing into the room,
Not knowing my pa's doom.
Ma's tears changed to a scream,
It was like a bad dream!
"Bob you vicious coward,
 You've shot Mr. Howard."
"I swear that I did not,
Not me who fired the shot."
Grabbing my pa's shotgun,
The worm began to run.
Momma took it from me,
Timmy just let it be!
Collapsed onto the floor,
Pa would be nevermore!

(The one-story, white painted framed cottage
with green shutters: St. Joseph
Courtesy Jackson County Historical Society)

CHAPTER I
IDENTITIES UNVEILED

<del>=■(O)■=</del>

Dateline: April 3, 1882
St. Joseph, Missouri

Headline:

PALM SUNDAY
RELIGIOUS SERVICES YESTERDAY
PALM SUNDAY DISTRIBUTION IN THE
VARIOUS CATHOLIC CHURCHS
DISCOURSE ELIQUENT OF REV. FRANCE,
SHIPPEN, DOWNS, AND OTHER CLERGY[12]

The shooter or shooters had no interest in the events that had transpired in the various Catholic Churches or other faith communities on Palm Sunday, but they did eloquently pray for their priestly reward the following day. They knew full well that the state's chief magistrate had offered $10,000 for the apprehension of the dead man. Immediately after the shooting, they went directly to the telegraph office and sent wire reports of the shooting to Governor Crittenden, Clay County Sheriff James Timberlake and Kansas City Police Commissioner Henry Craig. They boldly and proudly proclaimed having successfully fulfilled their mission by delivering justice to the State of Missouri. After detailing the account of their infamous deed, they surrendered to police.

Once city officials heard the startling reports stemming from 13th

---

12   *National Republican*, April 3, 1882, Washington City (D.C.).

and Lafayette Street, the undertaker, Coroner James W. Heddens, M.D. and the owner and editor of the *St. Joseph News-Press*, Jake Spencer, went immediately to the residence. A distraught woman met them at the front door. She identified herself as the wife of the slain victim, "Mr. Howard," and swiftly hurried back to her fallen husband, crouching over him, crying uncontrollably and begging reporters not to disclose anything to her children.[13] A brief examination was made of "Mr. Howard" and the corpse was removed to Sidenfaden's Funeral Parlor where Deputy Sheriff Tom Finch and six other deputies guarded it. After an autopsy, William Sidenfaden prepared the corpse and placed it on a board in the back room of the funeral home for a local photographer, J.W. Graham, to photograph. Graham had been ordered by City Marshal Enos Craig to take a postmortem image of the dead man. The body was affixed to a board by ropes under each arm to prevent it from sliding before it was stood upright as nearly as possible. Graham utilizing his eight by ten studio camera, lens and single plate-holder took the picture. Even in 1882, the economic value of the James name was not a novelty as countless books, dime novels and tales had already been written, published and read by a doting public.[14] The dead man was placed on an iced table and displayed for all to see, like an item for sale in a mercantile store.

---

13   *Liberty Tribune*, April 7, 1882, p. 2.

14   *Ibid.* The idea of taking the picture of Jesse James captured the fancy of twenty-six year old J.W. Graham, an employee at the local photo-studio owned by James W. Porch, a rising young Democrat lawyer. In the forenoon when Graham heard reports that the dead man may have been Jesse James (a story he later described as being "incredulous") he told his boss, R.C. Smith, the manager of Porch's studio, that they should promptly jump at the opportunity "to make some money by photographing" the corpse and "selling pictures of him." Eventually thousands of photos were sold. Smaller pictures sold for a quarter while larger prints brought a half-dollar. By November 1948, Graham had retired and was living in Buckner, Jackson County, Missouri, but even at that late date, he had retained the glass negatives of the pictures. Source: *Kansas City Times*, November 12, 1948; and Thruston, Ethylene, Ballard, Echoes of the Past, The Lowell Press, Kansas City, 1973, p. 434. The fatal bullet was removed during the autopsy and today is on display at the James home in St. Joseph.

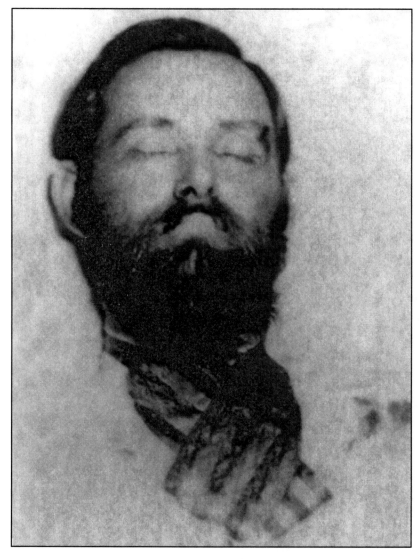

(Postmortem image of Jesse James)
(Courtesy Jackson County Historical Society)

News of the killing created the most intense excitement. Crowds soon gathered to view and identify the remains of the deceased husband and father. Dignitaries and politicians, including Missouri Governor

Thomas T. Crittenden and Jackson County Prosecutor William H. Wallace journeyed to St. Joseph to verify the corpse was the rogue, Jesse James.[15] It seemed truly amazing or simply doubtful that such a rascal was dead. Everyone had to visualize the corpse on the iced-table in St. Joseph. It was as if the circus had come to town. The identification of the decedent became the focal point of everyone's attention in the town (and it has remained the fulcrum focus for folks, frauds, fakes, freaks, foes, forensics, families, friends forevermore).[16]

Who was the dead man? What was his name? Could the victim really be the wanted desperado, Jesse James? Would the coroner's inquest unveil to "Little Tim" the real identity of his parents and the pedigree of his family? Maybe he would be provided an explanation for all the moves around the country (once his father had compared their plight to the biblical story of the Holy Family's flight into Egypt). Perhaps a reason would be uncovered for the utilization of so many aliases. Surely Tim's name would remain unchanged. Wouldn't it?

A coroner's inquest followed later that day in an effort to answer these and other puzzling questions, doubts and uncertainties. Would the coroner's jury reveal the "true" identity of the victim? Would it

---

15   Wallace, William H., Speeches and Writings of William H. Wallace and Autobiography, 1914. Neither Crittenden nor Wallace would have been able to identify Jesse James since both men had never laid eyes on him. For this reason, Wallace traveled by train to St. Joseph in the company of an unidentified person whom Wallace claimed would be able to positively identify the dead man, if he was in fact Jesse James. Ironically, at the time of the murder in St. Joseph, William Wallace was in the middle of a criminal jury trial in Jackson County at Independence. The defendants were all lads from Crackerneck who were on trial for allegedly committing the Blue Cut Train Robbery in September 1881. Hadn't Frank & Jesse James been accused of this train robbery, too? One of the defendants on trial was twenty-two year old John Bugler. The history of young Bugler's life made the train robbery charges against him most disheartening to the Jackson County community. This is because on the night of June 13, 1866 John's father, Henry Bugler, the jailer and elected marshal of the Jackson County Jail in Independence had been killed by guerillas in a jailbreak attempt. Henry was the first law official in the county's history to die in the line of duty. John who was about four at the time was also shot in the arm during the attack on the jail. Had the poor jailer's son truly robbed the train? Apparently, Wallace discovered that the boy had not, as after the prosecutor returned from his tour of St. Joseph, he dismissed all charges pending against the defendants, including John Bugler. The judge did not agree with Wallace as he personally thought Bugler was guilty. However, the judge reluctantly agreed to dismiss the case, but in doing so he admonished John Bugler to get out of town. Bugler walked out a free man; left the county; and never returned. Wallace said the dismissals were necessitated because of the "truth" he had learned about the Blue Cut crime while he was in St. Joseph. The boys on trial had not been at Blue Cut—it had been the James Gang.

16   Settle, William A. Jr., Jesse James Was His Name, The Curators of the University of Missouri, 1966, First Bison Book edition, 1977, at p. 118.

disclose the nature of the felled man's death and his killers? The hearing would certainly end all the rumors, innuendoes and speculations. Or would it? The press and public were clamoring to know.

On the afternoon of the murder, Coroner Heddens impaneled six men for the coroner's jury. They were W. H. Chouning, J. W. Moore, Warren Samuels, Thomas Norris, William Turner and William H. George. After the jurors were duly sworn upon their oath, Heddens began his inquest. The first witness to testify was the widow, Josie Howard. Would the truth finally be unveiled? Mrs. Howard could certainly end the rumors, reports and speculations surrounding the identity of the corpse.

Coroner Heddens, those assembled and the citizens of the world were anxious to ascertain the identity of the woman and the dead man. Heddens commenced his inquiry of the witness with the most innocuous of foundational questions: "Please state your name." Little did he or anyone else under the sun realize that the answer given would become a media frenzy and pulp-fodder that has lasted for one hundred and thirty years! Mrs. Howard holding back tears revealed the long-standing family secret. Softly but emphatically she declared, "I am Zerelda Mimms James" cousin and wife of Jesse Woodson James. Her stunning revelation prompted the most obvious follow-up question—the name and identity of the dead man. She somberly muttered, "My husband, Jesse Woodson James." No, she was not Josie Jackman, Josie Jackson, Josie Campbell, Josie Williams, Josie Lawson or Josie Howard. Her first name was not even Josie; she was Zerelda Mimms James. Her reply was stunning, moving, unbelievable, shocking and revealing.

The coroner next had to know who shot her husband. The widow Zerelda, pointing towards the Ford brothers, Bob and Charlie, angrily described them as men who had "wormed their way into the confidence" of her loving husband and adoring father. Those cowards killed her Jesse leaving her a widow and her children fatherless. Mrs. James had finally disclosed to the coroner's jury (and to the world) the identity of the victim, his family and the killers. She begged God to protect her and her young ones, and pleaded with reporters not to print her story for the sake of her babies—they knew nothing of her revelation and were unaware that their names were untrue.[17] She realized her children would no longer be protected from the family secret—the undisclosed truth in which she and her loving, late husband had kept within their bosoms could no longer be kept quiet. The emotional statement she gave, and quoted in the *Kansas City Times* on April 4th, exposed her inner soul.

> I can't shield them any longer. Even after they had shot my hus-
> band, who has been trying to live a peaceable life, I protected
> them and withheld their names, but it is all true. My husband
> is Jesse James, and a kinder hearted and truer man to his family
> never lived.

After Zerelda unveiled these sensational facts, the Coroner sum-moned the killers to the stand—the Ford brothers of Ray County, Missouri. Charlie testified first and was followed by his younger broth-er, Robert. Twenty-year old Bob confirmed he had pulled the trigger. During his interrogation, the younger Ford boy boasted his willing-ness to suffer the consequences of prison or death for his action and expressed no repentance for the killing.[18] The combined testimony of the Ford brothers was prideful, bold and arrogant. They told how they had met with public officials several months earlier to develop a plan designed to end the state's infamous nomenclature, the "Outlaw State." The derogatory term had become a thorn in the side of the law, the railroads and the Pinkerton Private-eye Agency. The Ford brothers had unveiled a government conspiracy in which they in duplicity with the law and state agencies, including Governor Thomas T. Crittenden, Sheriff Timberlake and Commissioner Craig had schemed to bring Jesse James to justice. Their goal had been to bring an end to the des-perado—and they, the Fords brothers, had achieved that end. By their success, the Fords proclaimed their entitlement to the reward.

---

17   *Ibid*, and *Kansas City Times*, April 4, 1882.
18   *The County Paper*, April 14, 1882, Oregon, Missouri.

(Robert Ford)

Once the Ford brothers had completed their testimonies, the Coroner recessed the hearing until the following morning. Charlie and Bob Ford were taken back to jail. Mrs. James (no longer Mrs. Howard or any other pseudonym) did not return to the little house on the hill. She and her two small children, along with her mother-in-law, were escorted to the World Hotel on 12th Street, a few blocks south of their rented house. Upon arriving at the hotel, the widow picked up stationery of the World Hotel and quickly dispatched a letter to Marshal Enos Craig asking him to return her late husband's personal property that had been obtained by a law officer after the murder. Reporters, investigators, politicians, police and detectives also gathered at the hotel.[19] There they all spent the night, while Jesse rested on ice. Even at that late hour neither Little Timmy nor his younger sister knew

---

19   The World Hotel had opened in 1858 under the name, 'Patee Hotel.' In 1860, it served as the headquarters for the Pony Express. From 1881-1883 the official name of the hotel was the World Hotel.

anything other than their father had been murdered and that their mother had testified at the inquest.

Dateline: Tuesday, April 4, 1882
Coroner's Inquest—Day 2

Headline:

CAPITOL CHIPS
AND DEPARTMENTAL SHAVINGS
ANOTHER FLOOD OF BILLS IN THE HOUSE AND
SENATE—WORK OF SOME OF THE COMMITTEES
AN APPROPRIATION FOR THE PURCHASE OF
SEED—OTHER MATTERS.[20]

Americans on the morning of April 4th were more interested in the news flooding across the wire about Jesse James than the various appropriation bills pending in Congress. Unlike the preceding day, the two little children joined their mother, and their one-armed paternal grandmother, Zerelda Cole James Simms Samuel, for the continuation of the coroner's inquest. By then, the little boy had been told the truth. He was not "Little Tim." He had the same name as his late father, and he was in fact the son of Jesse Woodson James. The murder of his father by Bob Ford had revealed to him his own identity, and had given him his real name.[21] Little Jesse must have questioned why his parents had concealed these truths from him for so long.

The *Kansas City Times* described the demeanor of the widow and children as they entered the chamber on the second day of the hearing. The *Times* reporter remarked that the murdered man's wife was a slender "neat and rather prepossessing lady," fair of face with a high forehead, blue eyes, light hair and bearing the stamp of having been well brought up with "marks of intelligence very strikingly apparent." The two orphans were said to be "a little boy and girl" who were "neat and intelligent" and "seemed to grieve over the deed which had in a

20   *National Republic*, April 4, 1882, Washington City (D.C.).
21   *The Kansas City Star*, October 20, 1898.

short moment deprived them of father's love and protection."

The first witness to take the stand on day two was Commissioner Craig. He conceded that the Ford boys had been working with his office, the Clay County Sheriff and other government officials and agents in capturing train robbers and putting an end to outlawry in Missouri. Craig had never seen Jesse James and this compelled the Coroner to summon someone other than a James' family member or Ford brother to identify the dead man. Heddens knew the witness had to be someone who wore the same moniker as Jesse James. No one was more qualified to respond to this assignment than the nefarious Vernon County horse thief, Dick Liddle. Without hesitation, reservation or equivocation, Liddle identified the dead man, confessed his own crimes and divulged the scope of the James gang. He had no doubt that the dead man was Jesse James.

Once Liddle's tangled testimony concluded, the matriarch of the family, Zerelda Samuel, testified. A black veil concealed her face, and she sobbed throughout her time on the witness stand. Mrs. Samuel "fighting back tears" identified the victim of the shooting as her sainted and badly persecuted son, Jesse Woodson James. Coroner Heddens asked her to identify the three people seated next to her. Lamenting bitterly, "the weather-aged woman" declared they were "my son's wife, Jesse's wife and his poor little children."[22] After responding to the Coroner's final question, the victim's mother stepped down and passed around the end of the reporters' table where she "suddenly spied Dick Liddle a few feet from her," and burst out yelling, "Oh, you traitor! Oh, you traitor! See what you have done? Oh may heaven send its vengence upon you for this! Oh, you traitor! Traitor! Traitor." The aged woman abruptly burst out, "Oh, you traitor! Oh you traitor! See what you have done? Oh may heaven send its vengence upon you for this! Oh, you traitor! Traitor! Traitor!" Dick Liddle cowered under the rage of the old lady and turned pale.[23] He defensively asserted not having been her son's killer. His assertion failed to relieve the grief or scorn of Mrs. Samuel; she considered Liddle as culpable as the Fords even though he had not pulled the trigger. To her, Liddle had been part of the conspiracy.

22 *Kansas City Evening Star*, April 4, 1882.
23 *St. Joseph Weekly Gazette*, April 5, 1882.

While other testimony was adduced at the hearing, nothing more significant was forthcoming. The Coroner's jury deliberated for only fifteen minutes and then swiftly announced its unanimous verdict:

> . . . That the body of the deceased is that of Jesse W. James and that
> he came to his death by a wound in the back of his head, caused
> by a pistol shot fired intentionally by the hand of Robert Ford . . .

The truth had been determined by the Coroner's verdict: the dead man in St. Joseph, Missouri, murdered at the hands of Robert Ford, was the long-hunted outlaw Jesse James. Their conclusion had to be true. Kansas City Mayor Daniel A. Frink pronounced his certainty that Jesse James was dead, and Governor Crittenden concurred: "Jesse James was killed by Bob Ford . . . too many people who knew him . . . came to identify him for there to be any possible doubt, so that is that."[24] The decision reached by the jury and the proclamations of the mayor and governor had settled the matter. For the family of the murdered man, he had not been an outlaw; he had been the loving husband, father, brother, son; he was their sainted Jesse Woodson James.

Following the Coroner's verdict, the widow, her two children and the victim's mother retired to the white cottage house where Jesse James had been killed. There they faced the task of gathering themselves and packing up their family belongings. While so engaged, a policeman entered the dwelling and picked up a purse belonging to the dead man's wife. The new 'little man' of the family summarily ordered him to put it down. The officer ignored the request so Jesse Jr. picked up a revolver, cocked it and aimed it declaring "that's mama's purse, damn you, put it down." Was he defending the family or becoming a chip off the old block?[25] Another oddity occurred while they were sorting through some personal items and "gathering . . . trinkets and playthings peculiar to a young boy." Young Jesse made a discovery—a pair of blue glasses. He

---

24   Crittenden, H. H., The Crittenden Memoirs, G. P. Puntam's Sons, New York, 1936.

25   The authority for this story was Marshal T. H. Richie who reported that the day following the murder little Jesse took the aggressive action. *Kansas City Journal-Post* reported the story on Sunday, April 3, 1938.

brought them to his aged grandmother proclaiming they had belonged to "Cousin Charlie." Mrs. Samuel sharply declared that Charlie Ford was no cousin; he was a worthless traitor who conspired to kill his father.[26]

The pain, misfortune and anguish suffered by the decedent's wife and his fatherless children never dissipated. In the short term, the family would face a funeral, an auction and yet another relocation. Over the long term, the poor widow never seemed to recover from her husband's death. She endured financial struggles and health problems while exerting efforts to rear small kids without a father. As the new man of the family, poor Timmy (now little Jesse) would be deprived of his own adolescence. It would become his fate to interrupt his education to provide the necessary financial support for his mother and young sister.

(Widow Zee, Jesse Jr. & Mary)
(Courtesy: www.LegendsOfAmerica.com)

---

26   *Kansas City Evening Star*, April 4, 1882; and *St. Joseph Weekly Gazette*, April 5, 1882.

Headline news stories around the country centered not upon the plight of the impoverished family, but rather upon the life and death of Jesse James. The storyline of the *Kansas City Journal* on April 4th read as if the murdered victim had been a friend or reputable community leader, not a notorious criminal at the center of a manhunt for nearly a generation:

GOOD-BYE, JESSE!

The St. Joseph *Daily Gazette* disagreeing with Reverend Miller's Palm Sunday condemnation that Jesse James was destined for the inferno of hell proclaimed the slain man had attained sainthood:

JESSE, BY JEHOVAH

The *Daily Gazette's* same by-line contained the truth, the whole truth, nothing but the truth!

JESSE JAMES, THE NOTORIOUS DESPERADO,
INSTANTLY KILLED BY ROBERT FORD.

HIS ADVENTUROUS CAREER BROUGHT TO
AN ABRUPT CLOSE ON THE EVE
OF ANOTHER CRIME.
FORD GETS INTO HIS CONFIDENCE AND
SHOOTS HIM FROM BEHIND WHILE
HIS BACK IS TURNED.

The evidence adduced through the Coroner's inquest, to many, created feelings of remorse or shock both locally and nationally. These view points considered the circumstances of the slaying to be fiendish and dastardly. Columns were written about a certain "universal loathing" over the manner in which he had been killed.[27] Several state

---

27   *Kansas City Daily Times*, April 7, 1882.

officials felt some personal regret over the nature of the deed. This is even true of Governor Crittendon who was fully aware that reports as far away as New York were writing that he had known in advance of the designs of the Ford boys to kill Jesse James.[28] This troubled him greatly (and would profoundly impact not only him but his progeny as well). Other opinions were dismayed over disclosures developed during the hearing. The *Milwaukee Republican* questioned how Jesse James could have been "shot down by a boy who had wormed into his confidence."[29] The best summation by those negatively impacted by the killing was expressed in the *Kansas City Daily Times*: "The general sentiment of the inner heart of all manner of men is that nothing in the recorded life of Jesse James equaled the infamy of the manner and mode" in which he had been slain.[30]

The most sensational commendation came from Major John Newman Edwards, a Confederate veteran who had served as adjutant to General Jo Shelby during the closing years of the Civil War, and later helped establish the *Kansas City Times*. Edwards had garnered a unique reputation for his inspirational storytelling about the James and Younger boys, especially their exploits he had covered in his book, *Noted Guerrillas*. The editor's writings and commentaries had helped inspire the "Robin Hood" legend of Frank and Jesse James. The former soldier described the death of Jesse James as a "murder plot" and boldly announced that no one "among all the hired cowards, hard on the hunt for blood money, dared face this wonderful outlaw." He accused Governor Crittenden of having placed a price upon Jesse's head by hiring a "band of cutthroats and highwaymen to murder him for money." Edwards' disdain and disgust over the way Jesse's life had ended reached an unambiguous climax:

Why, the whole State reeks today with a double orgy—that of lust and that of murder . . . Tear the two bears from the flag of Missouri. Put thereon in place of them, as more appropriate, a

---

28   *The Sun*, April 5, 1882, New York.
29   Good Bye, Jesse James, at p. 131.
30   *Ibid.*

thief blowing out the brains of an unarmed victim; and brazen harlot, naked to the waist and splashed to the brows in blood.[31]

Opposing views strenuously denounced the rabble coming from those who criticized the manner in which Jesse James had died. These writers and community leaders had grown tired of all these lamenting stories. Instead of protesting the actions taken by the governor and other government officials, they overtly expressed their approval. The *Weekly Graphic* stated that more should be done "until every bandit or defender of them were made to feel the full penalty of the law."[32] The *Rolla New Era* endorsed the handling of the outlaw's demise. The paper reminded its readers in its headline that his death had been positive for the state.

Jesse James, the Notorious Bandit Who has Disgraced Missouri By His Lawless Acts At Last Dead![33]

Many leading citizens shared the editorials expressed in the *Weekly Graphic* and *Rolla New Era*, including Colonel William E. Moberly (the namesake of Moberly, Missouri) an attorney in St. Louis and a Lieutenant Colonel of the First Missouri Militia and later of the Thirty-fifth regiment during the Civil War who declared the assassination to be just. "I am not a Democrat and would not vote for Governor Crittenden, but I'll stand by him on this matter every time."[34] In the wake of the guerilla's death, community advocates in Jackson County gathered at the Merchants Exchange Hall in Kansas City to reply to those who had been angered over Jesse's death. After debating several issues, the assembly promptly appointed three men, including former Congressman Abram Comingo of Independence, to draft resolutions

31 *Sedalia Democrat*, April 13, 1882; see also, Breihan, Carl W., <u>The Day Jesse James Was Killed</u>, Frederick Fell, Inc., Publishers, New York, 1961, at pp. 178 and 181.
32 *Weekly Graphic*, Kirksville, Adair County, Missouri, April 21, 1882.
33 *Rolla New Era*, April 8, 1882.
34 *The Republican*, April 14, 1882, St. Louis, Missouri.

of appreciation and gratitude to Governor Crittenden, Commissioner Craig and Chief Timberlake for having ended the reign of terror and bringing "Jesse to justice."[35]

There was no question that the circumstances relating to the death of Jesse James had produced diverse opinions locally, regionally and nationally. It still does today.

---

35 *Kansas City Evening Star*, May 8, 1882. A. Comingo had a most interesting career. After Comingo became a lawyer in Harrodsburg, Kentucky in 1847, he and his wife, Lucy, in 1848 moved to Independence. He formed a partnership with Sam Woodson and William Chrisman. He served two terms as mayor of Independence during the 1850's. In 1861 he was elected to the Missouri State Convention as an Unconditional Unionist where he opposed secession and cast his vote for the Union. In May 1863, he was appointed Captain and served as the Provost Marshal with the unenviable burden of enforcing General Thomas Ewing's famous or infamous Order # 11 that Ewing had issued after William Quantrill and his guerillas had raided and destroyed Lawrence, Kansas, killing some 185 men in August 1863 (some have claimed that both Frank and Jesse were among the guerillas). In 1870, Comingo, a Democrat, was elected to the U.S. Congress and served two terms. Coincidently, later in the year Jesse had been killed Comingo's Kansas City firm (Phillips, Comingo & Slover) served as legal counsel for the dead man's brother, Frank James.

CHAPTER II
THE FATHER'S FUNERAL & A FAMILY AUCTION

———◦《◉》◦———

Dateline: Thursday, April 6, 1882
Kearney, Missouri

Headline:

BILLIONS OF BATS.
IMMENSE GUANO DEPOSITS IN
TEXAS REACHED BY A RECENT
RAILROAD EXTENSION[36]

The billions of bats discovered by railroad workers in Texas paled in comparison to the emotional upheaval that was gripping the very hearts and souls of the widow and her orphaned children. Following the public viewing and coroner's inquest, a special train transported the remains of Jesse James to his mother's home near Kearney, Clay County, Missouri. Nearly two thousand people journeyed there to view the body of the notorious Jesse James.[37] On the morning of April 6th, the funeral cortege left the James house and took the body to the same Baptist church where the slain man had been baptized in 1866.

The press covered every minute detail of the funeral and quoted each word and lyric from the ceremony. By 2:00 p.m. the church was overly crowded as many were forced to stand throughout the service. Little Jesse, his mother, younger sister and grandmother sat beside the

---

36   *The Anderson Intelligencer*, April 6, 1882, Anderson Court House, South Carolina.
37   *Liberty Tribune*, April 14, 1882.

coffin situated at the foot of the altar. The services began with the sing-
ing of the hymn "What a Friend We Have in Jesus." Other prayers were
read out of the Old Testament. This was followed by the church pastor,
Rev. J. M. P. Martin, reading from the Book of Matthew, Chapter 24,
Verse 44: "Therefore be ye ready, for in such an hour as ye think not the
Son of Man Cometh." Pastor Martin's eulogy focused upon the theme
of "the willingness of Christ to forgive" and a warning to remain vigilant
as the "Lord comes like a thief in the night." He made no mention of
the life and times of Jesse James; nothing was said about his past criminal reputation; no word was announced about his killing. Instead the
minister focused upon the urgency and necessity of preparing to meet
God—no judgment was made or passed by Pastor Martin in either support or opposition of Jesse James.[38] The preacher's final request to the
gathering, he said, was made at the behest of the mother of the departed
soul. "Only family and close friends are permitted to return to the James
homestead for the burial services." Pallbearers J.D. Ford (no relation to
the Ford brothers), Deputy Marshal J.E. Reed, Sheriff Timberlake, James
Henderson, Benjamin Flanders, William Bond and Charles Scott then
carried the body out of the church to the awaiting horse drawn hearse.[39]

The family and "close friends" followed the funeral procession
back to the James Farm, some four miles from the church. The passage
to the final resting place consumed over an hour as the hearse "drove
slowly." Upon arrival, the casket was carried into the house for a private
family viewing. A lengthy period of time expired before the two hundred and fifty dollar metallic coffin was carried back into the open air
and placed upon supports where guests were "invited to a last look at
the outlaw's dead face."[40]

Rev. Martin conducted a short graveside memorial followed by a
final hymn. Before the body was lowered into the ground, the sobbing
widow stood next to her young, fatherless children and "cast herself upon

---

38   *Kansas City Times*, April 7, 1882.
39   *Liberty Tribune*, April 14, 1882, Liberty, Missouri; *Weekly Graphic*, April 14, 1882, Kirksville, Adair
     County, Missouri; and *St. Louis Daily Globe-Democrat*, April 7, 1882.
40   T*The County Paper*, Supplement, April 14, 1882. Elizabeth Beckett, the Administrator of the Clay
     County Historic Sites, including the James Farm in Kearney, Missouri, advises that the government
     had purchased the casket. E-mail from Ms. Beckett to author dated February 2, 2012.

the coffin" begging that her "Jesse" not be taken away from them.[41] The body was then lowered and "buried in a corner of the beautiful yard . . . beneath a giant coffee bean tree . . . covered by flowers."[42] The burial spot next to the family home had been selected to allow his mother to tend to his grave and "to keep anyone from stealing it away."[43]

Antagonists argued that his body should have been dug deeper and covered with rocks piled up high to assuage fears that somehow the dead man "would rise from the grave to rob and kill again."[44] Even in death, Jesse James was not permitted to rest in peace. The inscription on the tombstone read:[45]

Jesse W. James
Died
April 3, 1882
34 yrs. 6 mos. 28 da
JAMES

When memorial services concluded, the James family privately assembled in the home of the family matriarch, Zerelda Samuel. It had been the childhood home of little Jesse's father and his Uncle Frank (and the place where Pinkerton Agents had gone in search of the James boys on January 26, 1875). The Pinkerton mission on that fateful January evening proved disastrous. Instead of capturing the boys, the Pinkerton Agents under cover of darkness had cast a turpentine bottle into the house that produced horrific results! Archie, age eight (half-brother to Frank and Jesse), was killed and the boys' mother lost half her right arm—both victims of the explosion. Were these horrible memories recalled the night of the funeral? What the family actually

41 *Ibid.*
42 <u>Jesse James My Father</u>, at 115.
43 *Liberty Tribune*, April 7, 1882.
44 *Liberty Tribune*, April 14, 1882.
45 The following was the original inscription on Jesse James' first gravestone at the family homestead. According to Elizabeth Beckett, a new tombstone replaced the initial one and bore the following words: *In Loving Remembrance of My Beloved Son, JESSE JAMES, Died April 3, 1882, Aged 34 Years, 6 Months, 28 Days, Murdered by a Traitor and Coward Whose Name is Not Worthy to Appear Here.* E-mail from Ms. Beckett to author dated February 3, 2012.

discussed that evening is not recorded. They certainly prayed.

The family was deeply entrenched in the faith of the Southern Baptist Church. Young Jesse's paternal grandfather, Robert James, a native of Kentucky, had been a Baptist minister and an original trustee of William Jewell College in Liberty, Missouri. His late father, Uncle Frank and all the other James children had been baptized in the faith of Reverend James. Jesse Jr. never knew his grandfather. Rev. James had gone to California to save souls where he tragically died in 1850. Or had he gone west to avoid the mother of his children?

It is probable the family gathered to reminisce about the martyred Jesse James. Little Jesse surely had many questions. Was his actual date of birth clarified for him? Did he learn that he had been born Jesse Edwards James on August 31, 1875 (not December 31st) in Nashville, Davidson County, Tennessee—the first born child to Jesse and Zerelda "Zee" James?[46] He was not a junior, as father and son did not share a common middle name. His father's middle name was Woodson while that of his son's was Edwards. Young Jesse's parents had chosen the middle name "Edwards" in honor, tribute and recognition of the Civil War Confederate veteran, author, editor, publicist and co-founder of the *Kansas City Times* (and to some the apologist of the James-Younger Gang), John Newman Edwards.[47]

As they conversed that evening, did they discuss that poor Jesse James had become united in death with his twin sons? Three years after Jesse Jr. was born, the family had moved to Waverly, Humphreys County, Tennessee, where Zee gave birth to twins named Gould and Montgomery. Tragically and to the devastation of their parents, they did not survive and died in infancy. Following their death, the James family returned to Nashville, where on July 27, 1879, Zee gave birth to their last child, Mary Susan; her middle name was given in honor of the sister of Frank and Jesse James, Susan.

---

46 Settle, at p. 129, gives the birth date as December 31st, while Jesse Jr. in Jesse James My Father, at p. 5, gave his birth date as August 31st. At least they both agreed on the same year, 1875. The mother of Jesse Jr., Zerelda Mimms James, was named after her mother-in-law, Zerelda Cole James Simms Samuel.

47 Throughout his life, Jesse Edwards James was frequently referred to by either his childhood alias "Tim" or by "Junior." In keeping with the legacy of junior, this book will hereinafter refer to young Jesse, as Jesse Jr., to distinguish him from his father, Jesse Woodson James.

Maybe Jesse Jr. shared thoughts of some of his own childhood memories. One of his earliest recollections dated to Valentine's Day when he was about five and while the family was residing in Nashville. His father's friend, Dick Liddle, had been staying with the family while the "bandit" was out of town. On that evening, young Jesse (then Timmy) heard noises on the front steps of their house. Liddle, hearing the same sound, immediately grabbed a double gage shotgun and fired one load through the door and then ran outside and disengaged another round. No one was injured, but the dramatic scene left an indelible image in the mind of little Jesse, Jr.[48] The traumatic incident would prove not to be the last time in which Jesse James exposed his children to criminals staying in the James household.

Little Jesse never questioned his parents' constant moves around the Midwest. It was certainly fresh in the little boy's mind that only two years before his father's death, the family had left Tennessee and moved to Kansas City where they first lived with his mother's sister and her husband, Charles McBride. Jesse Jr. may have recalled his father returning home after being away "on business," and announcing that they would be moving "to another town."[49] It proved not to be to another town but to another house in K.C., the Doggett House at Sixth and Walnut. There the James stayed for about two or three days before moving again to a residence on Woodland Street between 12th and 13th Streets. Other locations in which the family resided in Kansas City included a house on Troost Avenue between 10th and 11th Streets and on 9th Street between Michigan and Euclid. One could hear young Jesse inquiring how his late father had been injured since he had a noticeable limp and utilized a cane. To the little boy it surely could not have been a disguise.

Dialogue that evening perhaps included the family's unfortunate final move to St. Joseph, the city of death. Toward the end of 1881, the family departed Kansas City and moved to a new city. They first traveled through Leavenworth in route to Atchison, Kansas, where they rented a house. These plans were thwarted when Jesse James thought

48   Jesse James My Father, at p. 5.
49   *Ibid*, at p. 7.

he had been recognized, and out of precaution, he resettled his young family in St. Joseph on November 9th. They first rented a small house, but within two months Jesse James grew anxious once again. On Christmas Eve, he moved them to the one story, white painted cottage with green shutters on Lafayette Street. It was a perfect setting for those who desired neither revelations nor strangers. The house insulated the family from outsiders, but ironically not from insiders. It proved to be the last home in which the infamous or heroic Jesse James, dependent upon a person's personal bias then as it is now, and his family resided together—the spot where "the dirty little coward who shot Mister Howard," had "laid poor Jesse in his grave."

One can only surmise little Jesse's emotions, thoughts and feelings as he had listened to the funeral hymns, prayers and admonitions of Pastor Martin. He would have countless days to recall the instructional words of the minister: to be constantly and vigilantly prepared for the coming of Christ and death. As the young boy went to bed that night, memories, questions and queries had to have swirled through his mind. The son of the bandit slept in the childhood home of his late father, while the bandit himself lay outside his window "under the daisies."[50]

Stories circulated "here and abroad" as to the whereabouts of the victim's brother, Frank James. Reports funneled in that Frank was seen "skulking" about the woods in every town in Missouri seeking revenge. The victim's wife had insisted that she had not seen or heard from him for a long time.[51] Others disagreed. Some sources claimed on the day of his brother's funeral, "Frank James was in the house, having arrived on Tuesday night" so "he could in this way alone view the body with comparative safety."[52] The *St. Joseph Weekly Gazette* reported that on the day of the murder "Frank James was in the city determined on vengeance and had viewed the corpse at the undertakers."[53] The *Richmond Democrat* concurred by declaring "Frank James, who was always the shrewdest member of the gang, is . . . no doubt today in

50 *Weekly Missouri Republican*, April 13, 1882, St. Louis, Missouri.
51 *Liberty Tribune*, April 7, 1882, p. 2.
52 *The County Paper*, Supplement, April 14, 1882.
53 *St. Joseph Weekly Gazette*, April 5, 1882.

this section of the country."[54] Others insisted that Frank was either in Omaha, Leavenworth, or Kansas City. A news story out of St. Louis reported Frank had been seen in that city.[55] Those who personally knew Frank were convinced that he was still back east perhaps in Indiana, Baltimore or Nashville, Tennessee. James family members merely proclaimed that brother "Frank would let nobody know."[56]

Of all of the stories and tales of the older brother's location, the most sensational claim was that Frank had traveled the day after Jesse's funeral to the State Capitol in Jefferson City and murdered Governor Crittenden. The assassination story lit up the Associated Press wire like lightning during a spring storm in western Missouri. In response to this firestorm, the Governor's Press Secretary Finnis C. Farr replied quickly and firmly. "The report is nonsensical. The Governor is well."[57] Nevertheless, the "search" for Frank was becoming as engaging as the death of his younger brother. Did the Ford boys feel some apprehension that Frank would bestow his vengeance upon them?

As for Bob and Charlie Ford, Buchanan County Prosecutor O.M. Spencer had the brothers indicted on April 17, 1882 on the charge of first-degree murder. On arraignment before Judge Sherman, the killers immediately entered pleas of guilty. The judge promptly sentenced them to death by hanging; the date set was May 17th. Following their death-sentence, the Ford brothers laughingly and confidently walked out of the courtroom and returned to their jail cells with the full knowledge that they would soon be pardoned by Governor Crittenden. Their assessment was correct as later that evening the governor issued full pardons to each of them.[58] The mortal life of Jesse James was over. He was dead, but his memory would never die. His killer and co-conspirator had been allowed to go free. Many speculated that someone someday would come forward to avenge the murder of poor Mr. Howard. Would it be Frank or a total stranger? Perhaps it would be from a bullet to the coward's head or a shotgun blast to his belly.

54   *Richmond Democrat*, April 13, 1882, Richmond, Ray County, Missouri.
55   *Weekly Missouri Republican*, April 17, 1882.
56   *Weekly Missouri Republican*, April 13, 1882, *St. Louis Daily Globe-Democrat*, April 7, 1882.
57   *The Sedalia Weekly*, April 11, 1882.
58   *Omaha Daily Bee*, April 18, 1882; *St. Louis Daily Globe-Democrat*, April 19, 1882.

Dateline: Thursday, April 10, 1882
Lafayette Street, St. Joe

Headline:

GENERAL SHERMAN
HIS ARRIVAL IN THE CITY OF TOMBSTONE
BRILLIANT RECEPTION OF THE HERO OF ATLANTA[59]

By his death "Jesse James left a wife that'll moan all her life, the children that he left will pray," or so goes a chorus line from the "Ballad of Jesse James." The lyrics were not too far from the truth. The family was left mournful and penniless. Zee had no funds to feed her children, pay the rent or satisfy their creditors. She was forced to sell everything they owned. Following the funeral, she and the children returned to the city of their calamity. Zee took charge of her late husband's effects and prepared for a public auction.[60] When they arrived at the dwelling on Lafayette Street, they were greeted by a reception of relic seekers who had been attracted to the house like it was the tomb of a martyred saint or the grave of a general or hero.

The public auction was held at 2 o'clock on April 10th at the house in which the elder James had been murdered. Handbills had been previously circulated advertising that all the family's personal goods and one pistol were to be offered for sale. Thousands of people gathered at the home of the fallen man. Mr. Haire, the widow's attorney, charged an admission fee of ten cents for anyone to get a glimpse of the home or to bid on sale items. The proceeds were intended for the benefit of the widow and her children.[61]

The large crowd attending the auction included the Irish born, Oxford educated play- write, author, editor, poet and lecturer Oscar Wilde. He had been in the United States on a lecture tour in which he had been criticizing Americans for being "great hero worshipers and always taking heroes from the criminal class." Ironically, when

59 *The Tombstone Epitaph*, April 10, 1882, Tombstone, Arizona Territory.
60 *Weekly Missouri Republican*, April 13, 1882.
61 *Liberty Tribune*, April 14, 1882.

Wilde heard the report of the killing of the noted bandit, he, too, made the "pilgrimage" and was at center stage for the auction.[62]

The multitude assembled for the auction did not generate large revenues. Some proved to be artifact hunters while others purchased such items as worthless furniture, the rickety husk-bottom chair in which Jesse James had been standing at the time of the shooting, a small revolver and an old valise. Sadly, the puppy brought home days before the murder was among the auction items sold bringing one of the highest prices paid—$15—the last gift Jesse Jr. ever received from his father. Overall bids were very low and the public sale proved unprofitable for Zee and her two children.[63]

The majority in attendance was not attracted by a desire to purchase personal property. They were more interested in touring the house and seizing souvenirs. Collectors were seen ripping apart pieces of the house, removing planks from the fence or pocketing items lying around; two cartridge belts were stolen. Oscar Wilde witnessed the events and recorded in a letter what he observed that morning from his hotel window. They assembled, Wilde wrote, at "the house of the great train-robber and murderer, Jesse James, mourning over his death and buying relics" as if he had been a saint. He saw the "crowd of people" pulling the house "all down." Wilde's editorial viewpoint on criminal hero worship in America, including his own, had been vindicated.[64]

The press added commentaries about the posterity and future significance of the house as well. The *Kansas City Daily Times* on April 4th opined that the house would "go to ornament the pages of history when the chronicles of this great and mighty country are written and handed down to posterity. As one of the few places of interest, it will be an object of curiosity to the people of this great country." This prediction was as true then as it is today. Hundreds upon hundreds of curiosity seekers came to the house on the day Jesse was shot, thousands gathered for the auction, and the interest in the house has

---

62 Yeatman, Ted, at p. 272; The Best Writings of the Notorious Outlaw Jesse James, editor Harold Dillinger, The Globe Pequot Press, Guilford, Connecticut, 2007, unnumbered page in preface.

63 Breihen, Carl, at p. 182; see also, *Weekly Missouri Republican*, April 13, 1882.

64 Yeatman, Ted, at p. 272; The Best Writings of the Notorious Outlaw Jesse James, editor Harold Dillinger, The Globe Pequot Press, Guilford, Connecticut, 2007, unnumbered page in preface.

continued for over 130 years. In some ways, the residence has become like a shrine to honor and pay tribute to Jesse James—to some, a hero; to some, a martyr; and to others, an infamous scoundrel. Regardless of the reasons why they came to the James home, they did, and have continued to do so to this date.

(The Jesse James Auction: "Selling Little Timmy's puppy")

Zee and her small children suffered considerably. Even after the auction, they had little more than the clothes on their backs. There was no buried treasure; there was no "trust" fund; no secret bank box or account existed. The orphaned family was forced into an impoverished life while Jesse Jr. was thrust into a premature adulthood as the new "man" of the fatherless family. The small James boy at such a young age would now begin experiencing life under his true identity—the son, and oldest child, of the famous criminal and outlaw, Jesse James.

Dateline: Thursday, April 13, 1882
Kansas City, Missouri

Headline:

A MILLION <u>FOR</u> EDUCATION
THE GENEROUS GIFT OF JOHN P. SLATER
A CONNECTICUT MANUFACTURER GIVES $1,000,000
FOR THE EDUCATION OF THE COLORED PEOPLE IN THE
SOUTH—EX-PRESIDENT HAYES, CHIEF JUSTICE WAITE
<u>JOHN A. SLATER AND OTHERS TO BE TRUSTEES</u>[65]

It was chiefly from the generosity extended by the widow's family in Kansas City that she and her young, destitute family had a roof over their head. They arrived in the city on April 13, 1882 and took up temporary residence with her sister, Mrs. McBride, on East 17th Street.[66] That same afternoon, a reporter from the *Kansas City Journal* found Zee at her sister's house and requested an interview. The grieving widow was dressed in mourning attire of "pleasing appearance" with blond colored hair. Though clearly distraught, she consented to being questioned. The journalist described her two "tender years" children as a boy possessing "more intelligence than lads his age" and a little girl who resembled her mother. During the dialogue, Zee referred to the Ford boys as traitors, but when asked about her late husband, her voice cracked with emotion and tears filled her eyes. She spoke of the deep seeded love she and Jesse had for one another. She adamantly insisted that rumors of her brother-in-law Frank James being in Missouri were simply "absurd." She emphatically declared not having seen him since the previous September when Frank had visited her and Jesse at their home on Troost Ave. in Kansas City. No, she did not have millions of dollars of ill-gotten money; such claims were simply "not true." They only had enough funds to relocate to Kansas City where she would be staying with her sister for the "present."[67]

---

65   *New York Tribune*, April 13, 1882.
66   *Weekly Missouri Republican*, April 14, 1882, St. Louis, Missouri.
67   *Ibid.*

Thereafter, their financial plight forced Zee and her two children to move in with her single brother, Tom Mimms. "Lots of people thought my father left us rich, [b]ut nothing could be further from the truth," Jesse Jr. would later write.[68] If not for "Uncle Tom," it would have been unimaginable what would have happened to the family.[69] Zee and the kids received aid from other relations, especially her mother-in-law and other James' kinfolk who lived on the "other side" of the Missouri River. Yet, their combined efforts were not enough to help the widow James overcome her husband's death. For the rest of her life she suffered. She donned only black clothing; she never remarried; she seldom socialized unless with relatives; she became a recluse; she suffered long-term illnesses and melancholy; but she held steadfast to her Christian values. Her only pleasure was her two children—children of her poor dead husband.

The new life of Jesse Jr. was drastically and instantly thrust upon him by his father's death. How would the bandit's past impact his son? Perhaps the immortal line from Act III, Scene V of Shakespeare's *Merchant of Venice* would prove to be a haunting foreshadowing of his future: "The sins of the father are to be laid upon the children."

---

68   James, Stella Frances, In the Shadow of Jesse James, edited by Milton F. Perry, The Revolver Press, 1979 at p. 8.

69   *Ibid.*

CHAPTER III
GROWING-UP IN AN ADOPTED CITY

———◄◉►———

Datelines: 1883-1897
Kansas City, Missouri

Headlines:

<u>**1883, HAPPY NEW YEAR**</u>
NEW YEAR'S CEREMONIES
<u>*AT THE WHITE HOUSE*[70]</u>

<u>**GREETINGS OF THE SEASON**</u>
TO THE CITIZENS OF OREGON
<u>*AND HOLT COUNTY*[71]</u>

O ver the course of the ensuing fifteen years, the impoverished condition of the dead man's widow and children made celebrating the holiday seasons very challenging. Their financial difficulties fell directly upon the shoulders of the fatherless boy, which directly compromised his education. He attended so many different elementary schools, including Morse, Woodland, Linwood and Webster, that it paralleled his childhood residences. One classmate, Emmet O'Malley, described young Jesse as hardworking, industrious student, but his schooling was subordinate to earning an income for his family.[72] Jesse ultimately graduated from Central High School in Kansas City, but his class attendance was an on again, off again part-time experience. In "years that boys generally attend school" Jesse Jr. "was at work earning wages for the support of my widowed mother and the education of my fatherless sister."[73] The

---

70 *Sedalia Weekly Bazoo*, January 2, 1883.
71 *The Holt County Sentinel*, December 31, 1897.
72   Meriwether, Lee, <u>Jim Reed Senatorial Immortal</u>, Mound City Press 1948, at p. 23.
73 *Kansas City Journal*, June 14, 1899.

bandit's son had become the surrogate head of the family.

When Jesse Jr. was eleven years old, he took his first official job. It was a part-time position at the Bee-Hive Department Store in Kansas City. He worked there for about one year until he answered an advertisement in one of the local newspapers. The article announced an opening for an office boy at Crittenden & Phister Real Estate Company, a local real estate company. The boy promptly filled out the application. Ironically, one of the partners of the firm was Thomas T. Crittenden, Jr. It had been his father, Governor Crittenden, who had issued the reward for the capture of the applicant's outlaw father and uncle back in 1881. It is quite likely that at such a young age the lad failed to understand the familial relationship between the firm's partner, Thomas T. Crittenden,

(Thomas T. Crittenden, Jr.)

Jr., and the former chief executive who had issued the "Wanted Poster" (a man many considered, at least partly, responsible for the death of Jesse James). There was no question that the former governor's son realized the strange coincidence. He offered Jesse Jr. the job, but it was conditioned upon the approval and consent of the young boy's mother and paternal grandmother. The perspective employer knew the James family had always considered his father as culpable as the Ford Brothers in having murdered the child's pa. Despite their bitterness, mother and grandmother allowed little Jesse to go to work for the son of the former governor.

Jesse Jr. reportedly enjoyed working for Crittenden. He garnered "lots of experiences and some wonderful friendships."[74] The young boy stayed with Crittenden's company for over one year before taking a clerk's position at the Germania Life Insurance Company. On June 12, 1891, and only three months after having gone to work for Germania, the "head of the family" was hired as a timekeeper and stock taker at the Armour Packing Co. where he remained employed for the next six years. The position not only provided an employment opportunity, but also a chance to play baseball for the company team. Jesse was a good athlete. He was a member of the local YMCA and had become noted for his talents in the new sport of basketball—but baseball was his best sport. One of his co-workers and teammates on the Armour Baseball Club was the future Chicago Cubs Hall of Fame shortstop, Joe Tinker.[75]

In 1893, Jesse Jr. like all Americans greatly wanted to attend the social and cultural event of the Century—the Chicago World's Fair, known as the World's Columbian Exposition. It was an extravaganza to celebrate and mark the 400th Anniversary of the discovery of America by Christopher Columbus. Despite the economic downturn in the country that year, it seemed as though everyone longed to attend the six-month event in the "White City." The fatherless boy was not alone in his desire to make the pilgrimage to Chicago. Millions of tourists flocked to the City on Lake Michigan, and Jesse Jr. struggled to find a way to journey to the utopian village created for the momentous occasion. To make the trip, he was compelled to sell "an old coat, a belt and a few other items that belonged to his father to the manager of the Libby Prison Museum."[76]

74 James, Stella, at p. 10.
75 *Ibid.* Tinker was part of the famous double-play combination: Tinker to Evers to Chance. In 1908, Tinker and his well-known infield partners proved to be a key component and reason for the Chicago Cubs winning the World Series that year—the last world championship ever won by the Cubs.
76 Ventimiglia, Jack, "Miles", Jesse James in the County of Clay, The Friends of the James Farm, Kearney, Missouri, 2001, at pp. 95-96, and citing Crittenden, Huston, H., "*The Crittenden Memoirs*", G. P. Putnam's Sons, New York, 1936, at pp. 249-250. The venue in Chicago became known as the White City, a reference to the architectural design and motif of the structures contained within the village—all of which were painted white (not to mention becoming the location of the largest serial killer in American history, some of whom claim took over fifty lives—for more reading on the Fair and the murders, see, Larson, Erik, Devil in the White City, Vintage Books, a Division of Random House, Inc., New York, 2004). As to the Libby Prison, it had been a Confederate prisoner of war camp in Richmond, Virginia. The museum however was located in Chicago, Illinois where it housed Civil War artifacts, and it was in

The hard work ethics and perseverance of Jesse Jr. gained him the attention, and perhaps affection, of Thomas T. Crittenden, Jr. He saw Jesse Jr. as a promising young man. Or was it a sense of personal guilt for his father's prior deed? Because of the affiliation and friendship that had developed between the two men, Crittenden sold land to Zee and financed the construction loan for a new family home located at 2402 Tracy Avenue, located on the east side in Kansas City. Mother and Sister Mary were totally dependent upon the young man, including the associations in which he had made from his various jobs.

The boy was a knight in the eyes of many community leaders. He had supported his mother and sister, and had even rescued the elderly. On November 9, 1897, he had come to the aid of an old man who had been knocked down by an assailant. Jesse Jr. fought off the culprit and turned him over to the police.[77] By the end of the same year, Jesse's income had allowed his little sister to remain in school. He hoped that by the end of the 1898 school year she, too, would graduate high school from his own alma mater.

Much had changed for Jesse Jr., his widowed mother and young sister in those years after they had relocated to Kansas City following his father's death. Many things had also changed in their adopted hometown as well.

---

operation from 1889-1899. See, Chicago Historical Society Northwestern University Wet With Blood, at www.chicagohistory.org/wetwithblood/bloody/libby/index.htm.

77   Pence, Samuel, A., I Knew Frank I Wish I Had Known Jesse, Two Trails Publishing, Independence, Missouri, 1997, at p. 397.

CHAPTER IV

K.C. AT THE TWILIGHT OF THE 19ᵀᴴ CENTURY

———◦«(◦)»◦———

Dateline: Circa January 1, 1898
Kansas City, Missouri

Headline:

IT WAS A MERRY CHRISTMAS AND
NOW THE JOURNAL EXTENDS A
<u>HAPPY NEW YEAR TO ALL</u>.[78]

The *Journal* proudly ushered in the New Year on the 1ˢᵗ day of January 1898 to a city that boasted a population of over 160,000 and a reputation for commercial and economic growth. Its geographic area had so greatly expanded that the city extended from the Missouri River on the north to 49ᵗʰ Street on the south, and from the Kansas River on the west in the West Bottoms to Topping Ave. on the east. The State of Missouri, with two metropolitan cities both situated on great rivers on its eastern and western borders, like bookends, was politically at its zenith with seventeen electoral votes. St. Louis situated on the Mississippi River had a population of more than 575,000 residents, and it was the fourth largest city in the country (ranking only behind New York, Chicago and Philadelphia).[79] The hometown that Jesse Jr. had embraced, the city on the western border, was witnessing the sun's

---

78   *Kansas City Journal*, January 1, 1898.
79   Missouri Secretary of State, Winn, Kenneth, H., "IT ALL ADDS UP: Reform and the Erosion of Representative Government in Missouri 1900-2000." <u>Official Manual of the State of Missouri</u>, 1999-2000, at p. 30.

setting on the Gilded Age and the rising on what Ray Stannard Baker described as the age of the "Great American Renascence."[80] So much had changed since the summer of 1882 when Jesse Jr., his widowed mother and little sister had taken up residency in the city.

By 1898, the natural terrain and the Missouri River valley had fostered Kansas City's expansion into two separate and distinct business centers. The formation and advancement of both districts were directly tied to the river. The older area, originally called "Kawsmouth" or "French Bottoms" (and by 1898, the "West Bottoms"), was nestled in the valley of the confluence of the Missouri and Kansas (or Kaw) Rivers. Francois Chouteau had first established this region in the early 1800's as a prominent junction for the western river mountain trade and the fur trapping industry. The eastern edge of the West Bottoms was fenced-in by a large commanding bluff in which the downtrodden and poor lived in squalor, while its northern border and western borders were guarded by the Missouri and Kansas Rivers. By 1869 the northern river boundary proved no longer to be a barrier. That summer, the Hannibal Bridge ("or the "immortal bridge") opened thereby linking the northern bank of the Missouri River to the Bottoms, and the Bottoms to the American Continent.

The city's other business district was nestled along the southern banks of the wide Missouri River. It held a commanding, panoramic view of the West Bottoms to its west and the Missouri River to its north. Like the Bottoms, this area's economic history was directly connected to the river. Frenchman Gabriel Prudhomme (spelled "Predom" in the original land patent) originally owned the land, but after he was killed in a tavern fight it developed into a commercial port. With the advent of steamships navigating the 'Ole Muddy River,' the natural limestone rock and configuration of the terrain formed the perfect location for a riverboat landing. The levy was initially called Westport Landing and later became known as the Town of Kansas. It served as the drop-off point for all trade traveling up the Missouri River or for goods and provisions that were freighted some four to five miles south

---

80   Traxel, David, Crusader Nation, The United States in Peace and the Great War 1898 to 1920, Alfred A. Knopf, 2007 at p. 3.

to the outfitting community of Westport.

Since the 1850's, city fathers had implemented drastic measures to modify the physical terrain of the city in an attempt to encourage economic development. By the turn of the century, the hills, cliffs, bluffs and gullies that had once majestically rose and fell, and rose and fell again along the southern bank of the Missouri River had been leveled, cleared and excavated. It had required perseverance and energy to remove each obstacle encountered during the massive earth-moving project. The result of these Herculean efforts produced a construction boom of buildings, grain elevators, skyscrapers, factories, theaters, industrial towns, parks, paved streets, boulevards, cabled streetcars and residential houses. Kansas City was the second largest railroad center in the United States consisting of approximately fifty thousand miles of tracks. These rails connected the city to almost every part of the country, and proved to be a leading reason for the city's expansion and growth. Kansas City was no longer just a river town; it had become a railroad metropolis.

The Civil War (for the James family and others who had struggled for the "cause" it was known as the War of Northern Aggression) had ended nearly thirty-five years earlier, and Kansas City was no longer the jumping off point for western migration. With its abundant natural resources and its strategic location in the heart of America, it had become a leading meatpacking, cattle town, and hub for railroads darting across the continent. The city had also experienced a substantial growth in manufacturing and industry. Factories, mills, grain elevators, and smelters in the West Bottoms stood as sentinels over the Missouri River. The extensive railroad lines, train junctions and crossings supported various factory towns, such as Manchester, Sheffield and Leeds, a coal mining community. These advancements were integral to the expansionism and growing expectations of a city that had earned its new reputation as the 'Pittsburgh of the West' and as such the new gateway to the west.[81]

Those who traveled south and crossed the Hannibal Bridge by

81 Manchester is located about 40 Hwy. and Raytown Road; Sheffield was located near 14-35 and Independence Ave; and Leeds is located at approximately Raytown Road and Stadium Drive (south of the K.C. Truman Sports Complex).

train found their destination point on Union Avenue in the heart of the West Bottoms. There stood Union Depot, a mammoth, ornate Victorian-styled station that had first opened on April 7, 1878. It was described as the "handsomest and largest railroad depot west of New York." Everything was available on the cobblestone-paved thoroughfares of the bottoms. Pedestrians along Union Avenue, Mulberry Street and St. Louis Avenue had to dodge electric streetcars. These avenues were lined with "saloons, curio shops, news stands, cigar stands, and everything to attract the tourists."[82] For men, the 'soiled doves' provided services for hire every day or night of the week within the various bawdy houses that lined the alleyways.[83] The area also served as the center for the grain and cattle markets, stockyards, factories, slaughterhouses and milling operations.

(The West Bottoms, Electric Cars & Union Depot)
(Courtesy Jackson County Historical Society)

There was a convenient "escape" route from the odoriferous stench that emitted from the packing plants, stockyards, and those seedy

---

82   Haskell, Harry, Boss-Busters & Sin Hounds, Kansas City and Its Star, at p. 2, The Curators of the University of Missouri Press, 2007.
83   The term "soiled dove" was another Nineteenth Century word for prostitute.

joints that lined the avenues. A magnificent lofty-cabled car ascended and descended from Union Depot and directly over the roof of the Wabash Freight House. The line connected the West Bottoms to the city's other commercial district located above and beyond its eastern bluffs. The descent or ascent dependent upon the direction traveled consisted of an incline or decline of over eighteen feet for every one hundred feet traveled. A passenger certainly skilled in Shakespearean prose metaphorically compared the trip to the bluff's bottoms to traveling down Pike's Peak causing her *"hair to stand on end like quills upon the fretful porcupine."*[84]

Like the older Bottoms the younger business district, too, was a thriving business community. It began at the levy on the Missouri River (formerly the landing or Westport Landing) and included the city's second train depot, Grand Central Station, located at 2nd and Wyandotte Street, which had opened in 1890. Grand Central initially opened for passengers traveling between Independence on the east and Argentine, Kansas on the west, but by the end of the 1890's, the railroad line had expanded southward to the Gulf of Mexico. Train travelers disembarking at Grand Central had a compelling southern view of the city's new skyline and the famous Hotel Savoy. This part of the city had evolved into the government and commercial business center.

By 1898, this second business district had begun to supplant the West Bottoms in promoting new businesses (floods in the bottoms had been a constant irritant for decades). A public market near city hall attracted farmers and their families for miles. Commercial business grew with the construction of impressive "skyscraper" buildings such as the seven-story New England Building, the seven-story Board of Trade and the ten-story New York Life Building. Marquee hotels, such as the Hotel Savoy, Midland Hotel, Pacific House, Lynch Hotel, Centropolis Hotel, Coates House Hotel, and old Delmonico's provided the finest in accommodations to travelers and business guests to the city.

A commitment to a strong governmental infrastructure and legal system had been at the foundation of the history of Jackson County

---

84   The young traveler was quoting the "Ghost" of Hamlet's father: Hamlet: Act I, Scene V.

since it was first established in 1826. While Independence remained the County Seat, a position it held since 1827—and still does, Kansas City had matured and developed into the county's de facto governmental capitol. The federal courthouse, a three story, two columned Victorian structure located at Ninth and Walnut had opened in 1884. Two blocks away stood the Jackson County Courthouse at the corner of Missouri Avenue (6th Street) and Locust. The building and its accompanying turrets made an imposing sight. A few blocks to the west stood the ornately constructed City Hall at the corner of Fifth Street and Main. Both buildings began serving the public in 1892 and each personified the city's governmental control over the county.[85]

The court system received an educational boost when the Kansas City School of Law was chartered in 1895. The following year the doors to the law school opened where classes were held inside the New York Life Building on 9th Street. It had been founded as a lawyers' school as practitioners of the profession and members of the judiciary voluntarily taught evening classes. The law program was designed to allow students to work by day and study under the direction of lawyers and judges by night. Its curriculum was initially a two-year course of studies with lectures and classes being held in the evening and after the close of business. In 1897, a third year program was added to award the degree of "Masters of Law." Applicants for admission were required to be proficient in the English language and to possess the equivalent of a high school diploma.[86]

Kansas City had grown into an urbanized community. Electric lights had been installed throughout the city, and with its population explosion and business expansion several telephone exchanges had been added. Civic Leader Robert Gillham had played a pivotal role in establishing the city's streetcar and cable car system. With well-over twenty thousand daily passengers, it ranked second only to San Francisco. The public transportation lines traversed from the river on the north towards Westport in the south at ground speeds of up to

---

85   The original Jackson County Courthouse in Kansas City had been destroyed by a tornado in 1886.
86   Whitney, Carrie, W., Kansas City, Missouri: Its History And Its People 1808-1908, Vol. 1, The S. J. Clarke Publishing Co., 1908 at pp. 471-472.

nine miles per hour. Charles Dudley Warner, a well-known contributor of the *Harper's New Monthly Magazine*, wrote that no city had been built up as solidly as Kansas City or had grown more substantially. To Warner, the "most exciting feature of the city was how the cable cars climbed such steeps that plunged down such grades and penetrated and whizzed through crowded thoroughfares" keeping "the rider in a perpetual exhilaration."[87]

(New York Life Building 1890's)
(Courtesy Jackson County Historical Society)

Leading civic-minded professionals and business leaders shared a common commitment designed to achieve the goal and theme of the Commercial Club: "Make Kansas City a Good Place to Live In." Meetings were held at the University Club, Kansas City Club, Chamber of Commerce and other similar venues. The purposes of these organizations were to promote philanthropic causes, contribute to parks and public improvement projects, foster economic development, and establish a national reputation for progressivism.

These community activists and leaders possessed significant wealth and notoriety. They included the millionaire philanthropist, William Volker; the lumber baron, R. A. Long; the great public benefactor,

---

87   Montgomery, Rick and Shirl Kasper, <u>Kansas City An American Story</u>, Kansas City Books, Kansas City, Missouri 1999 at p. 122.

Col. Thomas H. Swope (who in 1896 had given the city the park that bears his name to this day); the Baron of Brush Creek, William Rockhill Nelson (the owner and founder of the evening *Kansas City Star*); landscape and design architects, George E. Kessler and Henry Van Brunt;[88] and a smelting plant owner, August R. Meyer (born in St. Louis to German immigrant parents). Meyer accomplished as much by his public speaking as Nelson did by his *Star* editorials. Through donations from these philanthropists coupled with revenues raised by voter approved bond initiatives, tax levies and condemnation proceedings, the city had created funding sources to enhance public parks, such as Swope Park and Troost Park; to design and construct a comprehensive boulevard system that utilized the atheistic advantages of the regions natural terrain; to construct sanitary water and sewer systems; and to build public facilities, including the newly opened public library at 9th & Locust, a fifty-room sanitarium at 11th & Locust for the infirm, and a convention hall projected to open by February of the next year (the Armour Meat Packing Company even offered to donate one of its prized Hereford's to be auctioned to the public to raise additional money for the convention center). These promoters were committed to a big city mental attitude. It was as if everything was up-to-date in Kansas City.

Residents of the city were afforded a large array of entertainment options. These ranged from sports and social events to theatre and opera house performances. The advancement of the park and boulevard system enhanced the popularity of baseball, football, bicycling, horse racing, swimming, shooting galleries and golf. Exposition Park proved a popular baseball venue. Readers anxiously and regularly followed reports of athletes and scores covered by the local press; everyone needed to know the outcome of the game between the Jayhawks of Lawrence and the Tigers of Columbia. Sports fans devoured the daily results

---

88 Harvard educated and a member of the American Institute of Architectural Van Brunt moved to Kansas City about 1887 where he continued his national renowned for his architectural design work. He was the only architect involved in the 1893 world's fair held in Chicago (known as the World's Columbian Exposition) not from New York or Chicago. The exposition was an international fair celebrating the 400th anniversary of Columbus' discovery of America. Larson, Eric, <u>Devil in the White City</u>, Vintage Books, a Division of Random House, Inc. 2004, at p. 78.

posted of horse races, bowling (or ten pin) leagues with their strikes (X) and spares (/), and most importantly box scores of every pro-baseball franchise, company team and social club. The first golf course, Evanston Golf Club near Fairmount Park, was a very rough course that had opened within the last couple of years. Rumor abounded that Frank James had been seen playing golf on the new course (but there had been 'iron-clad' stories back in 1882 that Frank had been in almost every town and city on the day his brother Jesse was killed).

The Kansas City community strongly supported the various opera houses, theatres and stage productions where entertainers from New York, Boston and San Francisco performed. The papers regularly advertised and promoted concerts, ballets, operas and other entertainment at the famous Coates Opera House, across the street from the hotel of the same name, the Gillis Opera House, and the Grand Opera House or at other venues and theatres in the city.[89] An advertisement announcing an upcoming concert by John Phillips Sousa was of particular interest and brought great excitement to an adoring public. Debating societies and lecture courses were extremely popular among the educated, high browed and religious organizations. Readers anxiously followed the intrigues of the "rich and famous" in the "high society pages" and tracked journalistic reviews of every theatrical show or performance. Who had been seen shopping at the prestigious Emery Bird & Thayer was a commonly raised question. This idol watching ranged from the gala events of the philanthropic, celebrities and social reformers to the gatherings of the F.F.V. (First Families of Virginia) and the festivities and parades of the Priests of Pallas.[90] Following the movements and

---

89 The last performance held at the opera house was "Heart and Sword." Fifteen minutes after its last performance on the night of January 31, 1901 the theatre was destroyed by fire.

90 The Priests of Pallas fall harvest festival originated in Kansas City on October 13, 1887. By 1898, it attracted enormous crowds. Newspaper reporters wrote about the celebration in a breathless fashion. Everyone was captivated by the annual weeklong event (even President Grover Cleveland while touring the Midwest had once attended). The theme of the extravaganza was to celebrate the harvest where goddess Athena and the priests of her court returned each year to the city she found destined for greatness. The marquee moment of the annual fall event was the lighted parade of floats that was highlighted by a float honoring Athena herself. The event was held from 1887-1912, and from 1922-1925 (the Jackson County Historical Society, in association with the Westport Historical Society, brought the excitement back to the city from 2006-2008. See, Spencer, Thomas, M., "Priests of Pallas: Kansas City's Forgotten Fall Festival," Jackson County Historical Society Journal, Autumn 2003, at p. 11.

doings of the city's elite and stars on the stages was magnetic and captivating to consumers.

Kansas City at the turn of the century also had its seedy side. Reformers proclaimed that the city remained "too wide open." Too many saloons were granted dram shop licenses to dispense rum, whiskey and beer at all hours of the day and night. They complained police failed to corral the 'soiled doves' who were allowed to prowl in protected "red light districts" in the West Bottoms or along the levy. The moral decay they protested was fully illustrated by an obsession with gambling. There were slot machines and other gambling devices, like roulette, in various saloons, taverns and businesses. Money was waged at prizefights, horse races or over billiard and pool tables and dog fights (outcomes of which were sometimes printed). Of the many games of chance played in the town, cards, especially faro and poker, remained the mainstay where it was regularly played in back rooms of taverns or over card tables in the local saloons. For the social elite they, too, enjoyed a new card game, Bridge. Surely, they wagered bets on Bridge. To the reformers, cards, whether gambled upon or not, was simply the "Devil's Ticket."

Newspaper owners and party affiliations dominated politics during the "Gay Nineties." Editorials covered every world, national and local issue and they were not hesitant to express opinions or criticism, both biased and non-biased. There were no ethical rules or requirements for newspapers, reporters or newsmen to remain objective. The print media was principally noted for its political allegiance, party preference or identification. Some were considered as nothing more than "organ" of a political party or boss. Political intrigue was reported and covered like baseball and football scores. The newspapers in Jackson County included the *Kansas City Journal, Kansas City Times, Kansas City World* (located at 1116-1118 Oak), *Daily Record, Jackson Examiner, Independence Sentinel*, (the latter two operated out of Independence) and the two-cent daily evening newspaper, located at 11th & Grand, and owned by William Rockhill Nelson, the *Kansas City Evening Star*. Nelson's paper had earned a reputation as one of the leading progressive daily publications in the United States, behind Joseph Pulitzer's *New York Times* and William Randolph Hearts' yellow journalist paper, the *New York Journal.* Journalist Charles Austin Bates opined that the *Star* was one of America's four greatest evening newspapers.[91]

The most significant part of the dynamics of the political process in Jackson County was the command and control of the voting boxes by political bosses. It was frequently stated that the art of politics was very much the art of corruption. Both wealthy businessmen (not all of them) and some everyday folks participated in bribery schemes to garner favors.[92] This was the case despite the crusading efforts of Nelson and other progressive journalists, including the clergy, who were clamoring to end the reign of bossism and dishonesty.

While members of the Republican Party had their clubs and societies, including the American Protective Association (known for its anti-immigrant, anti-Catholic sentiments), the governance of the county's Democratic Party centered upon two "well-oiled" political machines. Both organizations had strong, influential boss leadership who coveted their patronage clout. Jim Pendergast, a gregarious and bigger-than-life city alderman from the First Ward and owner of the Climax Saloon located in the West Bottoms, reined over one group. His adherents were known as the "Pendergast Goats." Joseph Shannon was the formidable leader of the other political association, and his supporters were identified as the "Shannon Rabbits." These two factional chiefs were loyal family men, Irish Catholics and operated polarized Democratic political operations. They could also be counted on to deliver strong voter turnout on election days—voters held in their pockets. The Rabbits and Goats may have battled during primary season but they generally, not always, united their political voting clout in defeating Republicans during a general election.

The Pendergast Goats ruled the West Bottoms and the north end area of Kansas City (near the levy), which by the late 1890's was

---

91 Haskel, Harry, Boss-Busters & Sin Hounds at p. 33.
92 Missouri Secretary of State, Winn, Kenneth, H., "IT ALL ADDS UP: Reform and the Erosion of Representative Government in Missouri 1900-2000." Official Manual of the State of Missouri, 1999-2000, at p. 29.

noted for its large influx of Italian immigrants. As emigrants made their entry into these sections of the city, the "Goats" were out in front providing much needed support and assistance. Their paternalism helped forge and cement strong loyalties. Shannon and his block employed the same "good will" tactics by providing aid and relief to newcomers, especially those of Irish descent. The electoral power of the "Rabbits" was principally situated in the southern portion of the city, including the newly annexed Westport area. The combined voting power of the Goats and Rabbits was so pronounced that Nelson and especially the editors of the *Journal* referred to them derogatorily as the "gangs."

In addition to their domination over suffrage, both political machines were supported and aided by significant legal talent. The Pendergast Goats touted the genius of James A. Reed, an up and coming star on the political horizon. Local politicians often denominated Reed the "Bosky Dell," a nickname referring to his speeches as often being "too flowery."[93] The Shannon Rabbits, too, had their accompaniment of mouthpieces. Foremost among their legal battery was another Irishman, Frank W. Walsh. Neither Reed nor Walsh had been strangers to one another. For years, they had stood at opposite poles battling one another in the courtroom or in political circles. By the start of 1899, they would find themselves pitted in an intensive, media-filled and public conscious case that would dwarf all of their previous political squabbles and legal battles combined.

On the state and local level, the press debated whether the governor of Missouri or the mayor and city council of Kansas City should control the city's police department. The "blue laws" prohibiting businesses from opening on Sundays were puritanically, vigorously supported or hotly challenged. Political reformation of the boss system was singularly the leading battle cry of Nelson and his *Star*. Numerous commentaries, pro and con, were expressed on the recently enacted Missouri law making train robbery a capital crime—punishable by death.[94] The city council's new "curfew ordinance" proved to be yet

---

93   Meriwether, at p. 22.

94   1895 the Missouri General Assembly had made train robbery a capital offense. Rev. St. 1899, §1955

another controversial bone of contention. Reformers championed this new law, which by 1898 had been enacted in most urban communities in the U.S. The purpose of the legislation was to keep juveniles under the age of sixteen from loafing, loitering or remaining on streets or other public places, without a lawful purpose (after nine o'clock in the summer and eight thirty in the winter). Fire station alarm bells sounded the city wide warning each evening as a constant reminder of the curfew hour. Those who failed to comply were removed to the police court for their "sin."[95] Antagonists to the "curfew ordinance" insisted that elected officials were interfering in areas where parents, not city fathers, should be the sole decision maker for their children. The debate rages to this day.

The leading national and international stories in January 1898 were diverse and ominous. On the home front, the U.S. was enjoying significant technological advancements in electricity, communications and manufacturing. Rail transportation moved citizens and products across the continent, and the country had been free of warfare for over thirty years. Despite these internal successes, the country faced serious obstacles including overcrowded cities, poor working conditions, strikes and labor disputes, farm failures and discrimination (especially, towards Blacks and immigrants). With mid-term elections scheduled in the fall, President William McKinley's domestic agenda would be carefully scrutinized and Congressional action would be closely monitored.

At the same time, controversial debate raged over American foreign policy. The leading issues were protective tariffs, immigration and annexation (particularly, Puerto Rico and the Hawaiian Islands). As war clouds began to encircle the globe from Europe to Asia, imperialism

---

(Missouri Revised Statutes, 1895). Missouri was not alone in making train robbery a crime punishable by death or imprisonment. In 1897, New Mexico Territory in 1897 adopted the same law (§1151 Compiled Laws of 1897). By the summer of 1900, the Missouri Supreme Court, *in dicta*, declared that the law making train robbery a crime punishable by death or imprisonment did not constitute cruel or unusual punishment in violation of the Constitution. State v. Stubblefield, 157 Mo. 360, 58 S.W. 337 (Mo. 1900). The New Mexico Territory Supreme Court concurred with the Missouri Supreme Court the following year in Territory v. Ketchum, 65 P. 169 (N.M. Terr., Feb. 1901).

95 *Kansas City Journal*, August 28, 1898; and also see, "The School Journal, Vol. 60," at p. 554 (1900) at google.books.

became the most dominant and divisive international issue to polarize the country. Political hawks, including Assistant Navy Secretary Theodore Roosevelt and Senator Henry "Cabot" Lodge of Massachusetts, along with the yellow journalist William Randolph Hearst, owner and editor of the *New York Journal*, led the cry for American expansionism and world domination (Free Cuba, *Cuba Libre* filled the headlines of Hearst's *Journal*).[96] These protagonists demanded U.S. intervention in the Philippines and in the Cuban nationalists' struggle to gain independence from Spain. They insisted America should intercede in that embattled island the same way in which France had aided the country during the American Revolution.

Antagonists to imperialism and warfare had strong political and civic supporters. The powerful Republican Speaker of the U.S. House Thomas Reed of Ohio, the famous Harvard psychology and philosophy professor, William James and Harvard President Charles William Eliot, among others, cautioned restraint and encouraged resistance to conflict. Even President McKinley hoped for a negotiated resolution to the Spanish crises and a movement away from the fever pitch of war. As the New Year opened, the relationship between Spain and America was deteriorating. Their animosity would soon reach a climatic explosion as a second rate American Battleship, the Maine, was being dispatched to the harbor in Havana, Cuba. The Maine that January was on a course to destiny.

These global and national issues did not impede the deep sense of patriotism and national pride Americans felt during the decade of the 'Gay Nineties.' The Pledge of Allegiance was written in 1892; "America the Beautiful" was first sung in 1896; Memorial Day (called Decoration Day) celebrations honoring veterans of the Civil War became annual events; Grand Army of Republic ("GAR") and other veteran reunions united the blue and gray in festivals of national reconciliation and peace; immigrants arrived by the

---

96 William Randolph Hearst has been compared to the modern day tabloid mogul Robert Murdoch. Mayer, Catherine, *Tabloid Bites Man*, Time Magazine, July 25, 2011, at p. 33. According to Mayer's article, Rupert Murdoch was "a cultural force the likes of which we haven't seen since William Randolph Hearst."

thousands looking for the "gold paved" streets of America; and John Fisk's best-selling book, *Manifest Destiny*, proclaimed it was America's destiny to rule the world.[97]

By the start of 1898, the future of Jesse Jr. looked as promising as the patriotism that enveloped America and the growth of his adopted hometown. Surely, nothing could stand in his way!

(The Kansas City Junction)
(Courtesy Jackson County Historical Society)

---

97   Thomas, Evan, The War Lovers, Roosevelt, Lodge, Hearst, and the Rush to Empire, 1898, Little, Brown & Company, New York, 2010, at pp. 51 & 54.

CHAPTER V

THE ENTREPENURER KNOWS THE GOOD & BAD

⟶ ✦ ⟵

Dateline: January 15, 1898
Jackson County Courthouse

Headline:

BLOODSHED IN HAVANA
SEVERAL RIOTERS WOUNDED
IN FIGHTS WITH GUARDS
HARD WORK FOR THE TROOPS
CREATIVE ACCESSORIES IN THE RANK OF THE RIOTERS[98]

The year 1898 was as pivotal a year in America's foreign policy (war with Spain and imperialism) as it would prove to be for Jesse Jr.—perhaps for him even more so than the tragic year of 1882 when his father had been murdered. As the year opened, Zee and her two children were living in a house located at 3402 Tracy Avenue, Kansas City. The purchase of the land and the construction of the home had been financed by young Jesse's former employer, County Court Clerk Thomas Crittenden Jr. The widow's daughter, Mary Susan, was scheduled to graduate from high school in the spring, and her son had entered into a new business enterprise; this time he went into commerce for himself.[99]

The new venture was a sundry shop that principally sold cigars and

---

98   *The Sun*, January 15, 1898, New York.
99   The *Kansas City Journal*, February 28, 1898.

tobacco products. It had opened for business on January 15, 1898. Like the James family residence on Tracy, the family's benefactor, Thomas Crittenden, Jr., provided the investment funding. The location of the endeavor, inside the Jackson County Courthouse in Kansas City, was significant and ironic. It, too, had been arranged through the connections of Crittenden and other community leaders. These influential men (all of whom had seemingly taken young Jesse under their wings) believed the site of the business inside the ornate building would not only enhance expected earnings, but would make life easier for the James widow and her children. Perhaps Thomas, Jr. was continuing his attempts to undo a "perceived" wrong that his father had done to the young man's father back in 1882.

(Jackson County Courthouse - Kansas City: Circa 1899)
(Courtesy Jackson County Historical Society)

The first year of operations allowed Jesse Jr. the opportunity to continue meeting and rubbing elbows with influential business, political and community leaders. By the middle of 1898, the proprietor of the cigar counter met and befriended lawyers, judges and politicians. They had accepted him as a member of their society and considered him to have a promising and bright future. The young man even hinted about one day attending the new law school in Kansas City. It might have been said that by age twenty-three he had been like a phoenix rising above the dust and ashes of his family's checkered history. To most members of the city, he had triumphed over his late father's infamous and notorious identity and had altered the reputation and heritage of the James family.

While his entrepreneurial business allowed the young man to mingle with the elite, it also brought him into contact with those of questionable or even criminal reputations. Among these disputed figures were John F. Kennedy, William W. Lowe and Andy Ryan, the younger brother of Bill Ryan, a former member of the James Gang.[100] Jesse's relationships with such nefarious individuals proved not to be the only challenge or question to the otherwise good reputation Jesse Jr. had garnered. Kansas City Police Chief John Hayes reported young Jesse frequented saloons and houses of ill repute in the levy section of the city. Chief Hayes had previously arrested the bandit's son for kicking in the door of a bawdy house near the corner of 7th & Main.

(K.C. Police Chief
John Hayes)

Charles Finley, whose parents had been former slaves of the James family before the Civil War, chimed in with another unflattering remark. Finley had known the James boy for years, as he had helped the widow James nurse her two children after their father's assassination. He described young Jesse as being "a smart little fellow" but possessing "powerful mischievous" ways.[101] Of the negative sentiments expressed about Jesse Jr., it was his connection with John F. Kennedy, alias the "Quail Hunter," that proved the most compromising.

Jack Kennedy had been no stranger to the downtown courthouse; it was there Kennedy had first become acquainted with the young proprietor. He spent hours visiting the tobacco vendor over the cigar stand

---

100 Bill Ryan had the most dubious distinction. He was the first member of the James Gang to be prosecuted. In 1881, Jackson County Prosecutor William H. Wallace successfully convicted Ryan for the September 1879 robbery of the Glendale Train in the eastern part of Jackson Co., not too far from Crackerneck. For his crime, Bill Ryan received a 25 year prison sentence.

101 *Kansas City* Journal, August 16, 1907; Little, L. A., <u>Vintage Kansas City Stories, Early 20th Century Americana as Immortalized in the *Kansas City Journal 1907-1909*</u>, at p. 38, Vintage Antique Classics Publishing Co., 2009.

where they developed a "warm friendship."[102]

Kennedy had a long history and reputation for robbing trains and for admiring everything related to the James-Younger Gang. He reveled in their countless stories from the guerilla years of the Civil War through their escapades in the outlaw state. Kennedy's pedigree was the hills of eastern Jackson County, in an area known as "Crackerneck," where he had been born in December 1868 to John and Bridget Kennedy.[103] This region of the county was situated within a mile of the site of several train robberies all laid at the feet of the James Gang, including the Glendale Robbery in September 1879 and the Blue-Cut Robbery in September 1881. Crackerneck was a rough timbered district six miles southeast of Independence and had reportedly served as a noted hideout for both Confederate guerillas during the war and for the James-Younger Gang throughout their outlaw years. Most of the lessons Kennedy had learned about train robbing and the exploits of the James-Younger Gang came from the dime novels he read and the stories he heard as a child growing up in Crackerneck.

Whether it had been the heritage of Crackerneck, the history of train robberies, including the Glendale and Blue Cut, or its tradition as a hideout for the James-Younger Gang, Kennedy grew-up awe struck about anything related to the gang. He had developed an admiration and respect of everything related to their infamy, especially Jesse James. Many said that John F. "Jack" Kennedy didn't want to be like his hero but instead wanted to be the Jesse James. From 1889 to 1899, Jack chose to closely associate himself with family members, friends and acquaintances of both the James and Younger's.[104] As examples of his affinity towards the outlaws, in 1896 he courted Margaret Ralston, the sister of Ann Ralston James—the wife of Frank James. After their romance ended, he turned his affections in December 1897 to Rett Rose whose mother, Emma, was the sister of the Younger Brothers (by 1898 Cole and Jim Younger remained incarcerated in the state

102 *Kansas City Journal*, October 15, 1898.

103 Today the area is best known as the junction of I-470, Hwy 291 and 40 Hwy.

104 The origin of the district's name of "Crackerneck" was a derogatory reference to poor white settlers from Georgia, called 'crackers' who had first settled the area. *Kansas City Star*, January 10, 1937, Sec. C., I. Rabas, Chuck, Jack "Quail Hunter" Kennedy, Independence, Missouri. Joann Eakin, 1996.

penitentiary in Stillwater, Minnesota for the Northfield Bank Robbery on September 7, 1876, while their brother, Robert, had died of consumption, tuberculosis, while imprisoned for the same crime).[105]

Jack Kennedy was no stranger to the business operations of railroads. His familiarity and "inside" knowledge of the industry was first acquired when he worked as a railroad fireman. Following a railroad injury in which he had severely injured a foot, he became a train engineer working for the Southern Pacific Railroad. Kennedy's interest in trains, robberies and the band of thieves took on new practical dimensions in 1889. In that year, he personally met the former James Gang member, Bill Ryan, alias Whiskeyhead and Tom Hill. Bill had not only been a former member of the desperado band, but his brother, Andy Ryan, had been Kennedy's childhood friend. Following Bill Ryan's early parole release from prison on April 15, 1889, he immediately departed Missouri and landed in the Lone Star State.[106] It was in Texas while Kennedy was working for the Southern Pacific that he met Bill Ryan. The two soon developed a close friendship. Their meeting changed Kennedy's life forever—to a life of crime! From 1889 through 1895, Jack and Bill traveled from Texas to California allegedly robbing trains and trying to find qualified members to form the next generation of the James-Younger Gang. The two men returned to Jackson County in August 1896.

By 1898, Kennedy had been accused of several train robberies, one murder and other miscellaneous crimes. He and "Whiskeyhead" allegedly robbed the Chicago Alton train at Blue Cut in Jackson County near Crackerneck on October 23, 1896; apparently, Bill Ryan wanted to revenge his conviction or had forgotten the eight years he had spent in prison for the same crime. One month later on November 20, Jack was the prime suspect in the unsuccessful attempted robbery of a streetcar carrying about sixty passengers in route east from Kansas City to their homes in Independence. The following month, two days before

---

105 Most James scholars agree that Frank & Jesse James had been in the raid and were the only members of the gang to have escaped safely. Cole Younger in his book, Cole Younger, By Himself published in 1903 denied the James brothers had any part in the robbery (Cole's book provides other fictional tales as well). Margaret died of a brain tumor when she was about thirty years old.

106 See, Footnote #100.

Christmas, Kennedy and Ryan along with two other men, George Bowlin and James Flynn, were said to have held up another train at the Glendale Station; Blue Cut and Glendale Station were certainly popular stops for thieves to make train withdrawals! This felony resulted in charges being filed against Kennedy as Bowlin and Flynn turned state's evidence against him. No charges were filed against Ryan as neither Bowlin nor Flynn was able to positively identify him; they only knew him as an "old man" named Jennings. Kennedy's trial began on April 20, 1897, but it resulted in a hung jury, and the case was rescheduled for the October Criminal Term on October 12, 1897.

Six days before Kennedy's retrial was to have begun the Chicago Alton train was stopped and robbed by red lantern waiving thieves. Kennedy along with William W. Lowe, a former railroad switchman for the Santa Fe Railroad, and a third unknown man were considered the main culprits. With more criminal clouds circling over him, Kennedy's second trial for the Glendale train heist went forward, started on time and lasted five days—an acquittal and another victory for him. The verdict elicited a pronounced remonstration by Jackson County Prosecutor Frank Lowe (no kin to the bandit W.W. Lowe) who boldly asserted and accused Kennedy and his confederates of jury tampering.

Kennedy's acquittal only seemed to embolden his brashness. On November 12, 1897, the Missouri Pacific was robbed at the Elm Park Station near Independence around 9:00 p.m. The gang disguised in dresses recovered less than three dollars because the express safe was empty. Four men, the Ryan brothers, Bill and his younger brother, Andy, W. W. Lowe, and who else, Jack Kennedy, were the initial suspects, but no charges were filed. The next crime laid at Kennedy's feet occurred less than one month later on December 8th, but it was not a train robbery. Instead a grocery store located at 17th & Campbell in Kansas City was robbed and the owner, Emma Schumacher, had been shot and killed. Kennedy's name next circulated in the papers after the January 4, 1898 train robbery of the Pittsburgh and Gulf passenger train No. 4. This time Kansas City Police did not seriously consider him as a usual suspect as the crime's motes operandi failed to follow his typical pattern, and he was not prosecuted.

On January 28, 1898, Kennedy earned his lifetime alias, "Quail Hunter." On that evening, Pinkerton Agent George Leak observed two horsemen riding on ice-covered streets near 17th and Pennsylvania in Kansas City. As the men approached, Leak saw one of the horses slip on the roadway causing its rider to tumble, striking his head against the curb and rendering him unconscious. The other confederate fled from the scene. Agent Leak quickly approached the fallen man and discovered he was wearing a false red beard that had been "twisted" by the fall. Inside the man's hat, Leak found a mask; his frock coat contained a sawed-off shotgun, .44 Navy Colt revolver, cartridges and broken red lantern. When the "victim" regained consciousness, Leak realized it was Jack Kennedy and promptly questioned him about the arsenal and disguises. The notorious Kennedy mildly brushed off the inquiry and proclaimed he had been in route to go "quail hunting." Jack's new nom deplume "Quail Hunter" had been coined, and it remained his alias the rest of his life.

On February 6, 1898, the Quail Hunter was indicted for the murder of Emma Schumacher. During Jack's incarceration in the Jackson County Jail, he had some inimitable visitors. For reasons not readily ascertainable, these included Jesse Jr. and his late father's mother, Zerelda James Samuel. Their visits raised plenty of eyebrows in the courthouse and caused rumors to circulate around the city. Suspicions took on epic proportions when Jesse Jr. testified in the murder trial as an alibi witness for the Quail Hunter. The result of the case—another acquittal for Jack Kennedy!

Why would Jesse Jr. and his grandmother visit the Quail Hunter? Was the Quail Hunter good friends with the James family? What would be the reason for young Jesse befriending someone of Kennedy's reputation? How did he know the whereabouts of Jack Kennedy at the time of Emma's murder? Jesse Jr. should have changed his surname to a less notorious one. Certainly, a different last name would have enabled him to avoid any appearance of impropriety.[107] On a broader note,

---

107 The American Weekly, The Truth; Vol. 17, Number 605, November 23, 1898,

hadn't the young man tried to improve his family's reputation? While these questions were being discussed and debated, Kennedy who was being held yet again in the county jail for another alleged crime was released; insufficient evidence was the reason for the discharge. What would next be on the "Quail Hunter's" criminal menu?

at p 21.

CHAPTER VI

THE LEEDS GANG AT WORK

Dateline: September 23, 1898
Leeds Factory & Coal Town

Headline:

PRESIDENT MCKINLEY, HAVING
RESTORED PEACE, IS COMING
WEST TO LOOK AT PROSPERITY[108]

The United States may have prospered from its victory over Spain, but a few enterprising souls continued to seek prosperity the old fashioned way—robbing trains. On the evening of Friday, September 23, 1898, the southbound Missouri Pacific Train No. 5, and seven-car passenger train, including a combination baggage and express car, was robbed at gunpoint.[109] The train filled with a large number of passengers and suspected riches had left Union Depot in the West Bottoms around 9:15 in route to Wichita, Kansas and Little Rock, Arkansas. The holdup occurred in the unincorporated section of Jackson County, Missouri, known as Leeds, located about six to seven miles southeast of Downtown Kansas City. Known for its coal mining industry, Leeds was a well-traveled railroad junction with a telegraph station and post office that had been in operation since 1890. The surrounding circumstances of the train robbery may be said to have more closely paralleled

---

108 *Kansas City Journal,* September 23, 1898.
109 *Kansas City Journal,* September 24, 1898.

an account of the 'Gang That Couldn't Shoot Straight' than the escapades of a well-trained professional gang in operation.

(Missouri Pacific Railroad)
(Courtesy Western Missouri Manuscript Collection)

On that night, two masked men broke into the small telegraph office situated at the rail junction known as the "P. & G. Junction," the "Brush Creek Junction" or the "Belt Line Junction." It was a point in which the Pittsburgh & Gulf line intersected with the tracks of the Missouri Pacific. As the desperados entered the wire-room and approached D. M. Hissey, the telegraph operator, one man shoved his Winchester rifle into Hissey's stomach and ordered him to throw up his hands. One thief was described as a tall man who wore a cloth tied over his face and carried a revolver and wire pliers. The other desperado was said to have been much shorter, brandished the rifle and disguised himself with a black mask. As the Winchester toting bandit pointed his rifle at the telegraph officer, his cover slipped down his face. Hissey saw the "big red nose" and the upper part of his face. At the same time, the taller man had difficulties cutting the telegraph wires with his pliers, so he changed course and selected a much cruder maneuver. He smashed the switchboard with his revolver. Finally, he was able to destroy the telegraph line.

While Hissey was being restrained, the Missouri Pacific crossed the junction and came to its customary stop. The shorter man, while brandishing his rifle at Hissey, directed him out of the telegraph office and down the track line to the halted train. Once again the scoundrel's mouthpiece fell down over his chin, but Hissey was unable to make a "very good identification." When Hissey and the two crooks reached the stopped train, approximately seven other masked thieves were waving red lanterns, swearing most horribly, and ordering the engineer, Charles Slocum, and the fireman, G. L. Weston, down from the engine. Hissey and Slocum were then compelled to detach the engine and express car from the passenger cars. After complying with this mandate, the gang leader demanded Slocum and Hissey to get into the remaining passenger cars or they would be killed. The other members of the band of outlaws were forcing the train's flagman onto the engine and express car. Soon the engine, coal and express car left the junction and disappeared down the track line.

During the ordeal, the express messenger, Edwin N. Hills, had been working inside the express car. It was not until after the engine pulled away that he realized it was not attached to the passenger cars. When he looked outside, he saw several masked men and realized for the first time the train was being robbed. Hills unsuccessfully attempted to hide inside the car. The criminals then came to the side entrance of the express car and started beating on it with their guns demanding him to unbolt it or they would blow open the door. Hills' realizing he had no other option opened the gate whereupon three masked men immediately entered carrying sacks over their arms. The shorter man still carrying the Winchester continued to experience problems with his disguise; it once again slipped down his face. Hills tried to get a good look at him, but in a flash the butt of a revolver struck him over the head, and he collapsed to the floor. By then, the train began moving down the track line. It did not come to a stop until it was about one mile west of Swope Park, 1,300 acres city-park given to the city in 1896 by Col. Thomas H. Swope.

Up to this point, the crime scene was not much different than any regular James-Younger train robbery (other than the constant dropping of the shorter man's mask and the crude destruction of the telegraph line). When the crooks realized they could not open the express car's safe, they selected a more drastic method—dynamite. Hadn't Jesse James previously utilized dynamite? The comparison would end right there. Seven sticks of dynamite were placed on top of the safe and the fuse was lit. Hills' was ordered to stay in the car as the bandits leaped out of it. Begging and pleading for his life, Hills was finally allowed to leap out as well.

In what seemed to have been an eternity, there was no explosion; apparently, the fuse had failed. Hills worried he would be ordered to re-enter the car and relight it. Instead, he was told to uncouple the express car from the engine. As he was doing so, he saw a flash and heard one of the bandits yelling, "Get away." Panic stricken, Hills jumped up and began running down the track line side by side with the robbers, all of whom were stampeding as fast as they could.

Seconds later the dynamite exploded. The safe was blown to kingdom come! The magnitude of the explosion was so great that the report was heard eight miles away, as far away as Fire Station #18 at 25th & Prospect.[110] The gang had blundered—too much dynamite. They had destroyed not only the safe but the entire express car as well. A mass of debris was scattered over a two-mile radius, including dozens of invitations to the wedding of Albert Hamilton Denton and Alice Emily Young scheduled for September 27th in Arkansas City, Kansas. Twisted iron and tangled mass of baggage, clothing and the "express matter and timbers burned like a gigantic spent fire cracker or a huge bit of 'punk' . . . while the great iron safe . . . was shattered as if riddled by a

---

110 *Ibid.*

thirteen-inch shell." Everything had been blown to smithereens.

Shortly thereafter, one of the gang members handed Hills a card with directives and instructions to give it to authorities. The card had been a printed campaign card that read: "Vote for Robert W. Green, Republican nominee for county collector of Jackson County." The reverse side of the card contained the following penciled statement:

We the masked knights of the road, robbed the M. P. train at the Belt line junction tonight. The supply of quails was good. With much love we remain.
We are ex comspert to.

The hand-written salutation read, "with much love we remain, John Kennedy, Bill Ryan, Bill Anderson, Sam Brown and Jim Redmond." One of the robbers had to have known some Latin, very poor Latin at that, as the last line "We are ex comspert to" should have stated: "we are ex conspectus." In other words, "we are out of sight."

Nearby at 43rd and Indiana and within close proximity of the train robbery was a bordering house where the Hollenbeck family and several borders resided. Mr. Hollenbeck, a dairyman by trade, boarded a number of men employed by the Brush Creek Coalmine, located nearby. The blast from the explosion rattled the house's windows, but it did not create any real excitement to those residing inside the residence. This is because the members of the Hollenbeck household and neighbors were accustomed to such sounds coming from any of the many coal mines in the area; blasts were hardly anything new in Leeds. What they later ascertained became a revelation.

The blast had first awakened Mrs. Hollenbeck. Hearing loud noises, she looked outside and saw a buggy galloping "just like a fire horse" past their house west towards Indiana Ave. Private William Wain of the Third Regiment, a boarder at the Hollenbeck home, had also been arrested from his slumber. Rushing out of the house to render aid to the presumed injured miners, Wain was passed by another horse drawn buggy going at a "furious gait" and going in the same direction as the one that Mrs. Hollenbeck had seen—west towards Indiana Avenue. Wain did not follow the buggy but took a short cut through a pasture towards the coalmines. He then heard sounds from horse hoofs galloping eastward through the woods and in the opposite direction from the two buggies. Another tenant, William Wotox, was disturbed in his sleep as well. About fifteen minutes later, he saw a horse and buggy rushing rapidly by, and he overheard somebody in the vehicle yelling, "Look out; that horse will fall."[111] No one in the Hollenbeck residence slept well that night.

A farmer living in the Leeds community also bolted from his bed following the detonation. He went directly downstairs to investigate the incident. When he opened his front door, there stood a lonesome-looking dog that was "whining piteously." The farmer knew the dog was not from the neighborhood. Taking pity upon the canine, he opened the door to care for the lost hound. Whose dog was it? Why had the dog come to his old farmhouse? Would anyone claim the animal?

The farmer, Private Wain, Wotox, the Hollenbecks and all other residents of Leeds soon discovered the truth. There was no explosion in the coalmine. No miners had been injured at all. The Leeds train had been held up and the express car had been blown into a tangled mess.

The following morning, the *Kansas City Journal* headline read:

CAR BLOWN UP.

The *Kansas City Star* gave a mocking account of the explosive train robbery and described the calling card entrusted to Hills as "A Merry Little Train Robber Joke."

> The dull explosion that was heard throughout the south-eastern part of the city last night was the work of train robbers. It was not much after ten o'clock when the robbers dynamited the express car . . . That they did not blow off their own clothing was a wonder, for the car was razed, the great iron safe was

---

111 *Kansas City Journal*, February 26, 1899.

shattered, and, for a distance of two miles, waybills and papers and fragments of baggage were scattered along the track. The party of masked bandits, thinking that they had cut the telegraph wires to Kansas City, used no stint in the application of dynamite.

The final cynical note suggested by the press was that the thieves and their volatile evening had garnered a sizeable reward—twenty-nine silver dollars. The coins were found by sure luck as they had been shot into the air and scattered along the track line. It is humorous to consider this 'sophisticated' gang of robbers searching a debris field stringing out over two miles in the late night hours for "silver dollars."

CHAPTER VII
THE INVESTIGATION BEGINS

═══◄◉►═══

Dateline: September 24, 1898
City-Wide

Headline:

IS ROOSEVELT OUT

SAID TO BE INELIGIBLE FOR

GOVERNOR OF NEW YORK.[112]

It was said that the police launched a countywide investigation immediately after the Leeds robbery in an attempt to give a knockout blow to the gang of thieves. Every patrolman was notified and anyone found upon the roads of Jackson County that evening was questioned as to his whereabouts at the time of the train heist. The Leeds crossing, the explosion site near Swope Park, the post office and telegraph station were all searched and examined for clues and evidence. Nothing was to be left to chance. Crowds gathered to observe and search through the debris hoping to find a souvenir or perhaps "silver coins."

The following morning, the primary focus was rounding up all possible suspects, including the "usual suspects." At the top of the list was John Kennedy, the "Quail Hunter." Kennedy was suspected of complicity for the most obvious reason. He had been released from jail just two weeks before the robbery. Suspicions mounted as all efforts to locate the "Quail Hunter" at his residence or at his usual haunts had

112 *Kansas City Journal,* September 24, 1898

been unsuccessful. Once Kennedy realized police were on his trail, he came forward and professed his innocence. He provided names of a "string of witnesses as to his whereabouts between the hours of 6 and 11 o'clock" on the night of the Leeds robbery. The bulk of his alibi witnesses were family and friends from the Crackerneck area. Jackson County Marshal Chiles believed the "Quail Hunter" was not a participant in the train robbery and told reporters he was convinced Kennedy would be able to "establish that fact easily."[113]

Another suspect of the holdup was Andy Ryan, the brother of whiskey drunk, Bill Ryan. On the morning after the robbery, police discovered Andy Ryan sleeping on a cot at the #3 Firehouse located at 14th & Pennsylvania in Downtown Kansas City. When questioned by authorities, young Ryan adamantly denied having any knowledge or involvement in the crime. He further proclaimed he had not seen or heard from the "Quail Hunter" at any time that evening.

Dateline: September 26, 1898
Rewards Issued

Headline:

CUBANS ARE STARVING
PRESIDENT GOMEZ MAKES A PLEA
TO PRESIDENT MCKINLEY FOR ALL
FOR HIS HUNGRY SOLDIERS[114]

By September 26th state and local officials were starving for the apprehension of suspects involved in the Leeds robbery. That day, pleas for the arrest of the conspirators had been made public when Governor Lawrence Stephens offered a reward of $300, while the Jackson County Court offered another $500. The proclamations were not in the form of "dead or alive" posters, but were issued for the capture and conviction of any one of the robbers. An offer of $800 was a handsome sum. It would certainly bring about a thorough and exhaustive investigation

113 *Kansas City Journal*, September 26, 1898.
114 *Paducah Daily Sun*, September 26, 1898.

destined to lead to convictions. Who would not want to recover that kind of money in 1898? Every lead would surely be pursued. No one in Missouri could get away with this kind of crime. Not in 1898!

The rewards attracted detectives and private eyes (many hired by the railroads) to Kansas City like bees to honey. It was reported that as many as twenty-six railroad detectives arrived in the city to aid in the investigation. Shortly after the arrival of these investigators, it became unquestioned that the role of the Kansas City Police Department would be subordinate to these experts. Leading the investigation was Thomas Furlong of the Furlong Secret Service Agency. Furlong's chief assistant was Del Harbaugh. Others, including Railroad Detective John DeLong and the manager of the Pinkerton Agency, J. H. Schumacher, soon joined these "gum shoes." They had been hired by the Missouri Pacific Railroad to bring to justice the men responsible for this horrific transgression.

(Hotel Savoy: Circa 1898—Courtesies of Mr. Don Lee owner)

After making initial inquiries, Furlong and Harbaugh promptly established their command post at the Hotel Savoy located at 9th & Central and only a few blocks from Grand Central Station. Interested reporters begin to closely cover the clandestine events and meetings that were transpiring within the hotel. The movements of detectives inside the hotel were described as "exceedingly mysterious." Bellboys were constantly "delivering telegrams to the sleuths" and the "doors to their private apartments" were "locked and the keyholes stuffed with paper."

Despite their limited roles in the investigation, both Kansas City Police Chief Hayes and County Marshal Chiles made frequent and daily visits to meet these private detectives in their hotel rooms at the Savoy. Chief Hayes told investigators that his police department considered Jack Kennedy as the primary suspect. The chief reported that despite the "Quail Hunter's" protestations to the contrary the Jackson County Prosecutor Frank Lowe had positively seen Kennedy in Kansas City on the day of the robbery. Hayes also announced a witness had come forward who wished to remain anonymous for his own safety. The informant told police that he had seen Jack Kennedy board the 12th Street streetcar at 11:30 on the night of the robbery.

The sleuths traveled to the vicinity of Leeds in search of clues at both the robbery and explosion sites. There were many folks, including railroad employees, passengers, the Hollenbecks, Private Wain, Mr. Wotox and others, who needed to be interviewed. One witness shared the story of a local farmer finding the wayward dog on the night of the robbery. Detectives were convinced that this story contained significant clues and potentials. They concluded that the "strange creature . . . seemed to spring" from "the explosions" and surely belonged to one of the crooks.[115]

Detectives immediately took the hound into custody where it was delivered to Chief Hayes at police headquarters. Hearing the story, Hayes decided it would be a "good plan" to find out to whom the dog belonged. An officer was detailed for several days to take the "strange creature" around the city to see if he would find his way home. The

---

115 *Kansas City Times*, March 1, 1899.

canine was turned into a "blood hound" as it was taken to vicinities in which suspects were known to live, including the residences of Andy Ryan, Jack Kennedy, W. W. Lowe, Charles Polk, and to the area of 34th and Tracy, near the James house. The dog's search near the home of the Jesse Jr. caused eyebrows and questions to be raised. Why had the canine canvassed the neighborhood of the James family? Surely, no one in that family was under investigation for the Leeds incident. The search and find services proved fruitless, and Chief Hayes "gave the dog clue up in disgust." The orphan dog was not returned to the farmer but became a refugee at police headquarters.[116]

While the "Quail Hunter" remained a prim suspect, three arrests were made in St. Joseph, Missouri, within days of the robbery that brought welcomed news to authorities in Kansas City. The men were identified as James Morgan, James McAlear and John Ryan.[117] According to St. Joseph Police Chief Broder, the three appeared to fit the description of the train robbers. More significantly to the chief, they had been observed acting suspiciously, carrying over four hundred dollars in silver and flaunting their money about town. St. Joseph Police began shadowing the men earlier in the afternoon and saw them going from place to place, exchanging silver for paper currency. A fourth man was still wanted in the conspiracy, and though police felt confident they had the right suspects in custody, all three men appeared overtly nervous but stubbornly refused to speak or admit any involvement in the Leeds crime. Arrest warrants out of Jackson County were issued for the St. Joseph suspects for their return to Kansas City. Both Chief Hayes and Detective Halphin were confident that the arrested men in St. Joseph were among the bandits of the Leeds robbery.[118] Despite these arrests, the investigation made little further headway in locating or identifying other suspects of the train robbery.

Reports of other suspects were streaming in across the "wire." In addition to the men seized in St. Joseph, Constable Withers of Mayview, Missouri, had arrested two suspicious characters in his town.

---

116 *Ibid.*
117 *Kansas City Journal*, September 26, 1898.
118 *Ibid.*

Withers said the captured men were seen carrying large sums of money, Winchester rifles and large caliber self-acting revolvers just like the ones reportedly used in the heist at Leeds. Stories abounded and circulated that Chief Hayes had traveled to Mayview to bring the two men back to Kansas City for questioning. Neither man was ever transported to Kansas City; it was determined that they were merely vagrants and tramps possessing only nine and three dollars respectively.[119]

The media frenzy intensified when reliable reports began circulating stories of a new suspect in custody. Rumor had it that a former railroad switchman was being held at the Hotel Savoy. Reporters had a field day fueling speculations surrounding the investigation. Some even made an unsuccessful "search" of the hotel for the prisoner. Local papers raised numerous questions. Why were private eyes conducting ad hoc, covert meetings behind closed doors inside the Savoy? Was there a detainee at all? If so, who was the mystery person? In what private chamber of the Savoy were Pinkerton Agents concealing him? Was talk of someone being held nothing but a ruse? Had the robbers' trail grown cold? Were they "sweating" the man inside the hotel for information about the crime? Did the crooks really get $25,000 not just a mere $29? If the Mayview boys were innocent, what about those arrested in St. Joseph? Where were they? Inquiring minds needed to know.

As national media stories focused upon the hero of San Juan's eligibility to run for Governor of New York, the local press scrutinized the events at the Hotel Savoy. It soon became certain that someone was in fact being held "under lock and key" inside the hotel. Theories evolved but it was undisputed that whoever was being detained had to have been under intense scrutiny and interrogation within some private quarter in that hotel.

---

119 *Kansas City Times*, October 2, 1898.

Dateline: September 27, 1898
1001 W. 16th Street, K.C.

Headline:

ONE HUNDRED LIVES LOST IN FLAMES
DEAD BODIES MARK THE PATHS OF
TERRIBLE FOREST FIRES IN WISCONSIN[120]

Dead bodies may have been burned to death in Wisconsin, but one body had been arrested in Kansas City. The facts were revealed that around noon on Tuesday, September 27th, police seized William W. Lowe at his boarding house at 1001 W. 16th Street in Kansas City without benefit of an arrest or search warrant. Lowe had been considered a suspect from the outset. As a former Santa Fe railroad switchman, he knew the workings of the railroad industry and was closely connected with Jack Kennedy. Both he and the "Quail Hunter" had been no strangers to law enforcement as they had been implicated together in numerous prior train robberies and other criminal mischief. Of most significance was the fact Lowe had been in Kansas City the night of the robbery. Chief Hayes reported that evidence found in Lowe's apartment included some cartridges of the same caliber as those discovered in the buggy hired at Self's Livery Stable on the night of the robbery. Hayes also dis-closed that two other pieces of substantial and significant evidence had

William W. Lowe

---

120 *Kansas City Times,* September 27, 1898.

been found during the search of Lowe's apartment. However, neither Hayes nor anyone else was revealing anything about these discoveries. There would be time for disclosures.

The 'mole' that led detectives to Lowe was as interesting as the investigation itself. Lowe's own wife had been the source. Within a couple of days of the robbery, she, and her five-year old son, had gone to police headquarters. Her explanation for becoming a witness against her husband was simple: she had grown "tired of his ways" and she was worn out about how he had continuously boasted about the train robbery at Leeds. According to police, Mrs. Lowe said her husband came home around 11:30 p.m. on the night of the heist and told her how he had helped hold-up the train and had "blowed her to hell and never got a cent."[121] Efforts made by the press to interview Mrs. Lowe proved pointless. Police had cautioned her not to talk to anyone. Her only public comment was that she had told the whole story and "would not lie for anyone" not even her husband. As for Mrs. Lowe, her safety demanded she be disguised in men's clothing, secreted away from Kansas City and concealed in St. Louis for her own safety. Was Mrs. Lowe telling the truth or just wanting to get rid of her husband? Could anyone truly believe her story? Hadn't Mrs. Lowe previously criticized her husband for having befriended Jack Kennedy? Were reports of her filing for divorce meritorious? Didn't Lowe have an iron clad alibi? The press needed answers but no one was responding.[122]

Immediately after his arrest, Lowe was concealed and "locked up" at the Hotel Savoy as an accomplice and co-conspirator in the Leeds train robbery. Railroad detectives allowed no one to see or communicate with him during the period of his incarceration. Not only was Lowe denied an opportunity to talk to anyone, he also refused to give any statement to law officers. Within a few days of being captured, Chief Hayes ordered Lowe to be transferred to the police station on Southwest Boulevard. The directive had been made out of fear that some of Lowe's friends might make an attempt to have him

---

121 *Ibid.*

122 Mrs. Lowe's intentions to divorce her husband proved to be true. The story of her filing divorce papers was reported in the *Saline Republic* on March 10, 1899, at p. 3.

"released." Neither police nor private investigators were going to let Lowe get away.

Following Lowe's arrest, reporters and editors began to conduct their own investigation. Why should private eyes and cops be the only ones benefiting from the reward? The press core also reached its own conclusion: The capture of Lowe without benefit of an arrest warrant was unprecedented and illegal. Editorial commentaries compared Lowe's interrogation to the inquisition; he was being "sweated" by police. Reporters were convinced of this fact. Hadn't Lowe's neighbor, an attorney named H. A. Yonge, provided a credible alibi defense? Mr. Yonge had seen Lowe on the night in question, and he claimed that the only way Lowe could have been involved in the robbery was for him to have gone to Union Depot, boarded a train and ridden to the scene of the crime. Time would not have allowed for this to happen. Most significant to journalists was the obvious: Lowe's wife was prejudiced and biased against her husband. This was unquestioned, as another neighbor of Lowe, Mr. D. L. Ruggles, provided substantial proof. Ruggles told how the Lowe's "were not happy together" and were constantly fighting. He spoke about Mr. Lowe's vulgar disposition and having overheard Mrs. Lowe once proclaim she "would do anything to get rid of him." The consensus of the fourth estate was that the state's case against Lowe was clearly "weak" and police were simply "grasping at straws."[123]

Detective Thomas Furlong made the most sensational discovery after Lowe's arrest. A search of Lowe's coat pockets had unearthed something monumental—two letters. The correspondence found was tantamount to locating the "holy grail." The "Quail Hunter" purportedly wrote one letter, and none other than Jesse Jr. authored the other one. Furlong and his men now had circumstantial evidence directly linking the cigar-store owner to the train robbery. Once Furlong found the letters, Lowe's interrogation became more intense, and he was exhaustively questioned about the correspondence from James. Lowe merely avowed that Jesse Jr. had written it several

---

123 *Kansas City Times*, September 27, 1898.

months before the robbery. This answer was unsatisfactory and at that moment "Furlong then and there tried to get" Lowe "to say that James was in the robbery."[124]

The public had to know about the treasure trove discovered in Lowe's pockets. The only information being leaked to the press was that a momentous discovery of evidence had been made. No one in law enforcement would reveal the nature and extent of what had been found. The only comment made was that whatever had been found would certainly form important evidence and lead to the arrest of a popular suspect. A neighbor of Lowe, Mrs. H. A. Yonge, gave reporters the sensational information. She explained how she had overhead detectives reading a letter written by Jesse Jr. The contents she recalled was something to the effect Lowe was to meet James "on Seventeenth Street at around 7 o'clock," but admittedly she paid no attention to the date of the note.[125] The most significant part of the search and seizure was it had directed police to a new suspect: the son of Jesse James.

---

124 *St. Louis Post-Dispatch*, February 19, 1910; *New York Times*, February 20, 1910.
125 *Kansas City Star*, October 2, 1898.

CHAPTER VIII
CHIP OFF THE OLE' BLOCK?

―――《◉》―――

Dateline: September 30, 1898
Undisclosed K.C. Police Station

Headline:

AN END TO STRIFE
BLUE AND GRAY CELEBRATE
TOGETHER AT TOPEKA[126]

Wow that letter was significant! It brought tremendous strife to Jesse Jr., like reopening the war wounds of his late father.

On September 30th, detectives took Jesse Jr. into custody for questioning. The young man knew better than to give any statement to law officers. Had he learned this from his father or from working at the courthouse? Several futile attempts were made by detectives to obtain a confession, but he stoutly and steadfastly maintained his innocence. After an undisclosed length of time, he was released from detention. However, he was given an injunctive warning: not to leave the city, as his freedom was subject to an ongoing investigation. Investigators were certainly proud of their dual achievements. Not only had they discovered a letter from Jesse Jr. to W. W. Lowe, but they had also taken him into custody for questioning.

By late that evening, news of the tobacco vendor's arrest began to <u>reverberate around</u> the community. Everyone, especially reporters,

126 *Kansas City Journal*, September 30, 1898.

demanded an explanation. Despite being apprised of Lowe's arrest, "the letter" and the interrogation of Jesse Jr., newspapers were nevertheless very cautious and deliberate not to specifically implicate the James boy in any wrongdoing. This was in part because the press had already concluded the case was weak. More philosophically, no one wanted to believe that the young man had followed the path of his late father. News articles continued to pay tribute to his good name, reputation, hard work ethics and respectable habits. It was as if the media could not or did not want to believe he had gone the way of the notorious Jesse James.

After being implicated in the Leeds robbery, Jesse Jr. considered his arrest as nothing more than a vendetta of the Pinkerton's. He believed that the only reason he was suspected at all was because his name was against him. He knew it was for this reason, and only this reason, that the railroad detectives had conspired to go after him. Jesse was also well aware that he would need to affirmatively respond to the rumors, accusations and innuendoes; he knew just the way to go on the offensive. He would soon be invoking a long-standing tradition of his late father: releasing alibi stories and letters to the public.

Dateline: October 1, 1898
Cigar Stand

Headline:

**COLORADO FOREST
REGION IS DOOMED**
**UNLESS IT RAINS VERY SOON
AND A GREAT DEAL OF IT**[127]

The long-standing positive regional reputation Jesse Jr. had garnered had certainly been receiving a deluge of rain. He could not hide or seek shelter otherwise his business could be doomed. The following day he returned to his cigar store to transact business as usual.

Around three o'clock that afternoon, a reporter found him behind

---

127 *Wichita Daily Eagle*, October 1, 1898.

his counter reading a newspaper. The newsman approached the sales-man and asked him for an interview. Whereupon an impromptu press conference was held. As Jesse Jr. answered each question, a large assem-bly gathered to listen to the exceedingly cool and collected purveyor of tobacco products (and his popular chewing gum). The reporter described him as having dark eyes and not only handsome, but seem-ingly aware of it. During the dialogue, the suspect remained confident and self-assured even after the subject of the letter reportedly found in Lowe's coat pocket became a topic of discussion. He neither confirmed nor denied the letter story, but with a wink and scratch of his head, he decreed having no recollection of writing "any letter" to Lowe. If he had, it was not written recently. He did not deny knowing "Lowe and Kennedy" but he also asserted he knew "about 5,000 other people in this town, and I sometimes write letters, but you can put it down that I have not written a letter to Lowe that the police have ever got their hooks on, and I am almost positive I have not written a letter to him."[128]

Jesse Jr. simply smiled when he was questioned whether he was surprised at being identified as a suspect. He voiced no concerns or apprehensions about the allegations, but he failed to understand how knowing Lowe or Jack Kennedy could place him under suspicion as a member of the Leeds gang. When a reporter further pressed the issue of his friendship with the "Quail Hunter," he grew defensive. "I am a good friend to John Kennedy and I don't give a damn who knows it! I don't care what the police suspect. I know where I was that night, and so do they. They can suspect all they damn please, for all I care!"[129] The young man then willingly provided a detailed account of his where-abouts on the night of the robbery. He even insisted that those wishing to hear the story should take out their pad and pencil. Like his father before him, he wanted to ensure that the press and public had the en-tire, true alibi tale. After completing his tale and with a glimmer in his eye and brashness in his tone, he declared:

---

128 *Kansas City Times*, October 2, 1898.
129 *Kansas City Star*, October 1, 1898.

I'm a pretty looking train robber. I am, and I am surprised at Chief Hayes and his sleuths for not blaming me with everything in sight. It's tough on a fellow to be the son of a man like my father is said to have been.

This was not to be the last time Jesse Jr. would provide an alibi statement. He dispatched a letter to the editors of all local newspapers accounting for his activities on the evening of the train robbery. The alibi published in the *Kansas City Journal* on October 12, 1898 read as follows:

I was at home at 3402 Tracy avenue on Friday night of the train robbery until 8 o'clock, when I went over to Thirty-third and Troost avenue with my mother and some relatives to the street car lines. The relatives were my aunt, Mrs. Allen Parmer, and two little daughters, who live near Wichita Falls, Tex., and who were on their way home after a visit with us.

I carried their baggage to the cars, where they, in company with my mother, went onto the depot. On the car that carried them was Mr. and Mrs. Levens, whom we know and who spoke to me. I did not go to the depot because I never leave my grandmother alone in the house.

After placing the folks on the car, I stopped in at Hill & Howard's drug store. This was along about 8:30 o'clock, I should judge. The store is on the corner where we went to take the street car. Here I had a glass of ice cream soda. Mr. Hill, one of the proprietors, waited upon me and in the store at the same time were Charles Hovey and a number of the cable men that I know. I stayed there talking for a little while, possibly half an hour, but not more than that, and then started home. Mr. and Mrs. Bunch, neighbors of ours, saw and spoke to me as I was going home. There was present at the house my grandmother and my sister. I did not go out again, but went to bed about 11 o'clock my usual time.

I am a young man trying to make an honest living for my mother and sister, and it seems hard that I should be obliged to defend myself this way. Newspaper notoriety is something that I try to avoid, but I would like for all who have an interest in me to see the parties I saw that night and they will find that my statements are correct.

JESSE JAMES[130]

His oral statement to the press on October 1st and his letter published on October 12th were consistent. Each was made with a concerted effort to establish a sturdy and credible alibi defense. He had given his statements for two obvious reasons. He wanted to put closure to the slanderous and libelous reports circulating, and he had provided investigators, police and detectives with names and evidence to assuage their suspicions. Surely, Mr. and Mrs. Levens would be questioned about his alibi assertions. Wouldn't the police and detectives interview Mr. Hill and Mr. Hovey. Certainly, those he identified as seeing him at or about the drug store the night of the crime would be questioned to verify his story. Shouldn't the Bunch Family be interrogated as well?

---

130 *Kansas City Journal*, October 12, 1898.

CHAPTER IX
SWEATING OUT SUSPECTS

<hr>

Dateline: October 4, 1898
Kansas City Police Station No. 3

Headline:

THE PAGEANTRY OF PALLAS
PALLAS IN A MERRY MASQUERADE[131]

The commentaries made by Jesse Jr. brought him no merriment! The police considered his claims to be nothing more than a masquerade. Detectives had no interest in questioning the names disclosed by their marquee suspect. Instead they were going to continue their exhaustive examination and persistent clandestine interrogation of Lowe. Even after Lowe had been transferred from the Hotel Savoy and sequestered within the No. 3 Police Station, he was constantly queried about his relationship with Jesse Jr., the role in which young James had played in the robbery and the identification of all other accomplices to the crime.

On October 4, Detectives Sanderson and Harbaugh arrested Harry Milton as another suspect in the robbery. Had Lowe identified Milton? Milton, a Santa Fe train switchman, was arrested at his job in the Maple Leaf yards in Kansas City, Kansas. According to sleuths, Milton had been suspected from the outset because he had been seen on the Twelfth Street car traveling westbound about an hour or two

131 *Kansas City Star*, October 4, 1898.

after the train hold-up. After this information was unearthed, investigators turned to Lowe's wife once again. She was asked if her husband had ever identified Milton as being in the robbery. "Yes, he told me that two persons from Independence were in it and he mentioned the name of one." When she was asked if one of the men was named Milton, she replied in fact it was one of the names her husband had given her. Police confirmed that Milton's arrest was also supported by the testimony of Mr. Self, the liveryman from whom one of the robbers had hired a team on the night in question.[132]

Following his capture, Milton was ushered to "one of the outside police stations" where he was detained until other arrests were made in the case. Chief Hayes stated that Milton had been among several others who remained under surveillance, and that his apprehension was likely for purposes of "shaking him down." The Chief further insisted that there would be a number of additional men taken into custody within the next couple of weeks.[133]

The steamroller effect of the investigation seemed to wane and slow to a crawl. Leads and clues became less plentiful. Chief Hayes conceded to the press having nothing new to report. The *Kansas City Times* protested the sluggish search for evidence and boldly proclaimed police had "neglected to arrest a single suspect or sweat" any of "Quail Hunter Kennedy's friends in connection with the Missouri Pacific holdup."

Limited new information was compounded by an annual civic activity. The press interpreted it as a lackadaisical attitude on the part of police and detectives. The explanation given by Chief Hayes was more pragmatic. His office had become "so busy with other matters" on account of the Priests of Pallas that his department had to focus upon patrolling streets and not solving crimes. The weeklong carnival-like pageantry of the Priests of Pallas had become as much a part of the fabric of the city by the turn of the Century as the American Royal today. The Chief also reluctantly conceded his force simply lacked the ability and manpower to give any further consideration to the train

132 *Kansas City Star*, October 5, 1898.
133 *Kansas City Times*, October 5, 1898.

investigation. The *Times* complained that events surrounding the Priests of Pallas had interfered with serious police duties, including solving the Leeds robbery.[134]

Dateline: October 9, 1898
Kansas City Police Headquarters

Headline:

SPAIN'S EMBLEM ABSENT
NOT AMONG THE FLAGS WHICH
WAIVED IN HAVANA YESTERDAY[135]

When the exhilaration and flag waving of the Priests of Pallas concluded, police and railroad detectives returned to their absent emblem: solving the Leeds crime. By October 9th, the cumulative effects of the interrogation and examination of Lowe proved successful as Detectives Furlong, Harbaugh and police garnered, perhaps squeezed, a full and complete written confession from him. Chief Hayes quickly reported that Lowe had not only confessed to the crime, but had identified five of the six members of the "gang" who had robbed and blown up the train on the evening of September 23rd. Chief Hayes was disappointed that Lowe had categorically denied the 'Quail Hunter' had anything to do with the robbery. In addition to having implicated himself, Lowe had pointed fingers at Jesse Jr., Andy Ryan, Caleb Stone and Charles W. Polk. As to the identity of the sixth man, Lowe had informed detectives that he had not known him, but only knew him by the name of "Evans." The press pondered why Lowe had ventured into such a capital crime without knowing all the conspirators.

The intensity and intrigue of the criminal investigation had resumed center stage in the local and national print media. For the dime novelists, the story line offered an encore presentation of the old James-Younger gang. Why not? The James-Younger names had captivated audiences and tickled the fancy of readers for years; they still

134 *Ibid.*
135 *The Times*, October 9, 1898, Washington, City (D.C.).

do. The newspapers covered the daily intrigues of the interrogation of Lowe and the reports of Jesse Jr. having been an accomplice in the train robbery. Speculative rumors and claims were raised that Lowe had been promised immunity for his confession and "finger-pointing." What had Lowe demanded as consideration for implicating Jesse Jr. as a member of the Leeds gang? Surely, Lowe would not give up the son of the bandit without gaining in exchange his own personal immunity and freedom. Why not name Jesse Jr.? Lowe knew him; he had a letter in his pocket from the boy; James had befriended the "Quail Hunter;" the lad and his grandmother had visited the "Quail Hunter" in jail; and the store owner had previously provided alibi testimony for Jack Kennedy. Some or all of these thoughts and queries undoubtedly flowed through Lowe's mind during his inquisition, and perhaps culminated in his identification of Jesse Jr. as a co-member and leader of the gang.

For Chief Hayes, his detectives and the gumshoes hired by the railroads, Lowe's confession had been the product of nothing more than effective law enforcement. The Chief categorically denied having forced the confession. He and other law officers were confident Jesse Jr. had been an accomplice and gang-leader in the crime based upon the confession and his known friendship with the "Quail Hunter." Chief Hayes boasted having considered the young James boy a suspect from the moment he first learned of the robbery. This he said explained why he had dispatched detectives to the James residence the night of the robbery. He wanted to "shadow" his every movement that very evening. The letter from Jesse Jr. to Lowe was simply the icing on the cake to the police chief. Why would the son of the infamous Jesse James, a noted crook and train robber, be any different than his father? For the chief and detectives, Lowe had told the truth, the whole truth, and nothing but the truth.

CHAPTER X
CHARGED & ARRAIGNED

Dateline: October 11, 1898
Westport

Headline:

ANOTHER FLAG RAISING
STARS AND STRIPES WILL FLY FROM
SCHOOL BUILDING IN THE REPUBLIC OF HAWAII[136]

Waving Lowe's full written confession in hand, police and the rail-road detectives went directly to the tobacco stand in the county courthouse on October 11th. They found Jesse Jr. working behind his counter engaged in a conversation with a well-known local attorney, William H. Wallace, the former elected pros-ecutor of Jackson County. Wallace, like many other attorneys, had become acquainted with the proprietor at his cigar store. Had Wallace also taken young Jesse under his watchful eye? When officers arrived to take their leading man into custody, Wallace intervened, pleaded and admonished

William H. Wallace

136 *Evening Bulletin*, October 11, 1898, Oahu, Hawaii.

that without a warrant the arrest was illegal. His appeal was to no avail.

Ironically, Wallace in his days as Jackson County Prosecutor had been quite successful in bringing an end to the "outlaw" reputation of the State of Missouri. He brought down Bill Ryan, a member of the James gang (brother of Andy Ryan and friend of the Quail Hunter), back in 1881; he traveled to St. Joseph and identified Jesse James, back in 1882; he had prosecuted the boy's uncle, Frank James, back in 1883, effectively but unsuccessfully; and he had an unblemished record. Despite the former prosecutor's well-known and celebrated identity, his pleas for Jesse Jr. were ignored. Police and detectives, not hesitating for any further explanation, took the purveyor of tobacco products into custody.[137]

It is an over simplification to describe his arrest as being out of the ordinary. Two weeks earlier he had been questioned and then released. When finally "captured" at his business, a place he had been operating since January 15th, police did not allow him to secure his stock or business inventory. Even after he attempted to give his keys and cash receipts totaling over fifteen dollars to William Wallace for safekeeping, police seized them. There had been no warrant issued. The suspect was summarily removed from the courthouse and transported by cable car to Westport where he was secreted in an unknown location before being transferred to Police Station No. 5 in Westport.

The headline news the following day was simply sensational. The story line of the *Kansas City Journal* was unambiguous:

JESSE JAMES
SON OF THE NOTED BANDIT KING UNDER ARREST
IS A SUSPECTED TRAIN ROBBER
APPREHENDED BY DETECTIVES AT THE COURT HOUSE
NOW LOCKED UP AT WESTPORT

---

137 In the later part of the 19th Century, William H. Wallace traveled to England where he met an eminent British gentleman. The Brit asked Wallace a question: "Do you know who is the most famous man America has produced?" Wallace, after pondering the question provided the man with the standard names of Washington, Lincoln and Jackson. "No!" The Englishman declared to Wallace. "He was Jesse James. We hear more about him over here than all of the rest put together." See, *Kansas City Star*, August 7, 1938 (Some things never change!).

The *Kansas City Times* in keeping with the mystic of the James' family heritage, not only captured the story, it included photographs of father, son and Uncle Frank on the front page as well. The Jesse James story was not to die; his story deserved to be retold, again and again and again.

After his arrest, Jesse Jr. was initially installed in Acting Lieutenant Mike Kennedy's room, located above the jail in the police station in Westport, where two other suspects, Andy Ryan and W. W. Lowe, joined him. Several law enforcement visitors came to the room where Jesse Jr. was being detained. Their sole purpose in the "visit" was to gather and collect the "truth" from the bandit's son. Kansas City Police Chief Hayes and Detectives Keshlear, Bryant and Boyle questioned him for hours. After completing their interrogation, Railroad Detectives Harbaugh, Delong and Furlong took their turn sifting through their web of questions. When the "inquisition" was concluded, Chief Hayes and railroad sleuths, along with Andy Ryan in their custody, returned by cable car to the police station downtown. That night, Jesse Jr. and the confessor, Lowe, remained "locked-up" together in an apartment above the jail in Westport. Chief Hayes categorically denied that young Jesse was "locked-up." He proclaimed that the young man had only been "watched" over by police and allowed the full use of the telephone at the police station. Whether Jesse Jr. was "locked-up" or "watched," he remained "detained" until further order of the court.

Local and national editorialists doubted, queried and questioned the integrity of both the arrest of Jesse Jr. and Lowe's confession. The *Salt Lake Herald* quoting the *Los Angeles Times* opined that the "Kansas City Police were relying more on a name than on a deed coupling the son and namesake of the famous Jesse James" with the hold-up.[138] The *Kansas City Star* objected to W. W. Lowe being "continually harassed by detectives," and that Detective Harbough had guaranteed Lowe "the lowest penalty" and "a permanent job on the railroad" after his prison sentence if Lowe confessed and implicated Jesse Jr. Rumors were rampant that Lowe's testimony was tainted, the result of being worn-down

---

138   *Salt Lake Herald*, October 7, 1898.

and coerced by detectives, or the byproduct of bribery. Later, when Lowe was interviewed after his confession, he conceded being extensively questioned to the point of teetering on the "brink of insanity" and pressured into implicating Jesse Jr. in the crime.[139]

Not only was Lowe's confession spurious in the minds of many, the methodology utilized in arresting Jesse Jr. brought protestations from leading members of the judiciary and community. Western District of Missouri Federal Judge John F. Phillips (the same John Phillips who had successfully defended the young man's uncle, Frank James, in 1883) came forward publicly denouncing police procedures. Former Governor Thomas Crittenden (the same governor who had issued the wanted poster for Frank & Jesse James in 1881) vigorously proclaimed it had been a crime greater than the train robbery itself. Mr. Finnis Farr (the same man who had been secretary to Governor Crittenden when Jesse James was killed in 1882) categorically compared the arrest to a kidnapping. Farr had known Jesse Jr. since his childhood and had previously served as his lawyer. In an interview with a reporter for the *Times* on October 12th, Farr argued that police and detectives had coerced Lowe's confession by holding him for two to three weeks without benefit of a warrant, and that the only reason Jesse Jr. was arrested was because of his name. "If the boy had been named George or John he

R. L. YEAGER.

would not have been arrested. His name is against him." Farr assured the reporter a writ of habeas corpus would be filed in court immediately to secure the release of his client. President R. L. Yeager of the Kansas City School Board echoed these sentiments. Representatives of Armour Packing Company came forward in support of their former

---

139 *Kansas City Journal*, October 12, 1898.

employee by declaring a commitment to stand firmly behind his integrity and honor.

There were countless editorials expressing intense dismay and deep regret against those questioning or challenging the integrity of the police investigation. The *Courier* of Lincoln, Nebraska was insensed over criticism being leveled at Chief Hayes and questioned whether Jesse Jr. or Chief Hayes would be going on trial. Sarcastically, the *Courier* stated that if Jesse Jr. was acquitted he would be set free and "awarded a martyres crown" while Hayes would be drummed out of office to "walk the streets in disgrace."[140] The *Kansas City Journal* sang a chorus line to the views expressed in the *Courier*. To these critics, the defendant did not deserve any treatment other than that of any common thief. They were convinced he committed the crime; he was no different than his father; police and detectives only exercised their legal duty; it had been nothing more than good law enforcement in accordance with standard operating procedures.

Dateline: October 12, 1898
Judge Henry's Courtroom

Headline:

PRESIDENT MCKINLEY
ARRIVES IN OMAHA[141]

At 2:00 p.m. the day following his arrest, Jesse Jr. arrived at the courthouse for his first court appearance. Inspector Halphin and other Missouri Pacific Detectives delivered him to Circuit Court Judge John W. Henry. The irony was unavoidable as the courtroom was located on the second floor in the same building in which the suspect ran his business. Although the court proceeding lasted less than ten minutes, it proved to be controversial. Chief Hayes first explained to Judge Henry that Jesse Jr. had been arrested and held in connection with the Leeds' train robbery. Jackson County Prosecutor Frank Lowe informed the

140   *The Courier*, Lincoln, Nebraska, October 22, 1898.
141   *Wichita Daily Eagle*, October 12, 1898, Wichita, Kansas.

judge that charges had been presented to the grand jury earlier that morning. He insisted that the defendant should remain incarcerated because significant evidence existed to convict him. Judge Henry then read the formal charges against Jesse Jr.

Immediately after Judge Henry had completed reading the information, the defense team leaped into action. Farr's threats made the preceding day to file a writ of habeas corpus had proven to be no mere words. He and School Board President Yeager filed the writ, and demanded the release of their client. Yeager told Judge Henry that his client had been arrested without benefit of a warrant—an illegal act in derogation of local, state and federal law. Prosecutor Lowe objected vehemently to Yeager's assertions. He proclaimed the state's arrest of Jesse Jr. had followed "customary" criminal procedures. Judge Henry appeared disturbed and flustered by the prosecutor's objection. The judge examined some law books and pondered the motion and writ before "firmly" declaring the "custom" followed by police and detectives was "not authorized by the law, either the state law or the federal law." He ordered the young man to be released calling the arrest a "damnable outrage."

Judge Henry's ruling did not conclude the courtroom haranguing between prosecutors and defense attorneys. As Jesse Jr., his attorneys and friends retired to another room in celebration, Joseph Keshlear served the arrest warrant. The state had finally done it right. The detective then led "his prisoner" to Justice Spitz where a bond hearing was held that lasted about fifteen minutes. Bond was set at $2,500 and a preliminary hearing was scheduled for the following Monday, October 17th, Finnis C. Farr and E. F. Sweeney, the cashier at the First National Bank (Sweeney a wealthy man lived in a country estate on Lee's Summit Road that he called the Glendale Mansion), endorsed the surety bond and Jesse Jr. was discharged from custody. This time he, his lawyers and several friends adjourned to the entrepreneur's cigar stand downstairs, where he resumed business operations and received the "courthouse gang."

The *Kansas City Journal* expressed disgust the following day about the preferential treatment community leaders had provided to Jesse

Jr. The *Journal* reported five thousand dollars had been raised by the "courthouse gang" to prevent him from going to jail with additional monies being raised to retain investigators and detectives to prove his innocence. The *Journal* took critical aim at Yeager and others by ridiculing and criticizing how "presidents of school boards and bank cashiers" had rushed to the aid of the "son of the most notorious bandit in the history of the United States." The actions of "President Yeager of the school board" were "wide of the mark and sent a terrible message to students in the district and would cause young students to believe that train robbery was not a big deal."

In addition to the "courthouse gang" raising funds for the defense of Jesse Jr., others came forward proffering aid and assistance. David Ball, a perennial Democrat gubernatorial candidate from Pike County, Missouri, offered to represent Jesse Jr. *pro bono*. Jesse Jr. first declined Ball's offer of free legal representation claiming he already had defense attorneys. In the end Jesse Jr., told Ball he was not in a position to turn down any help. The legal team hired to represent the defendant did not agree with their client on this point. They promptly turned Ball away claiming his proposal was to get his name in the papers and not out of an interest in defending the case.

The James family did not remain silent. They expressed their shock, dismay and disgust over how "poor" Jesse Jr., the mainstay of his mother, had been treated and arrested. Mrs. Samuel first learned of her grandson's arrest that very evening at the train station in Kearney. She was preparing to board the southbound train to Kansas City for a visit with her daughter-in-law and grandchildren when a newsboy entered and bellowed, "Read all about the train robbery—Jesse James arrested." The aged mother of the late bandit was in torment when she arrived at Union Depot to meet the distraught mother of Jesse Jr. It was at the station that she heard about the unorthodox arrest. She was incensed her grandson had been taken into custody on "mere suspicion" and grew angrier when she discovered her "poor Jesse" had been secreted away to an apartment in Westport for questioning. She told reporters the arrest of her grandson was a "sham," extremely "irregular" and an "outrage." She compared police tactics to those followed by detectives, whom she admittedly detested, to that fateful night in January 1875 when Pinkerton agents had killed her baby, Archie, and had blown off half her right arm.

Mrs. Samuel and her granddaughter, Mary Susan, confirmed the alibi previously provided by Jesse Jr. Mrs. Samuel told reporters she was as guilty as her grandson for the Leeds train robbery and point-blank declared he had not been involved in the holdup. Why not? Because she had been seated next to him on the front porch of the family's home on Tracy that very night. She had remembered the event back in September so clearly as they had all commented about the loud explosion they heard that evening. Mary echoed the veracity of her grandmother's story. She explained her brother was home because he never was "gone long whenever" grandma visited, as she did that night. Mary added most of their neighbors knew he was there as well.[142]

(Zerelda Cole James Samuel
Mother of Jesse James & Grandmother of Jesse Jr.)
(Courtesy Jackson County Historical Society)

---

142 *The Courier*, October 12, 1898.

From the eastern side of the State, there were reports of yet, another James family member coming forward to stand behind "poor" Jesse. His famous or infamous Uncle Frank James purportedly had sent his nephew a letter announcing his intentions on traveling to Kansas City to support him throughout the ordeal. Frank at the time was living in St. Louis, working as a theatre doorkeeper. Certainly, Frank's presence would be beneficial. He had his own practical experiences in the courtroom. Frank James after having surrendered to Governor Crittenden in October 1882, stood trial not once but twice, in 1883 for the Winston Train Robbery and in 1884 for the Muscle Shoals stage coach robbery. He had been acquitted both times. Frank James' presence would surely bolster the atmospheric excitement.

Unquestionably, it had been Lowe's "written confession" that provided detectives the central element for the subsequent arrest and incarceration of Jesse Jr. The *Kansas City Times* and the *Kansas City Star* on October 13th printed Lowe's full "confession" in its entirety. The public clamored to know every detail of what he had said.

LOWE TELLS HOW THE JOB WAS DONE

I planned this robbery myself, having gained information that on a certain date the Missouri Pacific would carry a large sum of money out of Kansas City. I went over the ground myself several times and marked carefully the exact spot where the engine of the east-bound Missouri Pacific stopped for the Belt Hue crossing at Leeds. I marked the exact tie, it being twenty-nine ties from a certain telegraph pole. On two occasions I took Jesse James out with me and we came back in the afternoon on freight cars.

Jesse arranged for one of the buggies at Self's bars, a friend hiring it for him and leaving it at a point just south of Jesse's house, where there is a small clump of timber. Polk obtained the other buggy at a livery stable near his house, 1712 Harrison street.

At 4 o'clock on the day of the robbery we got information that the big swag of money would be sent out that night. Jesse and I went out on a car together and got off near Goodlee & McMurray's liver stable thirty third street and Troost Ave. Jesse led me to the buggy, a one-seated affair with one horse attached to it and then went away. I drove around the block several times and finally met Jesse again. He had a sack with him and the masks and old clothing. We waited for Ryan, Polk, Evans, the big fellow and old man Stone. The latter went along to hold the horses. Polk handled the dynamite. He did not say, and I do not know where he obtained it. I do know that he procured it somewhere. James, Ryan and myself occupied the one-seated buggy, driving south on Troost ave to thirty-fifth street. We led and the others followed.

When we reached the little station James smashed the operator's telegraph instruments while Ryan covered him with a revolver. We took him along.

When the train came to a stand-still, James was the first man in the express car. Ryan covered the messenger and Polk attended to the dynamite. The first attempt to explode the dynamite failed and it was some time before Polk again was able to complete his preparations and explode the dynamite. Evans and I climbed into the engine and covered the engineer and fireman.

After the explosion, Evans ran out to look for money. He found a big package, which I suppose was money and placed it in the sack that Jesse had brought along. I do not know how much money Evans picked up, but we had information that there was $180,000 in the safe. What Evans got he kept, for we have not seen him since. Between us we found $20, which have not yet divided.

We were all pretty much exited after the explosion, but managed to gather our clothing, weapons, and masks together and burn them in the firebox of the engine.

We came back to town the same way we went out to the scene of the robbery.

There it was for the world to read and review—the confessor's confession. Jesse Jr. was no longer a subject of clandestine gumshoe meetings and Lowe was no longer the focus of intensive interrogation. The cigar man had been identified as the brainy leader of the operations and Lowe would be his two-faced accuser. To some in the press, Jesse Jr. was just 'a real chip-off the old-block.'

CHAPTER XI

AN INDICTMENT OR NOT

$$\Longrightarrow \equiv \Longleftarrow$$

Dateline: October 12, 1898
(Continued)
Grand Jury Room

Headline:

Dons Make A Bluff
Propose to Keep
Troops in Cuba Until
Treaty is signed[143]

Detectives were not bluffing in their desire to bring Jesse Jr. to justice. The morning after his arrest the Jackson County Grand Jury was convened and impaneled. The twelve male members of the Grand Jury were assigned the task of reviewing and considering evidence from prosecution witnesses, including the train's engineer, express messenger and victims of the robbery. Mr. Self, the owner of the livery stable where a buggy and horse had been leased on the evening of the robbery, was among those who testified.

Undoubtedly, the most sensational event of the day was the testimony provided by the first witness paraded before the grand jury—the tale of the confessor. Assistant Prosecutor Brady began by reading Lowe's written confession to the Grand Jury. Lowe spent the next three

---

143 *Kansas City Star*, October 12, 1898.

hours on the witness stand. His full, true confession admitted that not only had he participated in the robbery, but he helped plan it as well. Furthermore, he identified Andy Ryan, Charles Polk, Caleb Stone and Evans as co-conspirators. He just didn't really know the real identity of Evans. Lastly, he explained that the "Quail Hunter" was not involved whatsoever.

Brady's line of questioning then turned to the cigar and tobacco salesman. Lowe was not reluctant to assert that Jesse Jr. had been more than just a mere gang member; he had carefully orchestrated the robbery and was its leader. Lowe outlined how he and Jesse Jr. inspected the Leeds terrain several times in advance of the heist, with the last being made on Sunday, August 28th. It was Jesse Jr. himself who had smashed the telegraph wire, carried the double-barreled, breach-loading shotgun, and had been the first to enter the express messenger's car. Lowe's story only "scratched the surface" as to the various roles in which Jesse Jr. had played.

On day two, the grand jury heard testimony from several other witnesses ranging from railroad employees to "private eyes." The most thrilling part of the second day occurred when Mrs. Lowe testified. Detective Furlong brought her safely back from St. Louis the evening before, and he had her concealed a few blocks away from the courthouse at the Centropolis Hotel located at 5th & Grand Avenue. Mrs. Lowe, no longer masquerading in men's clothing, took the witness stand at around 3:00 p.m. Perhaps, she would have been more pleasing to the press if she had not dawned woman's apparel. The *Times* reporter described her as a "plump' yet "decidedly good-looking young woman." Mrs. Lowe was the last witness called by the prosecutor on the second day.

The third day of the proceeding was nothing more than a continuation of the two previous days. Scores of witnesses were once again presented until around 3:00 p.m. at which time the state rested. Prosecutor Brady told the grand jurors his office had provided complete, thorough and sufficient evidence, and that the hour had come for them to reach a decision. He asked for true bills of indictments to be returned against each man identified by Lowe, and especially against Jesse Jr. The jury then adjourned and went into executive session to deliberate, consider and ponder the evidence.

Time seemed to pass slowly while the grand jury deliberated. The press speculated on the outcome. One reporter had surmised that the first vote was eight to four for a "true bill." Another announced the count at ten to two for an indictment. The *Journal* was so confident that it boldly, but prematurely, announced an indictment had been returned against Jesse Jr. After several hours of deliberations and countless votes, the jurors retired for the night. Surely, there would be a verdict the following day. To everyone's disappointment the grand jury made a shocking declaration. There would be no verdict the next day. They decided not to deliberate over the voluminous evidence on Saturday, October 15th. They chose instead to use the day inspecting the two Jackson County jails, the new one in Kansas City and the old one in Independence.[144]

Much to the chagrin of the press and its adoring readers an entire weekend would go by without any formal announcement from the grand jury. Questions only mounted. Would Jesse Jr. be indicted? Would indictments be returned against Andy Ryan, Charles Polk and Caleb Stone? Who was the mystery man, Evans? Why did Andy Ryan remain in custody at the county jail while Polk and Stone had not even been arrested? Despite police having put the "thumbs" to Polk and Stone, they remained free to roam. Perhaps the grand jury did not want to return a "true bill" against Jesse Jr. Why not? Wasn't his preliminary hearing scheduled before Judge Spitz on Monday, the 17? If Judge Spitz determined there was probable cause against Jesse Jr., there would be no need for the grand jury to even make a decision. This may have explained the jurors' decision to tour the jails and not deliberate the following day.

While the press and community speculated, police and other law enforcement officials were convinced that Jesse Jr. would be indicted <u>and convicted.</u> The police boldly announced they had evidence to

---

144 The county jail in Independence had been in continuous operation since 1859. It discontinued serving as a jail in the 1930's, and became a museum in 1958.

prove beyond a doubt that Jesse Jr. had been with the "Quail Hunter," Jack Kennedy on January 28th, the night in which Kennedy had fallen off his horse in route to the famous quail hunt.[145] Police would only say they had a big surprise awaiting the attorneys for Jesse Jr. when the preliminary hearing opened in Judge's Spitz courtroom on Monday the 17th. When pressed for a hint, police would only say they had evidence that unequivocally linked Jesse Jr. to Kennedy on the night of January 28th, and to the Leeds train robbery on the evening of September 23rd. What was that evidence; when was it discovered; and who uncovered it? Was James-Kennedy the new James-Younger gang? Surely, answers to these puzzling questions would be revealed.

Dateline: October 17, 1898
Grand Jury Room & Judge Spitz Courtroom

Headline:

PORTO RICO OURS TOMORROW
Stars and Stripes to Be Raised at San
Juan, Betokening American Possession[146]

The stars and stripes over the Jackson County Courthouse waved majestically as snow and freezing-drizzle filled the air Monday, morning October 17th. Under such biting elements, Jesse Jr., his lawyers and the Grand Jury arrived at the Jackson County Courthouse around 9:00 a.m. Despite the inclement weather, a large, motley and diverse mass gathered inside and outside the courthouse. Their reasons for assembling were as assorted as the crowd itself. Some were assembled to learn if the grand jury had reached a verdict while most were hopeful to listen to witness testimony presented at a preliminary hearing. Some had simply arrived to celebrity watch with the hope of catching a glimpse of the celebrated James family or recapturing a moment of the enduring James gang legend. Many just came out of idle curiosity. The horde gathered that morning also included "old farmers with mud"

145 *Kansas City Times*, October 16, 1898.
146 *Kansas City Journal*, October 17, 1898.

from "Crackerneck still on their boots;" boys with "harmless 22-caliber revolvers" in their hip pockets; "former slaves" and their descendants who had known the James brothers before, during and after the war; old women "anxious to see the unfortunate boy;" and young ladies with "yellow curls and handsome complexions" clamoring to catch a glimpse of the son of Jesse James.

The multitude of observers anxious and thrilled to hear witnesses be examined by lawyers at the preliminary hearing left extremely disappointed. There would be no testimony on this date. The Grand Jury around Noon issued true bills of indictments against Jesse Jr., Andy Ryan and his older brother, Bill Ryan, Charles W. Polk, Caleb Stone, William W. Lowe, John F. Kennedy, the "Quail Hunter," James Flynn, George Bowlin and the mysterious "Evans," who remained unknown and unfound. It is undisputed that inside information had been previously leaked to the clerk of the criminal court. Clerk Thompson had already prepared arrest warrants for each man before the indictments had been publicly announced. Deputy Marshals lost no time in arresting Jesse Jr., as they walked directly down the hall where the defendant sat waiting for the start of his preliminary hearing before Judge Spitz. The now indicted man voluntarily surrendered to County Marshal Chiles at the county jail building in Kansas City about 2:00 p.m.

Deputy Marshals then returned Jesse Jr. along with Polk, Stone and Ryan at 3:00 p.m. to the courthouse to appear before Judge John W. Wofford to plead to their indictments. Counsel for Jesse Jr., R. L. Yeager and Finis C. Farr, entered not guilty pleas and requested a severance of the indictment so their client would be tried separately from the other co-defendants. Yeager also requested a bond reduction "and if possible" to "have the trial set for tomorrow" as "[w]e are ready and anxious to go to trial and the sooner it has been done away with the better." Judge Wofford promptly reduced the bond to $8,000. Various leading citizens in the community were prepared to serve as bondsman. Among those stepping forward to sign the bond were attorneys, Frank Walsh and Finnis C. Farr, and E. F. Swinney of the First National Bank. As to the speedy trial request, the court's calendar precluded the case from starting the following day, but it did allow for it to commence within a few days. The judge set the case for October 26, 1898. Nothing like a speedy trial!

The Grand Jurors requested a release from further service after the issuance of the indictments. Judge Wofford refused and charged them to take up bribery claims that had been circulating during the criminal investigation of the Leeds train robbery. The judge first pointed to the headline news stories that had alleged jury tampering in the Jack Kennedy

(Judge John W. Wofford)

trials. The judge next reminded them of Lowe's grand jury testimony in which he claimed Jesse Jr. and several other Leeds gang members had given him $7,000 to bribe jurors to acquit the "Quail Hunter." The judge was gravely concerned the acquittal of Kennedy had been a direct and proximate result of bribery. Judge Wofford clearly wanted answers (and heads) and told the grand jurors the newspapers had made a story of these allegations and he wanted to get to the bottom of it. Was he also playing to the press in an attempt to overcome the negative editorials written about him in a re-election year? He gave the grand jury the following directives:

> It is a serious thing to corrupt or attempt to corrupt a juror. Lowe has made these charges and you will have something at the start to work upon. Probe this matter to the bottom and find out where the fire is. Summon Lowe and every juror that sat in either of Kennedy's trials and question them closely. Summon the newspaper reporters who made the statements in their columns that Lowe said he spent money on behalf of Kennedy. You have not finished your work and I will not let

you go until you have done so satisfactorily to me.[147]

Who would the grand jury call first? Would it be Lowe or the "Quail Hunter?" Shouldn't they hear from Jesse Jr., the so-called moneyman? To the shock and horror of Lowe, he was the first witness grand jurors' wanted to interrogate. Would poor little Jesse be indicted on other charges involving these nefarious characters?

The train robbery indictment of Jesse Jr. renewed demands for him to consider an acting career. He received a least two offers from national theatre managers to perform on stage at the rate of $100 per week. The manager of the Gillis Theatre offered him a role in the new and upcoming production of "Daughter's of the Poor." He had an interest but declined to accept the part until he had spoken with his mother and Uncle Frank James. This was not the first time the theatrical industry had sought to capitalize on his family name. Three years before, producers of "The Great Train Robbery" had offered him the same weekly salary to perform on stage. They knew the appearance of the son of the bandit would promote ticket sales and substantially bolster revenues, but his mother emphatically vetoed the idea. Would his mother or Uncle Frank voice objections to the acting contract? If they objected, perhaps these offers would one day spark an interest for him to go into acting or enter the newly invented film industry.

---

147 *Kansas City Times*, October 18, 1898.

CHAPTER XII
WILL THE TRIAL BEGIN?

➤━━●●●━━➤

Dateline: October 26, 1898
Judge Wofford's Courtroom

Headline:

CONGRESSMEN WHO OPPOSED
PRESIDENT'S WAR POLICY HAVE
RICHLY EARNED THEIR RETIREMENT[148]

On Wednesday, October 26th, the Jackson County Prosecutor's "war policy" to retire Jesse Jr. from the tobacco industry was scheduled to begin in a courtroom immediately above his cigar shop. Reporters seemed more interested in the anticipated court appearance of Frank James, the "uncle of the youthful defendant," than upon the talents of the defense team aligned to defend Jesse Jr. Stories had surfaced earlier in the week that Frank was traveling from St. Louis. Would he be prominently seated next to his young nephew in the courtroom as a sign of support? The newspapers were convinced of the validity of these theories.[149] Throngs of onlookers, including many of Frank's old soldiers and "pards" had gathered at the courthouse and in the courtroom with excitement, curiosity, anticipation and even adoration for the expectant arrival of the elder James.[150] The crowd was not to be

---

148 *Kansas City Journal*, October 26, 1898.
149 *Kansas City Journal*, October 23, 1898; *New York Times*, October 27, 1898.
150 The *Kansas City Journal*, October 26, 1898.

denied. Frank's entry into the courthouse caused thunderous excitement to bellow throughout the building. Frank James had become the cynosure for all eyes to see. However, the "unwilling lion" appeared to pay no attention to the "manifest admiration" he received.[151] This would prove not to be the only courtroom appearance Uncle Frank would make in this case.

(Alexander "Frank" James)
(Courtesty of Jackson County Historical Society)

Procedurally, once the attorneys announced their readiness to begin the trial, the court process of selecting forty-seven qualified potential jurors, called veniremen, would begin. The selection process had a unique and acute overtone for both prosecutors and defense counsel. This is because new Missouri law had made train robbery a 'hanging offense.'

---

151 The *Kansas City Journal*, October 26, 1898.

The jurors would be selected from a list of one hundred and fifty. Names were placed into a jury wheel, and "Old Shack," an-aged employee of the country court, would then spin the wheel and randomly select forty-seven names. Once the forty-seventh man was identified, the lawyers would interrogate each juror to reach the final twelve. Each would have to answer a legion of questions, including his viewpoint on whether train robbery should be a capital crime, punishable by death.

Jackson County Prosecutor Frank Lowe was not hesitant to speak to the press that morning. The State he reported was in high spirits with its evidence well in hand. The prosecutor also proudly boasted having twenty-nine witnesses under subpoena to testify against Jesse James. Frank Lowe said he would dismiss the indictment against W.W. Lowe once the jury selection process was completed, and he would call the confessor as the State's first trial witness.

It was also theorized that the prosecution had another potential witness available to testify against Jesse Jr. This was co-indicted Charles W. Polk, a grandson of former Governor Polk of Delaware and a distant relative of former President James K. Polk. The rumormongers alleged Polk, ever since the indictments, had been held in the custody of Jackson County Marshal Chiles without the ability to post bond. The city buzz was that Polk had been repetitively questioned but had repeatedly refused to admit his involvement in the train robbery. The veracity of this gossip was uncertain, but it was unquestioned that Polk had remained under lock and key since the indictments on October 17th. Talk soon reverberated around the community that the day before the indictments Polk had given a full confession to Prosecutor Lowe and Inspector Halphin in which he had implicated Jesse Jr. in the hold-up. It was also questioned whether Polk, like W. W. Lowe, would turn on Jesse Jr. and testify against him at trial. Frank Lowe himself helped to circulate many of these pretrial rumors. He had been putting forth a great deal of strong evidence against Jesse Jr., and he hinted of additional evidence that was "even more convincing."[152]

Jesse Jr. seemed extremely confident. He had assembled and

---

152   The *Kansas City Times*, October 27, 1898.

retained extremely prominate attorneys to defend him. Finnis C. Farr, R. G. Yeager and John Atwood, a heralded criminal lawyer from Leavenworth, Kansas, were each considered to be among the best legal minds and advisers in the region. His confidence was further bolstered by the sense that approximately nineteen witnesses, including alibi and notable community leaders, were available to testify on his behalf. The strategy of the defense was principally twofold: establish the good moral character of Jesse Jr., and utilize Lowe's printed "confession" against the State. Specifically, the defense intended to assail Lowe's story by demonstrating it had been procured by illegal inquisition techniques of coercion, undue influence and threats. Farr told the press that Lowe's public confession had been nothing more than "a fabrication made for the purpose of shielding the men who had actually took part in the robbery."[153]

The defense insisted that Lowe's confession was the only admission of personal culpability obtained by the inquisitors. Finnis C. Farr attributed no stock or validity to reports Charles Polk had cut a deal with the Jackson County Prosecutor. Attorney Farr disclosed how Polk had sent two letters following his arrest. One had been sent to Farr personally and the other to Marshal Chiles. In both letters, Polk not only protested the manner in which detectives had interrogated and treated him while incarcerated, but he also unambiguously and vehemently proclaimed his innocence. To ensure full disclosure, Polk's letters appeared on the front pages of the *Times* and *Journal* on Sunday the 26th. The correspondence to Marshal Chiles read as follows:

> Dear Sir: I earnestly request you to deny access to me to everybody except my attorney, Mr. Farr, and such friends as I may request to see while I am in your custody. I appeal to you to protect me from being tortured or talked to by detectives.
> Very respectfully, CHARLES M. POLK

The letter to Farr was similar, except Polk more emphatically

---

153   The *Kansas City Times*, October 26, 1898.

denied any criminal involvement. The letter to Farr in part proclaimed:

> I am not a criminal, either by birth, education, associa-
> tion or inclination, and if I were, I am entitled to protection
> from outrage. I am under indictment, charged with one of the
> highest crimes known to the law. If I am guilty, I ought to
> be hanged. If I am innocent, I am entitled to my freedom,
> and the respect and confidence of my fellow men. I want a
> trial, and I beg you as my attorney to urge the matter by ev-
> ery means in your power. I know what the result will be, but
> above everything else, for God's sake, protect me from further
> outrage upon the part of the detectives . . . I told you the truth
> when I employed you as my attorney. I still declare to you,
> with increased feeling and emphasis that I am innocent of this
> crime, and I know nothing about it, or who was engaged in it
> . . . Relieve me from further annoyance by the detectives and
> get my trial set for the earliest day possible, and I will be more
> grateful to you than I can express.
>
> Very respectfully yours, CHARLES W. POLK

Apparently, Finnis C. Farr saw no conflict of interest in serving as defense counsel for both Jesse Jr. and Charles Polk. Likewise, he seemed to disregard any ethical consideration that the letter Polk had sent to him was privileged communication. Did Polk authorize its publication or did Farr believe that pretrial publicity of any nature was beneficial? Farr clearly considered both men guiltless and victims of a "Salem Witch Hunt" by detectives. Some suspected Marshal Chiles had leaked the story to the press. Nobody was talking. The odds on favorite for having provided the letters to the papers were the boys' mutual attorney, Finnis C. Farr. Their release to the press illustrated and solidified the defense theme that the law of sweating-out suspects had achieved each and every confession given in the case.

When the court convened that morning, Judge Wofford read the names of Jesse James, Caleb Stone and W.W. Lowe as all being indicted for the train robbery. The judge first inquired of Prosecutor Lowe as to the status of the case moving forward. Lowe told the judge that since the defense had asked for a severance of the James case from the other co-defendants, the state had selected <u>State v. Jesse James</u> as the initial case to proceed to trial. Prosecutor Lowe then announced the state was ready, and "the sooner it was over with the better."[154]

The judge posed the same question to defense lawyers. Mr. Farr and Mr. Yeager gave a puzzling response. They requested a continuance. Judge Wofford overruled this motion; they were getting their speedy trial. Jesse's attorneys then asked the judge for twenty minutes to consult with one another; this the court granted. As defense counsel left the courtroom to consider their options, Frank James sat motionless. He stared at the crowd "with his cat-like eyes, but never a feature relaxed. He looked stern and cold, even revengeful."[155] Perhaps, it had been Frank who had plotted the strategic maneuvers that the defendant's attorneys were utilizing to delay the case.

At the end of the allotted time period, the two attorneys returned to the courtroom "hot and flurried." They were armed with a motion to disqualify Judge Wofford based upon affidavits obtained from Charles H. Peacock, an Independence lawyer, and Frank McNiney, an elevator boy at the courthouse. According to these sworn statements, Peacock and McNiney both had overheard several remarks made by Judge Wofford revealing and demonstrating his "prejudice in the case against James, and was not the right man to preside at the trial." Did Judge Wofford hold a predisposition as to the guilt of Jesse Jr.? Some members of the media considered the affidavits as nothing more than a criminal defense maneuver to delay the case. It was presumed that these sworn statements were only produced once Judge Wofford had denied the defense request for the continuance. Although the judge strenuously denied the accusations, he felt an ethical compulsion to recuse himself and sustained the motion. Judge Wofford immediately reset the case for trial for Monday, October 31st. He then dispatched a letter to Judge Dorsey W. Shackleford, Circuit Judge of Cooper County,

154 The *Kansas City Times*, October 27, 1898.
155 *Ibid.*

Boonville, Missouri, requesting him to consider coming to Kansas City to preside over the trial.[156] If the defense had wanted to postpone the trial, Judge Wofford was not going to let it be a long one.

Published editorials and newspaper articles may have influenced the defense's decision to disqualify Judge Wofford as the trial judge. According to the *Kansas City Star*, Judge Wofford had demonstrated an "utter unfitness" as a criminal judge. The *Star* opined that in the seven years in which he had served on the criminal bench he had "never been free of scandal." The *Star's* sentiments against Wofford had the support of many community leaders, even Wofford's own party. Democrats at their nominating convention earlier that summer had been reluctant to put Wofford's name on the ballot for reelection. Although Wofford ultimately received his party's nomination, it had been accomplished by a very narrow margin. It is conceivable that Jesse Jr. and his lawyers, all of whom were Democrats, shared the same concerns about Judge Wofford, as had the press and other members of their party.

Those gathered to watch the trial were stunned by the courtroom gymnastics of Farr and Yeager. The press protested declaring that the defense had demonstrated a disposition to quibble, and it was certain the attorneys for Jesse Jr. did not want to go to trial. Some folks felt defense counsel had been caught off guard when Prosecutor Lowe announced the State was ready to proceed to trial. It appeared as if the defense had been out-bluffed by the prosecution in their game of criminal poker. The disqualification of Judge Wofford served as only a short reprieve. After the trial's brief postponement, Uncle Frank and his nephew left the courtroom together where they retreated to the defendant's cigar counter to smoke a cigar.

156　*Ibid.*

Dateline: October 31, 1898
Day 1 of the Trial, a 2nd Time
Judge Wofford's Courtroom

Headline:

WORK OF GHOULS
GRAVES IN ST. MARY'S
CEMETERY ROBBED[157]

Ghouls were not only polfering graves in a local cemetery, many "spooked" the courthouse in the early hours of Halloween desirous of witnessing the start of the James trial. They appeared more anxious to observe the spectacle of the courtoom events that morning than their children were to be beneficiaires of Halloween treats that evening. Would Halloween serve as the 'witching day' or 'vindication day' for Jesse Jr.?

Judge Wofford's courtroom was filled to capacity that morning. Uncle Frank, Jesse Jr., his attorneys, and Prosecutor Frank Lowe and his assistants were all seated at or near counsel table. After Judge Wofford ascended the bench, he quickly announced having heard no word from Judge Shackleford. He told those gathered that the projected time of the visting judge's arrival would be anyone's guess. The judge next instructed the defendant and legal counsel for both sides to remain within close proximity of the courtroom as he would provide regular updates on the status of Judge Shackleford's arrival from Boonville.

The balance of the day was spent waiting for the appearance of the outstate judge. At noon Judge Wofford returned to the courtroom and stated he still had received no word from Judge Shackleford; court was in recess for the noon meal. The judge resumed the bench at two o'clock, but he had no additional information on the whereabouts of the missing judge. Judge Wofford tendered the supposition that Judge Shackleford was probably out making campaign speeches in his own district since he was a judicial candidate for re-election.[158] No new trial

157 *Kansas City Journal,* October 31, 1898.
158 *Kansas City Times,* November 1, 1898.

date was set because no one knew the whereabouts or time table of the visiting judge.

It had been a long day for Jesse, the attorneys for both sides and an impatient audience. The defense and prosecution expressed their disappointment over the postponement of the trial, claiming they were fully prepared to proceed. Many in the gallery demonstrated their displeasure over the continuance. Those "panicky women" in the courtroom responded by rushing up to young Jesse "and shook hands with him and wished him well after the postponment."[159] The young bachelor was certainly the idol of the ladies.

The press raised several poignant questions over the next few days. What thoughts and questions crossed the young man's mind as he left the courtroom that afternoon? Did he relax knowing nothing would transpire for quite some time? How did he feel about remaining under the indictment pendulum? Would Judge Shackleford be re-elected in his district? If he lost who would preside over the trial? Who would assume the duties of Jackson County Prosecutor, the Republican or Democrat candidate? It was certain that neither Judge Wofford nor Prosecutor Frank Lowe would have any furhter involvement in the case. The judge had been disqualified and Frank Lowe had not been renominated by his party.

Leaving the courtroom that afternoon, the spirits of Jesse Jr. undoubtedly had to have been enhanced by the adorations he garnered from all the women. Certainly, the confidence he felt could not have been dampened by the day's events. By then, it had to have been clear to the young cigar store owner his future trial, as well as his life, rested in the hands of the electorate.

---

159 *Ibid.*

CHAPTER XIII
ELECTION DAY RESULTS

══╼◗◖╾══

Dateline: Wednesday, November 9, 1898
Election Day Results (K.C. & U.S.)

Headline:

ROOSEVELT WINS

ELECTED GOVERNOR OF NEW YORK

OVER TAMMANY'S MAN[160]

In the days preceding the fall election, both political parties engaged in their traditional wranglings by accusing each other of corruption and demogagary. Offensive and counteroffensive attacks were launched by party loyalists. The newspapers joined the fray with accusatorial finger pointing in assuming their customary partisan positions. Charles C. Yost, the City Assessor and Jackson County Republican Commmitte Chairman and the *Journal*, a political organ of the Republican Party, launched a viscious attack against Democratic candidates. Their rhetoric claimed Democrats were controlled by ruthless bosses, acted in concert with robbers and guerillas and sympathized with the city's criminal elements. They insisted that only by corruption at the polls could Democrats prevail on election day. Democrats and their leading puppet, the *Times*, asserted that opponents were abusive and slanderous. Republicans, they claimed, failed to address issues, spoke in generalities, created the financial crisis at city hall and could only

---

160 *Kansas City Journal*, November 9, 1898.

prevail by election fraud. The *Times* projected the good male citizens of Jackson County would elect only Democrats and throw Republicans out of office.[161]

The *Times* projection proved accurate. Voters on a cold, blustery, rain soaked day went to the polls on Tuesday, November 8th and delivered an "old-time majority" for Democrats in the State of Missouri.[162] The *Star* described election day as quiet and marked by unusual peacefulness.[163] The *Journal* vigorously disagreed and protested that "fraud had carried the day" resulting in "the same old result" with Democrats sweeping the local and county elections. The *Journal* boldly accused the city's political "gangs," the Goats and Rabbits, of "election fraud" and "political charades" in defeating Republican candidates.[164]

Locally and statewide Democrats celebrated the outcome of the election. They proudly announced city hall would no longer be under the domination of manipulators or reformers and good government had been restored by their landslide victory. The same sentiments were expressed in Jefferson City as Democrats seized control of the state legislature. While Republicans retained local majorities in St. Louis, their victory had been a "close shave" as its plurality was reduced from 16,000 to 3,600 votes.[165] The *Journal* on November 9th summarized its frustration over the outcome of the local and state elections: "Republicans Gain Nothing!"

National elections returns differed somewhat from the results in Missouri. Republicans since the Civil War had held slight majorities in the legislative branch of government while the executive mansion had been dominated by the Party of Lincoln.[166] Adhering to their postbellum campaign theme of waving the "bloody shirt" and accusing Democrats of causing the Civil War, Republicans withstood a loss of thirty-seven seats, principally from the southern states, but held onto

---

161 *Kansas City Times*, November 8, 1898.
162 *Kansas City Times*, November 9, 1898.
163 *Kansas City Star*, November 8, 1898.
164 *The Kansas City Journal*, November 9, 1898.
165 *Kansas City Times*, November 9, 1898.
166 From 1860-1912 the only Democrat to be elected as President of the U.S. was Steven Grover Cleveland (who had been the former governor of New York). Cleveland served two terms as President, 1884 and 1892.

Congress. President McKinley's party remained in the majority—but by a much narrower margin. Allegations that Colonel Theodore Roosevelt was not a legal resident of New York failed to hold back the maverick war hero from being elected as the chief executive of the Empire State. His success would become a rallying cry for Republicans in a year in which the party had experienced plenty of reverses. Would Roosevelt's victory be symbolic for the future? Republicans and their papers maintained that it would be. For Teddy, he intended to utilize his new elected post as a venue for something very personal to him. It turned into his own bully pulpit and lobbying platform for the Congressional Medal of Honor. Teddy certainly thought he deserved the tribute for the heroism he had displayed on San Juan Hill.[167]

The election having the most direct impact upon the trial of Jesse Jr. was that of Jackson County Prosecutor. Since the sitting prosecutor, Frank Lowe, had failed to receive his party's renomination, a new prosecutor would be taking over the case against the young man. The Democrats had nominated James A. Reed, a prominent attorney and political disciple of Jim Pendergast and his Goats. Reed was pitted against Republican George A. Neal. The electorate chose to retain the prosecutor's office under the control of Democrats; Reed was elected by a vote of 16,000 to Neal's 14,887—a majority of less than two thousand votes. Whether Jesse, a strong Democrat, voted his party-line for prosecutor or simply chose not vote is unknown. He certainly had to have questioned whether Reed would be as zealous as Frank Lowe had been in prosecuting the case. The dust had not settled over his election victory when the new prosecutor boldly and directly answered the question:

> Too many men in this town seem to enjoy immunity from the consequences of their misdeeds. As Public Prosecutor my aim shall be to see that no guilty man escapes, no matter or how powerful are his political friends.[168]

---

167   Before President Bill Clinton left the White House in 2001, he posthumously awarded the hero of San Juan Heights the Congressional Medal of Honor.

168   Meriwether, Lee, <u>Jim Reed Senatorial Immortal</u>, The International Mark Twain Society, Webster

(Prosecutor James A. Reed)

While Judge Wofford would not be presiding over the trial of Jesse Jr., he did hold onto his judicial position. Despite Nelson's *Star* editorials criticizing, chastising and condemning the judge, voters by a narrow margin retained him as chief magistrate of the Criminal Court. Judge Shackleford also carried his county by over 4,000 votes and the reelected judge from Cooper County would be available to hear the James case at the next criminal term. The only question was its commencement date.

In the Jackson County races for County Court Clerk, Marshal and Sheriff Democrat candidates were re-elected. The benefactor of Jesse, Jr. and his family, Thomas Crittenden, Jr., received a sound endorsement from voters and was retained as the County Court Clerk

---

Groves, Missouri, 1948, p. 22.

by a large percentage over his Republican challenger John B. Stone.[169] Incumbents Marshal Samuel H. Chiles and Sheriff Robert S. Stone, both of whom had been involved in the James investigation, held onto their positions over their Republican opponents. It was surmised that Jesse Jr. would continue to benefit from having his loyal friend continue in his position as the County Court Clerk.

Over the course of the next couple of months, the sensationalism of the expectant trial continued to mount. Nationally, the *Evening Time* of Washington D.C. on December 26, 1898, proclaimed it was shaping up to be "one of the most interesting trials ever held." Locally, the *Journal* described it as potentially "the most and far-reaching . . . in the history of Jackson County."[170]

While the Goats and Rabbits had united their efforts to carry the county and state for the Democratic ticket during the mid-term elections, there would be no party unity during the trial of Jesse Jr. Newly elected Prosecutor Reed and recently appointed Lead Defense Attorney Frank Walsh would be pitted against one another on the courtroom stage like gladiators in the Roman Coliseum. This marked neither the first nor the last time in which Reed and Walsh would battle on opposite sides in the courtroom (it served as a foreshadowing of a marquee criminal case in which the two lawyers would become hotly embroiled some ten years later—and in the same courthouse).[171]

---

169 In 1908, Crittenden was elected mayor of Kansas City.

170 *Kansas City Journal*, February 15, 1899.

171 In 1910, Frank Walsh defended Dr. Bennett Clark Hyde and James A. Reed prosecuted Dr. Hyde for the alleged murder of the "Great Public Benefactor" of Kansas City, Col. Thomas H. Swope (the donor of Swope Park). See, Monaco, Ralph, A. II, The Strange Story of Col. Swope & Dr. Hyde, Two Trails Publishing Co., 2010.

CHAPTER XIV
REED TAKES CHARGE

<hr>

Dateline: January 3, 1899
New York Life Building

Headline:

MORE <u>TROOPS TO</u> MANILA

CONFLICT WITH THE FILIPINOS

SEEMS IMMINENT.

<u>THE WAR OFFICE ALARMED</u>[172]

Even before he took the oath of office, the new Jackson County Prosecutor was imminently aware he had to promptly prepare for trial. It was set to begin on Monday, January 16th, and time was of the essence. Sitting in his prosecutor's office in the New York Life Building on 9th Street (the same building in which the law school held evening classes), Reed grew alarmed. His concern was that the men responsible for the Leeds train robbery could escape justice since they had all been charged under a blanket indictment. All of the criminal cases had been severed by the procedural defense move of the attorneys for Jesse James. This would result in each defendant receiving separate trials. Reed worried that if he failed to obtain a conviction against the popular James boy the acquittal would free all other defendants. To avoid this predicament, Reed had a special grand jury convened on January 3, 1899. He wanted to obtain separate indictments against each defendant. This

172 *The Times*, January 3, 1899, Washington City (D.C.).

way an acquittal in one case would not result in the dismissal of the other cases.

As James A. Reed was presenting evidence to the second grand jury, the bandit's son was working behind his cigar stand. Jesse Jr. had become a celebrity. The pavarotti press stood by watching his every move and commenting about the throngs of "good looking" girls that daily flocked to admire him. The "pretty girls" came "singlely, in couples, and in groups of five or six . . . all of them" to see the city's Don Juan. "Some of them are bashful about introducing themselves, but others walk boldly up and began a conversation on some pretext or other." Being a purveyor of tobacco products and chewing gum, it was certain that the girls would only choose gum. Not so! Two adventurous girls ventured in and wanted to look at clay pipes. Of course, the proprietor displayed a "handful on the glass showcase," and much to the dismay of the reporter, the two girls after a "merry conversation" with the store owner, lasting over half an hour, "bought four pipes."[173] Jesse had become the showcase of the town and the city's special feature.

The young man's pride over the out-pouring of affection by these damsels was interrupted the following day when word came of the death of Sam Ralston, the father-in-law of his Uncle Frank James. Ralston was well respected and considered to be "one of the best known characters" in Jackson County.[174] Rumors soon began circulating that Ralston's famous son-in-law would be coming to Kansas City for the services. The public excitement intensified with the thought of not just a James trial but a funeral in which the entire James family would be reunited. This would surely enable an adoring public to capture a glimpse of all the James members—not just the owner of the cigar store.

---

173 *Kansas City Journal*, January 2, 1899.
174 *Kansas City Journal*, January 5, 1899. Sam Ralston died of heart failure at his home in Independence on January 4th at the age of 89.

Dateline: January 7, 1899
Topeka, Kansas

Headline:

SPIRITED CONTEST OF THE
BICYCLE STARS
MILLER FORCED TO TAKE REST
ALBERT MEETS WITH AN ACCIDENT
AFTER RIDING 102 MILES—LATEST
SCORE OF THE CONTESTANTS[175]

Spirited and startling developments in the Leeds case came out of Topeka, Kansas (located about 100 miles west of Kansas City) that precluded Reed's office, police and detectives from any rest on Saturday, January 7th. Late that morning Chief of Police Strauss of Topeka, Kansas arrived at Union Depot. He was met at the station by local police and taken immediately to police headquarters where he and Chief Hayes were closeted for several hours. Following their closed-door session, Chief Strauss along with other detectives went to the Jackson County Courthouse to observe the movements of Jesse Jr. While the highly sensitive meetings were intended to be privileged, the press soon had the story, and reporters began to stalk every move of Chief Strauss and other Kansas City law officials.[176]

The surveillance by the press unearthed significant information not previously disclosed. Specifically, Kansas officials had evidence fastening the Leeds crime upon two eighteen-year-old Topekans, Chad Stowell and Seth Rosebrook, along with three other unidentified boys. According to the Under Sheriff of Topeka, Stowell and Rosebrook were inmates of the reformatory in Hutchinson, and it was there that Stowell had made a full and complete confession. Rosebrook had also provided insightful knowledge of the Leeds crime. Despite their youthfulness, the two boys had been career crooks. Much ink and pulp was consumed in describing their criminal pedigree and former residences,

175 *The Evening Times*, January 7, 1899, Washington City (D.C.).
176 *Kansas City Journal*, January 8, 1899.

including stints residing in Jackson County. They were said to have adopted their path in life by reading all the dime novels about the escapades of the James-Younger gang.[177] Were they just wanting the attention or notoriety of their childhood heros?

The wire out of Topeka on January 7th gave more complete and thorough details. It told how Kansas officials had long-possessed evidence that exculpated Jesse James from any alleged involvement or duplicity in the Leeds robbery. According to the report, Stowell had also bragged how he and his confederates had seized over $11,000 in the train heist, and then buried their ill-gotten gains in Gallatin, Missouri, a town some 75 miles northeast of Kansas City. Officials at the Hutchinson reformatory expressed diverse opinions as to the veracity of Stowell and Rosebrook. Most expressed their belief that the confessions and accounts given by the two boys corroborated so much of the details of the Leeds crime that they had to have been involved in the robbery to have known so much. The minority view was that Stowell and Rosebrook were frauds who had garnered their knowledge by reading newspaper stories.

Chiefs Hayes and Detectives Halphin and Harbaugh outwardly gave no credibility to the reports out of Topeka or Hutchinson. Hayes even denied that Chief Strauss had been to his office to discuss the Leeds robbery. Regardless of what Hayes was saying publicly, his actions as well as that of other investigators appeared to be the contrary. On the evening of the 7th, Chief Hayes traveled by train to Hutchinson, Kansas in the company of Detective Dell Harbaugh. When a reporter spotted them at the station, they proclaimed that Stowell's confession was fiction; the men currently under indictment in Jackson County, including Jesse James, were the real culprits; and their trip to Hutchinson was in search of the illusive "Evans," nothing more. While Hayes and Harbaugh were heading west to the reformatory, Chief Strauss and other officials were traveling east to Gallatin, Missouri. There they encountered "mysterious strangers" who for well over a week had been seen in or about Gallatin in search of buried

---

177 *Ibid.*

treasure. The diggers were said to be "persons with knowledge of the alleged confession of the boys in the Hutchinson reform school."[178] Was there really "gold in them thar hills?"

The story of the confession of the young men in Hutchinson was not a foreign topic to Jesse's lawyer, Finis C. Farr. It was evidence that he and Frank Walsh had not wanted leaked to anyone, especially to Reed and the press. When a reporter for the *Journal* spoke with Farr on the evening of January 7th, he "corrugated his brows and sat some moments in reflection, before agreeing to say anything further about it for publication."[179] Farr was greatly exercised and spoke of the revelation with great reluctance. The defense team, he said, had known for more than a month about the story and the identity of those who had robbed the Missouri Pacific train at Leeds. Farr confirmed that he was certain that at least one of the boys in the Hutchinson reformatory was involved in the robbery, and that they knew another three or four men who had taken part in the crime—all of whom would be called as witnesses. He adamantly insisted, "Jesse James was not in the hold-up. I know who did do it—they don't live in Crackerneck or Jackson County—but aside from that I know James was not in it. I am not relying on this discovey of the real robbers, wholly, in defense of my client. I think we will furnish evidence at the trial on which the real robbers will be convicted. I am sure that will be true, unless the premature publication of this dispatch from Topeka may make some of the plans miscarry." When pressed for more information, Farr snapped that there were "many facts that will be brought out at the trial that it wouldn't be discreet for me to divulge in advance. It is enough for me to say that we will have evidence at the trial that will pinch the toes of detectives and officials who have been so hot in pursuit of Jesse James."[180]

Jesse Jr. was at his cigar stand throughout the day and evening of January 7th. At around 9:00 p.m., he was asked about the news out of Topeka. Jesse confirmed that Chief Strauss had visited him earlier that day and had spoken to him. Yes, the Chief gave him the particulars of

178 *Wichita Daily Eagle*, January 8, 1899.
179 *Kansas City Journal*, January 8, 1899.
180 *Ibid.*

the confessions made by the reformatory boys. This marked the first time Jesse Jr. had heard of the news; "I am glad to hear it" but he refused to talk further about it or any other part of the case because his attorneys had instructed him "to express no opinions."[181]

Reed was the last to be questioned on the day of revelation. He wholly discredited the entire affair. When he was further pressed about the confession of the Hutchinson reform boys, Reed merely laughed. He had understood for some time that "the attorneys for the defense had been nursing some such scheme." Reed did not hesitate to affirm that he had spoken with Detective Harbaugh about the stories coming out of Hutchinson and Topeka, but Harbaugh had told him "they were merely some boys who had got hold of a few old masks and occasionally looted a freight car," but "aside from that there was absolutely nothing in it."[182] Nothwithstanding the allegations of the boys in the reformatory and their purported confessions, Reed was determined to proceed against Jesse Jr. and the other co-defendants named under the indictment. Not only was he not swayed by the recent developments, but he was insistent on resuming the presentation of evidence before the grand jury on Monday, the 9th. The new prosecutor wanted the co-conspirators re-indicted on the charge of robbing the Leeds train on September 23, 1898. There was no question that James A. Reed was determined to successfully prosecute Jesse James and the others charged with the crime.

Dateline: January 16, 1899
Jackson County Courthouse

Headline:

YACHT <u>PAUL JONES</u> LOST?
PLEASURE PARTY THOUGHT TO
<u>HAVE GONE DOWN IN THE GULF</u>
SEVEN WELL-KNOWN PERSONS IN THE
CENTRAL WEST ON BOARD—ONE WAS

---

181 *Ibid.*
182 *Ibid.*

REED TAKES CHARGE

Miss Taggart, Daughter of the Mayor of Indianapolis—Vessel was on a Three Days' Trips.[183]

On Monday morning, January 16th as the people in the western part of Kansas City boarded cable cars, streetcars, buggies, wagons or horses, they were greeted by another unseasonably "gulf-weather" type day. For the third day in a row, temperature was going to reach nearly 60 degrees. The climate had provided great pleasure to all who had enjoyed outdoor activities over the weekend, but this day the weather could have dipped to zero and no one would have cared. The expectant opening day of the James trial was about to begin. Or was it?

Jesse James woke in the early morning of January 16th to make the trek to the courthouse. He knew that his case would be taking center stage. Upon entering the building, a reporter for the *Journal* approached and asked him about the case. The defendant's only reply was. "I'm ready for trial." His attorneys heartedly agreed. Had they heard reports that the grand jury had just returned a second indictment against their client? Did they know the prosecutor was contemplating a continuance request? No, were their answers to both questions; they insisted that the case should not be further delayed.

Reed's morning had been fully occupied. He was continuing to sift through new developments in the case; the grand jury had just delivered separate indictments against Jesse James, Jr., Andy Ryan, W.W. Lowe, Caleb Stone, Jack Kennedy and Charles Polk for the Leeds train robbery; and his docket for the criminal-term was extensive. Neither Reed nor police would disclose the nature and extent of the recent discoveries.[184] Reed had been feeling overloaded, overwhelmed and overworked; he had been contemplating for several days requesting a continuance of the James case.

The first courtroom appearance of Jesse Jr. on the 16th was to enter a plea of not guilty to the second arraignment. Judge Shackleford

---

183 *The Sun*, January 16, 1899, New York.
184 *Kansas City Journal*, January 12, 1899. Andy Ryan entered a not guilty plea, and his case was set for trial in April. *Omaha Daily Bee*, January 17, 1899.

released him on bonds of $8,000 with Thomas T. Crittenden and Edward F. Swinney serving as his securities. After the arraignment and summary hearings on other criminal matters, Judge Shackleford then called the James case for trial. All eyes were on Reed as he approached the bench and promptly requested a continuance to the March criminal term.

This second court appearance of Jesse James that morning was unlike the earlier one; Reed's application for continuance was hotly contested. Reed's first justification for his motion was predicated upon the new indictment. Frank Walsh vehemently objected. His client had been re-arraigned; he had entered a plea of not guilty; Jesse had been released on bond; and they were ready for trial. If there were any criminal procedural formalities because of the new arraignment, Walsh was prepared to "waive all" of them. He further articulated his opposition by protesting, "We have received no notice that another indictment would be returned or that the prosecution would not be ready for trial. We have our witnesses here and are ready to go on with the case and very much desired that it be tried immediately."[185]

Reed realized that his initial reason for a postponement was not resonating well with the judge. He then turned his justification to the "startling developments in regard to this case" that had only recently "come to light." Walsh and the court asked how much time he needed to "inquire into" the new information. Reed requested "until the middle of March." The judge did not want any unnecessary delays and told Reed that "when a defendant is indicted the prosecution is in possession of sufficient evidence to convict him. I cannot give the prosecution time to hunt up evidence to convict after an indictment has been returned." This prompted Reed finally to disclose a portion of the newly discovered evidence. He told the judge that Bill Ryan, alias William Jennings, the brother of co-defendant Andy Ryan, and Jack Kennedy another co-defendant in the Leeds case, were both currently incarcerated in Springfield, Missouri accused of having robbed a Memphis train at Macomb, Missouri one week earlier. Reed explained

---

185 *Kansas City Journal*, January 17, 1899.

that he expected to secure evidence from the gang in the Springfield jail that would be damaging to the defendants in the Leeds case. Reed further argued that since the the Wright County grand jury would not be meeting until March a delay of the James trial until at least mid-March was warranted.[186] When the judge was informed that the preliminary hearing in the Kennedy and Billy Ryan case in Macomb was scheduled for later in the month, and well in advance of the February trial date, the visiting judge set the case for trial for February 20, 1899. Reed responded promptly to the new date. "If the court please, the prosecuting attorney is but human, and I have other cases besides this to look after." The judge was not moved and stated so: "The law has wisely provided that the prosecutor can employ assistants to work." In other words, hire more assistants and you've got one month.[187]

Reed simply did not believe one month was enough time. He then gave yet another reason for a two month delay: to clear the criminal trial docket. Reed argued that because the criminal court calendar was crowded with cases it would be better to clear it before taking up the James case, which he claimed would be drawn-out. The more the chief prosecutor pleaded for additional time, the more insistent the defense became in demanding an immediate trial. The persistent pleas of Reed were not sufficient to garner any further delay of the case. The new trial date, February 20th, was etched in stone, with the jury process scheduled to commence four days earlier.[188]

---

186 *Omaha Daily Bee*, January 17, 1899.
187 *Kansas City Journal*, and *Wichita Daily Eagle*, both dated January 17, 1899.
188 *Ibid*, 1899; *The Guthrie Daily Leader*, January 16, 1899; *Omaha Daily Bee*, January 17, 1899.

CHAPTER XV
THE TRIAL COMMENCES

Dateline: February 16, 1899
Office of the County Court Clerk

Headline:

MEMORY OF THE MAIN
STARS AND STRIPES HALF-MASTED ON
WRECK IN HABANA, HARBOR
WREATHS OVER SUNKEN SHIP[189]

The first round of the James train robbery trial was the selection of those who would determine his fate. On the morning of February 16th, "Old Shack," an iconic figure in Jackson County history, entered the office of County Court Clerk Thomas T. Crittenden, Jr. and ordered the jury wheel to be brought forth. For as long as anyone's memory could recall, "Old Shack's" main county duty was to oversee and supervise the county's criminal jury selection process. After the wheel was delivered to "Old Shack," he immediately "spun the jury wheel" in front of Assistant Prosecutor Johnson, Jesse Jr. and his defense team. The "spinning" continued until 150 men in Jackson County had been randomly chosen.

Anonymity was not the watchword for turn of the century American jurisprudence. The outcome of the selection process was provided to the press. Whereupon, the daily newspapers proceeded to publish

189 *The Richmond Dispatch*, February 16, 1899, Richmond, Virginia.

detailed information about the "list of the honored ones" so selected, including their names, addresses and known occupations.[190] It then became the daunting task and responsibility of the Jackson County Sheriff's Department to attempt to personally serve each man whose name had been drawn from the "spin of the jury wheel." The Sheriff's office had a very short time period (Thursday the 16th to Sunday evening the 19th) to perfect service upon the "honored ones." Each man served by the Sheriff or his deputies were mandated to report to court on Monday the 20th by 9:00 a.m.

The defendant's attorneys aligned to represent him included some of the greatest legal counselors in the community. Thomas Crittenden, Jr., purportedly coordinated the selection of these premier attorneys to defend his young friend; some opined he had even paid their fees. Crittenden, himself, made no secret of the fact that he was willing to expend his entire family fortune, if necessary, to prove the innocence of young Jesse.[191] The lead defense

FRANK P. WALSH.

counsel would be Frank P. Walsh, a young, well known, formidable attorney and member of the Shannon Rabbits faction of the Democratic Party in Jackson County. Serving as co-counsel with Walsh was R. L. Yeager, Sr., President of the Kansas City School Board, Milton J. Oldham, John H. Atwood and Finis C. Farr. The decision to include Farr had to have been by design or by the "shame" that had haunted the Crittenden Family since the death of the defendant's father, Jesse James (Finis as previously discussed had been the private secretary to Governor Crittenden at the time Jesse James had been killed). Their defense theory was firmly established: to prove that railroad companies dismayed over the numerous train robberies and inability of detectives

190 *Kansas City Journal*, February 17, 1899.
191 *Kansas City Journal*, January 8, 1899.

to solve them had conspired with Pinkerton Agents to lay the Leeds crime at the feet of the bandit's son. The memory of Jesse James could not be ignored.

The newly elected Jackson County Prosecutor James A. Reed led the prosecution's team. Reed knew full well the reputation of the defense attorneys allied against him, especially his long-time political and courthouse foe Frank Walsh. Reed, immediately after his election victory, had gone right to work preparing his case against Jesse Jr., though he only officially took office the first of January. To those bent on a conviction, Reed was considered well qualified to combat the James family and the reputation of those assembled to defend him. Several capable and proven prosecutors were available to assist Reed including Assistant Prosecutors Frank Johnson and Strother Howell. Reed, an ambitious politician, realized the prosecution of Jesse Jr. would be the largest front-page story of his prosecutorial career to date. A conviction would further his political appetite!

Dateline: February 20, 1899
Judge Shackleford's Courtroom

Headline:

THE ENTERPRISE THAT
BUILT CONVENTION HALL
IS BUILDING KANSAS CITY[192]

The state's enterprising effort to build its case against Jesse Jr. had been persistent, beginning long before the first indictments. Now there would be no further delays; no more postponements; the day in which the globe had anxiously awaited had finally arrived. Unlike his late father, but like his Uncle Frank, Jesse Jr. was going to stand trial for train robbery.[193] The criminal court in Jackson County was

---

192 *Kansas City Journal*, February 20, 1899.

193 Jesse James had been indicted in various venues for several crimes, including train robbery, but he never stood trial on any of the charges—Robert Ford had taken care of that minor detail! Frank James on the other hand stood trial twice. The first was in August 1883 in Davies County, Missouri for the July 15, 1881 Winston Train Robbery. After Frank was acquitted of those charges, he stood

held in Independence on the fourth Mondays in February with Judge Wofford presiding. However, the James' trial did not follow the statute; it convened on the third Monday of February in Kansas City, not Independence, and with a judge from another judicial circuit presiding.

After the disqualification of Judge Wofford, the Missouri Supreme Court formally assigned the recently re-elected Circuit Judge of the 14th Judicial Circuit of Cooper County, Democrat Dorsey W. Shackleford, to formally preside over the trial. The special appointment was forced upon the high court because every judge in the Jackson County Circuit (composed of James Slover, Edward P. Gates, James Gibson and John W. Henry) had recused himself after Judge Wofford had been removed. It was ethically appropriate for the judges on the bench in Jackson County to request a member of the judiciary from another circuit to handle the trial as each judge had become well acquainted with Jesse Jr. as a customer, as a courtroom witness or as a man with a name. By order of the Missouri Supreme Court, the duty fell upon the shoulders of Judge Shackleford.[194]

On February 20th at 9:00 a.m., 47 of the 150 veniremen had been served and assembled for the jury selection process. Like a beauty contest, it would be from these "honored ones" that the top twelve would be chosen as the finalists to serve on the jury. After the perspective jurors and counsels of record had gathered, Judge Shackleford convened court at the appointed time. He and the attorneys for both sides reached a prompt consensus—choosing the 12 men to serve on the jury would be concluded by day's end. After these preliminaries had been concluded, it was finally time for the much delayed and much awaited trial to commence.

Prosecutor James A. Reed began the selection by first raising general and specific questions to the forty-seven men gathered. The broad questions included background informational issues such as name, age,

---

trial in Muscle Shoals, Alabama in April 1884 for allegedly robbing the stagecoach express messenger on March 11, 1881. Frank James was once again acquitted. Frank James never stood trial for any other criminal charge, although many others charges did remain pending against him. Frank also never returned to Minnesota.

194 Later in August 1899, Judge Shackleford was elected to the United States Congress from Booneville, Missouri, and he would go on to serve seven terms in Congress (1899-1913).

address, occupation, marital status and even their political party preference. It is likely that Reed had concerns about the jurors being biased
for or against the political adversaries aligned in the case. He certainly
wanted to know if the jury panel was advocates of his political club,
the Pendergast Goats, Frank Walsh's Shannon Rabbits or Republicans.

Reed's questioning then focused upon the specifics of the case. He
asked whether any of the potential jurors had formed an opinion of
the charges, including the guilt or innocence of the colorful defendant.
Did anyone know or recognize the names of John F. Kennedy, the
"Quail Hunter," William W. Lowe, Caleb Stone, Charles W. Polk, James
Flynn, George Bowlin, William "Bill" Ryan, his brother Andy Ryan,
or Charles Milton. The prosecution had to know if any of them knew
other conspirators under indictment or who were under suspicion for
the crime. Reed explored the legend, memory and history of the James
Gang out of concern they would cast a shadow upon the trial—had
anyone known or heard of Jesse James? Reed, pointing towards the
brother of the late bandit, anxiously inquired if they knew or were familiar with Frank James. Had any opinion been formulated about the
defendant because of his familial relationships?

After Reed finished his examination, Frank Walsh took his turn
questioning those assembled as possible jurors. While Reed's line of
inquiry had been nothing out of the ordinary, Walsh's interrogation
proved to be the opposite. Like a director of an orchestra tuning up,
he started slowly and methodically, but concluded with a percussion
finish. His assessment began with their familiarity of the case through
pretrial publicity. Had they read any of the numerous newspaper accounts and stories concerning the matter? Did they know Detectives
Harbaugh, Halphin, Furlong, Tillotson, Keshlear, Bryant or the countless other law officers or private agencies involved in the investigation,
including Police Chief Hayes? Knowing that his client faced the death
penalty if convicted (regardless if anyone was injured or not), Walsh
needed to identify any potential juror who supported or opposed the
death penalty. Oddly and much to the amusement of the gallery and
press, Bernard Davidson, an undertaker, emphatically announced his

opposition to the death penalty for train robbery—Reed excluded him from the jury panel.

Walsh having fully resolved these issues to his satisfaction turned his focus to the theme of conspiracy; not a conspiracy to commit train robbery, but a conspiracy to convict his client. Had any member of the jury panel interacted or been approached, directly or indirectly, by detectives since their names had been "drawn from the wheel?" The responses provided by several panelists had to have been painful or uncomfortable for the prosecution to hear. Three veniremen, Eugene McEntee, Whitfield Woods and Christian D. Guy, each told similar tales: private detectives had approached them; they wanted to know if they had formed an opinion about the guilt or innocence of the defendant; of the three, only McEntee was selected to serve on the jury. This line of questioning served as the defense's initial salvo against the prosecution and to lay the foundation to their theory of conspiracy by the railroads and their team of investigators. Was reward money, blood money, more important than the truth? The next day the *Kansas City Star* reported that Walsh's interrogation on this point had been the most "sensational feature" of the jury selection process.

Jesse Jr. had been the center of attention throughout the full day's proceedings. The courtroom was filled to overcapacity levels. Everyone wanted to get a glimpse of him or any other James family member in attendance. The press described the young man as "the boyish looking defendant" dressed in a "neat fitting blue serge suit."[195] During the ordeal, he sat quietly in his chair near his attorneys. He appeared to be unconscious during the day's events, and his "nonchalant air" proved startling to the press and spectators.[196]

Those gathered in the courtroom were equally, if not more, enthralled to see the famous or infamous uncle, Frank James. Unlike his nephew, Frank remained extremely attentive to both the questions presented by the lawyers and the answers given by each possible juror. His cold gray eyes were elevated towards the judge and he carefully scrutinized every detail of the proceeding. Whenever any member of

195 *Kansas City Journal*, February 21, 1899.
196 *Ibid*.

the panel was questioned, Frank James was observed shading his eyes with his hand and scanning every face in the jury box as if the former fugitive had been reconnoitering his next train robbery. Frank James' attendance spurred the passion and memory of his late brother's life and death in the minds and hearts of those assembled. Walsh, a master of trial strategy, had undoubtedly prearranged, or at a minimum had voiced his approval of the uncle's presence. He knew full well of the popularity and good will the elder James had garnered in the community, especially since his two acquittals and subsequent exemplary law-biding conduct. Perhaps, the defense even considered that Frank's insight and personal experiences would be beneficial not only in the jury selection process, but also during the trial itself.

Questioning of the perspective jurors by the attorneys continued throughout the day. It did not conclude until 6:30 p.m. Once the lawyers had finished examining the forty-seven men, the judge admonished them not to discuss or talk about the case amongst each other or with anyone else. There was little concern that the hired private investigators would be approaching them with any more inquiries. The judge then told the jurors to return to the courthouse at 9:00 a.m. the following morning, Tuesday, February 21, 1899.

CHAPTER XVI
NAMING THE JURORS

━━━━━◄(◗)►━━━━━

Dateline: February 21, 1899
12 Men Selected For Jury Duty

Headline:

ROBBERS
OPEN AN EXPRESS SAFE
CHERRYVALE IN BROAD DAYLIGHT[197]

Robbing express safes was not unique to the State of Missouri. The Cherryvale robbers in Oklahoma just did not have the surname of 'James' for their thievery to reach national renown, like the one pending in Kansas City.

Missouri law in 1899, like today, authorized defense counsel and prosecutors the right to make their "strikes," a legal term used by lawyers and judges, to eliminate unwanted or potentially biased jurors. The criminal procedure, unlike today, allowed the defense team twenty-four hours to "strike" twenty names for cause. The defendant's attorneys proceeded to take nearly their entire allotted time to make their selection. One hour before the expiration of their time period, attorneys in tow with their client and his uncle returned to the courtroom around five thirty. Judge Shackleford soon followed and after he assumed the bench oral arguments were made by the defense as to which jurors they wanted struck from jury duty for cause. After their challenges

197 *The Guthrie Daily Leader*, February 21, 1899 (Guthrie, Oklahoma).

were presented and ruled on by the judge, the prosecution was allowed thirty minutes to remove fifteen additional jurors. Thereafter, Reed announced the names of the men his office challenged to serve.[198]

At the conclusion of this process, Judge Shackleford, like a master of ceremonies at a beauty contest, read off the list of the "honored ones" selected to serve on the jury. The judge promptly cautioned the jurors that they would be sequestered in a hotel until a verdict was reached. He further admonished them not to discuss the case with one another or anyone whatsoever. They were prohibited, the judge said, from reading any newspaper or other account of the court proceedings. He told the twelve men that would be staying at the Lynch Hotel throughout

Judge Dorsey W. Shackleford

the trial. Was there a smirk or smile floating in the back of the judge's mind when he considered the irony of selecting the Lynch Hotel as the living quarters for the jury since Jesse Jr. could be sentenced to death by lynching if he was convicted?

Unlike the secrecy of the identities of criminal jurors today, the twelve men, including his name, address, age, marital status, occupation and state of nativity, was listed in both local and national papers. Did the public have an interest in knowing about the men excluded from service? In the days of "yellow journalism" nothing was left out of print. The names of the thirty-five men excluded from jury service were not merely also listed but the papers provided an explanation as to why each man had been rejected by the defense or prosecution. The morning after the jury selection process had been completed the *Kansas City Journal* and *Kansas City Times* published the names and statistical

---

198 *Kansas City Journal*, February 22, 1899.

information of the twelve men chosen to compose the jury. The following is a verbatim account (including spelling) of how each juror was identified in the *Journal* article (if there is a discrepancy between the *Journal* and the *Times* articles, it is noted below each individual listed):[199]

King R. Powell, of 507 Grand avenue, 63 years old and a stationary engineer; a widower. Born in Massachusetts.

[Note: The *Times* article lists Powell as being married—Powell should have known if his wife was dead or alive.]

William Ewing, of 921 Highland avenue, a clerk, 29 years old; married. Born in Illinois.

Albert Miller, a confectioner employed at Eighteenth and Oak streets. He is 50 years old and is a baker.

[The *Times* indicated that Miller was unmarried but gave his age as 36—Surely, Miller knew his own age].

Eugene McEntee, of 526 Blemont avenue; is 36 years old, unmarried and is a bricklayer. He swore that he had been approached by detectives after his name was announced as a venireman.

[The *Times* article left McEntee's name off its list altogether.]

John J. Durrett, of 2707 Southwest boulevard; is a native of Missouri and is married. He is 58 years old.

[Note: The *Times* article listed Durrett as a farmer, age 50, married living in Lee's Summit; at least the two articles seem to have gotten his name and marital status right.]

William S. Rodgers, lives at 1536 Kansas avenue, laborer, is 32 years old, married and is employed as a laborer at Loose Bros.' factory.

[Note: The *Times* article states that Rodgers was unmarried—if Rodgers was married what would his wife have thought by the *Times* having listed her husband as being unmarried?]

Leonard Veugelen, lives at 909 East Fourteenth street; is 30

---

199 *Kansas City Journal*, February 22, 1899, and *Kansas City Times*, February 22, 1899.

years old, and is a meat cutter by occupation.

[The *Times* added his place of employment as being the Armour Packing Company.]

Samuel E. Spence, lives at 1815 East Eleventh street; is 33 years old, married and a laborer.

Joseph M. O'Connell, lives at 604 West Fourteenth street, and is 24 years old. He knows Detective Boyle. He is opposed to capital punishment.

William E. Mullins lives at 905 Linwood avenue; is 27 years old and is unmarried. He is employed as a dry goods clerk.

Joseph E. Broughal lives at 538 Jackson avenue and is a coal dealer. He is acquainted with Prosecutor Reed.

Harry G. Clark lives at 1418 East Twelfth street and is the local agent for Streets' Western Stable Car line. He is well known at the stock yards.

[Note: The *Times* article differs in employment; it lists Clark as an employee of the stock yards—at least both papers place him in the stock yards.]

The make-up of the jury was not typical for the twilight days of the 19th Century. Either there was only one farmer chosen, John J. Durrett of Lee's Summit (if you believe the *Times*) or there were no farmers (if you believe the *Times* or *Star*). The *Kansas City Star* was so overwhelmed by the make-up of the jury that it ran a bold black pointed font headline column that read:

"FARMERS BARRED"!
"Not one on the Jury that will try Jesse James".[200]

Apparently, the *Star* did agree with the *Journal* or disagreed with the *Times*. Did anyone really bother to ask John J. Durrett whether he was a farmer from Lee's Summit or whether he was not a farmer living in the city on Southwest Blvd? It is more likely that the papers didn't

---

200 *Kansas City Star*, February 22, 1899.

care one way or the other. Nonetheless, it was remarkable for a jury in 1899 to consist of either an eleven to one or twelve to none ratio of city folks to rural representatives.

The local newspapers over the next couple of days gave various but consistent favorable comments about the make-up of the jury. The *Star* on February 22 described the jurors "as excellent men, who will do their duty as their consciences see it." On the same day, the *Journal* announced that there was not a single "blemish upon the name and character of any of the jurymen." The following day the *Kansas City World* reported that prosecutors and defense attorneys all agreed that it was an "exceptionally fine" jury, with each "man of more than ordinary intelligence."[201]

Jesse Jr., during the final stage of the selection process, sat affixed next to his attorneys. He appeared much more interested in this phase of the case than the previous day's proceedings. Seated directly behind him was his uncle. While Jesse Jr. appeared to be very impressed and pleased with those chosen to serve on the jury, Frank James had spent his time examining "each juryman carefully, but did not commit himself."[202]

There was one final issue that needed to be considered by the judge and attorneys before concluding for the day. This centered upon the legality of holding court on February 22nd, the birthday of George Washington—a national holiday. James A. Reed wanted a speedy and prompt trial, without delays. He requested that the case commence the following morning. Frank Walsh agreed as he considered delays to be dangerous. He also informed the judge he had a scheduling conflict because of the high-profiled trial, Smith v. Lowry, set before Judge James Slover three days later on February 24. Walsh wanted to move forward to avoid the awkward predicament of being involved in two trials at the same time. After hearing arguments of counsel, Judge Shackleford said he would delay his decision until 10:00 p.m., and he instructed the attorneys to communicate with him at that hour.

The lawyers called the judge at the appointed time. The judge

201 *Kansas City World*, February 23, 1899.
202 *Kansas City Star*, February 22, 1899.

informed Reed and Walsh he considered it inappropriate for court to convene on a day set aside to honor the "Father of the Country." The judge expressed such a special day should not only take precedence, but he felt that having a trial on Washington's Day could violate the law—the judge would not permit either side or the press to argue he had violated the law. The case would not resume until 9:00 a.m. on Thursday, February 23rd. For Jesse Jr., the lawyers, gallery, press, the city and nation, they would all have to wait that much longer until the trial commenced.

CHAPTER XVII
LET THE EVIDENCE BEGIN

——————◦◦◦◦◦——————

Dateline: Thursday, February 23, 1899
The Confessor Tells His Tale!

Headline:

AT THE CONVENTION HALL
<u>DEDICATION BALL LAST NIGHT,</u>
KANSAS CITY WEALTH & BEAUTY
<u>WERE THERE</u>
A Magnificent Spectacle Fully 1,500
<u>People on the Floor At One Time</u>[203]

Kansas City on the evening of Washington's observance held a gala and much-anticipated event—the grand opening of the city's new spectacular convention hall. The next morning marked the actual commencement of the sensational, much-awaited and greatly advertised James trial. Judge Shackleford entered the courtroom at 9:00 a.m. on February 23rd and promptly ascended the dais. He looked down at the attorneys and asked if they were prepared to present their opening statements to the jury.

With an overcrowded courtroom, Jackson County Prosecutor James A. Reed approached the jurors. Standing directly in front of them, he patiently and calmly explained how the State would present compelling evidence beyond a reasonable doubt to prove Jesse Jr. was

203 *Kansas City Journal*, February 23, 1899.

in fact guilty of duplicity and participation in the Leeds train robbery. The defendant, Reed asserted, was not just involved in the crime, but he had been the gang leader. He analytically presented the prosecution's basis for their claims: Jesse Jr. had the opportunity and motive to commit the crime; he knew the Leeds area well; he possessed a reputation for bad acts and conduct; he had befriended characters of moral turpitude; and eyewitnesses placed him at the scene of the crime. Reed alleged that additional evidence linking the defendant to the robbery would be adduced through the confession and testimony of William W. Lowe. To Reed, the State had direct evidence of a conspiracy to commit the train robbery, all of which he laid at the feet of Jesse Jr. The prosecutor appeared confident and self-assured as he returned to his chair after completing his remarks.

(Kansas City Convention Hall Dedicated Feb. 22, 1899)
(Courtesy Jackson County Historical Society)

Frank Walsh's opening statement conceded a conspiracy. He asserted railroad detectives had acted in concert to convict his client. They wanted the son of the infamous bandit regardless of the truth.

Walsh proclaimed these men bent on destroying young Jesse had based their entire case upon the statements of "the self-confessed train robber, Lowe." Reed quickly objected insisting it was the trial of Jesse Jr. and not that of Lowe. A long wrangling over this point interrupted the flow of Walsh's presentation, but he was not to be deterred. He just detoured from the confessor and focused upon the emotional. Poor Jesse had been working since age eleven, "compelled to work for his living," attending just one year of high school, and spending "more than fifteen years" as "more a husband to his family than a brother and son." Reed protested vigorously over the relevance of the young man's poor, unfortunate background. His argument was to no avail as the judge overruled the objection, much to the displeasure of the prosecutor. Was the judge's unfavorable ruling an embodying signal of the judge's sentiments about the case? Reed must have feared it would.

The defense knew full well prosecutors strategically planned to convict Jesse Jr. by developing several circumstantial points. These theories included proving the young man frequented Leeds and associated with men of bad moral character. With this knowledge, Walsh made several admissions. He admitted his client had been to the crime area frequently, driving "out in a buggy or rode his wheel in order to see some school directors in the interest of his sister, Mary" who was seeking a teaching position "in one of the schools near Leeds." Walsh said this would be proven by "the testimony of the school directors whose integrity cannot be questioned."[204]

He likewise did not conceal the fact his client had met men of questionable morality. "We admit" Jesse knew Lowe, but this was not until "the confessor" had gone "to Jesse's stand after the Leeds robbery." Any testimony to the contrary was simply untrue and the defense was prepared to prove its falsity. Lowe was expected to testify that on August 28th, three weeks before the robbery, he and Jesse Jr. had both ridden "from the place near Leeds on a Missouri Pacific freight train" for surveillance purposes. Lowe, Walsh stated, would testify that on that day the name of the train "brakeman was Downer." The brakeman's name,

---

204 *Kansas City Journal*, February 24, 1899.

Walsh insisted, was not Downer, but Harry Vallee. Walsh told the jurors that Valle had been a former "schoolmate of Jesse's so that there could have been no mistake about" him having been able to positively identify "the accused if he had been on his train." The prosecution should produce Valle.

Frank Walsh also acknowledged that his client knew the "Quail Hunter." Again, he explained that Jesse Jr. "never knew Kennedy until the latter came to him and introduced himself . . . some time last summer." Kennedy, he explained, made frequent trips to the courthouse "to see other persons, and not Jesse" for such purposes ranging from answering criminal charges to meeting with "the assessor and the collector on many occasions." Walsh insisted young Jesse's acquaintance with Kennedy was merely as a tobacco customer. The question was not whether he knew men of suspect character, but the focal point he insisted should be upon how he had become acquainted with them.

Walsh then returned to his opening comments about the state's conspiracy. "We will show that the police placed Lowe under arrest and subjected him to what is known as the 'thirty-third degree' sweating process." His persistent interrogation resulted in the arrest of Jesse Jr. "The testimony will show that Harbaugh and several other detectives told Jesse" after he had been taken into custody that every man suspected of the robbery "had confessed and had implicated him." He told how his young client had been imprisoned in the Westport jail for several hours in an attempt "to coerce a confession from him" in the same sweating fashion interrogators had used to compel a confession from Lowe.[205]

At the conclusion of the opening statements, Judge Shackleford looked down from the bench and asked Reed to call his first witness. John J. Brown, a civil engineer, from Wichita, Kansas and an employee of the Missouri Pacific Railroad for about thirty years, was the State's first witness. Brown, an expert witness, was asked to identify a plat map of the area and list the distance from Thirty-fifth Street and Troost Avenue to the Belt Line crossing at Leeds. Brown explained he had

---

205   *Ibid.*

personally prepared the exhibit ("Exhibit A") and had calculated the mileage from Mr. Self's livery stable to the Leeds' junction. The media remarked that the direct examination of Brown had gone smoothly.

The attack upon Brown focused upon the defense strategy of developing the theme of duplicity by police and detectives. Brown admitted making the map, taking measurements and clocking the time on January 4th. Who had directed the mapping and charting? "Detective Harbaugh" was the response. Who showed Brown "where the fence" had been cut at the location of the robbery? Detective Harbaugh was the answer once again. Walsh then asked the Deputy Marshal to bring Detective Harbaugh into the courtroom. After Harbaugh entered, Walsh pointed towards him and asked: "Now, Mr. Brown, I would like to have you look at this gentleman, and tell me whether this is the Harbaugh who accompanied you when you visited the vicinity of the scene of the holdup." Brown confirmed that which Walsh already knew. Courtroom observers enjoyed Walsh's line of questioning as laughter broke out after Brown gave the name "Harbaugh" to the final question. Was the jury speculating why Harbaugh was so actively controlling the state's investigation? Were he and the railroads or James on trial? The *Journal's* commentary was more basic and pointed: "Brown failed to hold up during Walsh's cross-examination."[206]

The State's second witness sensationalized, shocked, surprised and silenced all assembled. The confessor, William W. Lowe, stocky-built with a high forehead, sandy hair, mustache and gray eyes, ambled to the stand much to the awe and amazement of everyone. Legal experts who had been following the trial had speculated that this key witness would be the last to be called by the state. By having Lowe testify at this early juncture, it appeared to observers that Reed had elected to present his most powerful evidence in the beginning instead of waiting until the end of the case.

Reed systematically and chronologically reviewed the facts and details of the crime during the first part of Lowe's direct testimony. It was like a tapestry flowing from the time in which Lowe and the James boy

---

206 *Ibid.*

had first met to the planning and execution of the raid. Lowe answered each question tranquilly and deliberately. He told how Jesse Jr. had even brought up the idea of robbing trains at the time the two had first met. He then described in great minuteness each and every detail of the robbery. Lowe was not reticent to assert how Jesse Jr. had been an integral part of it.

Lowe said the plot evolved from a series of meetings held at the James house. Lowe identified those in attendance as Andy Ryan along with three other men, "a man called Evans, who was a stranger to him, whom he had never seen before or since, and two other men, one an old man, who were introduced to him by Jesse; they were called Charlie and Harry."[207] To prove Lowe's familiarity with the house, Reed had him pencil-sketch its interior, describe the furniture, and identify the picture in the family parlor. The judge intervened before any answer was given and demanded an explanation from Reed on what difference it made as to the subject of the picture. Did the judge already know that it was the crayon image of the boy's late father? Reed argued that it proved Lowe had been in the house. Walsh chuckled and proclaimed an obvious point. "There have been many people in the house since the robbery."[208] Reed gained nothing by seeking information about the description of the drawing or the contents of the house.

According to Lowe, the cumulative effect of the meetings at the James residence concluded with the decision and the methodology on how the train robbery in Leeds would be committed. It had first been scheduled for September 1st, with Andy Ryan and Charles Polk serving as confederates. This date, he said, became unavailable, as Frank James had arrived in the city to visit his family. Lowe proudly boasted how he met the famous uncle at his nephew's cigar stand when the former bandit had been in town. The second date chosen, September 21st, was postponed because of rain. They then settled upon the night of September 23rd.

Reed proceeded to question Lowe about his history, pedigree and long-standing friendship with Jack Kennedy, Andy Ryan and even the

207 *Kansas City Star*, February 23, 1899.
208 *Kansas City Journal*, February 24, 1899.

LET THE EVIDENCE BEGIN

defendant. Lowe explained how he knew Kennedy and Ryan; they had all grown up together in the Crackerneck area of eastern Jackson County. Questioning then focused upon Lowe's knowledge of the relationship between Jesse Jr. and the "Quail Hunter." It dated back several months, Lowe said, prior to when he and Jesse had testified as alibi witnesses during the State's last criminal case against Kennedy, which had resulted in Kennedy's acquittal. Lowe insisted that it was during that time period that the three of them first planted the seed to rob the Leeds train.

Reed asked Lowe about his relationship with the defendant. Lowe stated they had first become acquainted the previous May in the courtroom of Judge Krueger. "What was Jesse doing over there?" Lowe was not allowed to answer the question as Judge Shackleford sustained Frank Walsh's objection. Reed, not deterred by the judge's ruling, solicited what he and Jesse discussed when they first met. "We introduced ourselves to each other and talked about Kennedy." This line of questioning went no further as the judge again agreed with Walsh. Reed finally was able to maneuver around the objections and obtained from Lowe a statement against the interest of the defendant. Lowe adamantly proclaimed when he had first met Jesse Jr. the young man had inquired of him how trains operated and the best way to rob them.

Reed turned his inquiry to the confessor's confession. Lowe acknowledged having given a full account of the Leeds robbery after his arrest. He could not remember the exact number of times in which he had told his story. No, he never dictated or wrote out his confession. Yes, he and the big man, Jesse Jr., the gang's leader, had been involved in the Leeds train heist. The other members of the outlaws he identified were Caleb Stone "the old man", Andy Ryan, Charles Polk, and someone named Evans. So, ended Reed's direct examination of the confessor.

Frank Walsh quickly assumed center stage. Like a well-rehearsed maestro of an orchestra with baton in hand, the lead defense attorney approached Lowe holding a copy of the *Kansas City Star*. He commenced a poignant cross-examination designed to prove the railroads' conspiracy to convict his client. He first focused upon the nature, extent and circumstances of Lowe's confession. Lowe denied ever giving a written statement, which played well into Walsh's plans. Walsh took out the October 12th edition of the *Star*. He waved the article in which the confession appeared, but Lowe's denial of authorship did not waiver.

Walsh was not deterred by these answers and denials. He was determined to demonstrate to the jury that Lowe's arrest and confession had been tainted through coercive measures. Like an artist painting a fresco, Walsh developed the intrigues of how Lowe had been sequestered at the Hotel Savoy, transferred to No. 3 Police Station, transported to the Westport Station and then removed to a hotel or boarding house in Westport where he took his meals at the Harris House. Throughout the entirety of his cross, Walsh obtained admissions that illustrated the relentless pressure Lowe had undergone by railroad agents and police to obtain the confession. Lowe acknowledged being held for fourteen days. He explained how police and detectives had repeatedly told him during "each visit they made" that "the evidence they had . . . was good, straight evidence. They kept getting after me stronger and stronger all the time. They brought my wife down to see me, and she told me she had told the police all she knew. They wouldn't let me see an attorney, nor no one else."[209]

Walsh next assaulted and challenged Lowe's creditability and reliability. This he handled artfully by utilizing every defense instrument. He illustrated how illogical it was for Lowe to assert that Jesse Jr. had inquired about the operation of trains and robberies on the occasion of their first meeting. Walsh also knew that it was too fresh in the minds of those who had heard Lowe's direct testimony to ignore he had clearly identified Caleb Stone as one of the train robbers. Surely, Lowe knew that Stone had been involved in the robbery. Wasn't Stone, the "old man," already under indictment for the crime? Walsh was aware Lowe had fingered Stone as an accomplice, but he doubted that Lowe would he be able to identify the man himself. To demonstrate this point,

---

209 *Ibid.*

Walsh had served a subpoena on Caleb Stone to compel his courtroom appearance, and he orchestrated Stone's seating arrangement. Stone was purposely sat at the end of the lawyers' table, and directly behind Jesse Jr. He began challenging Lowe's reliability by asking him to identify those involved in the crime "besides Jesse James, Ryan and Evan." Lowe promptly identified two men called Charlie and the "Old man." Walsh had laid his trap and asked Lowe to "describe them."

> Lowe: Charlie was about my size.
> Walsh: What sort of a looking man was the 'Old man'?
> Lowe: He was an oldish man.
> Walsh: Would you know him if you saw him again?
> Lowe: I don't know.

Frank Walsh, turning to Caleb Stone, asked him to stand for Lowe and the jury to see. Stone complied with the request and stood.

> Walsh: Is that the man?
> Lowe: I wouldn't identify him.
> Walsh: Do you think it's he?
> Lowe: I wouldn't say.
> Walsh: Does it look like the man?
> Lowe: I can't say; I don't know.
> Walsh: You saw the 'old man' plainly the night of the robbery?
> Lowe: I saw him there.
> Walsh: Did he have a mask on?
> Lowe: No.
> Walsh: And you don't know whether this is the man or not?
> Lowe: No.

By conceding his inability to verify or pick out Caleb Stone in the crowd, Lowe had been cornered. Reporters described Walsh's demonstration of the confessor's inability to identify Caleb Stone as the most "dramatic incident" of the day.

Walsh point blank asked whether any guarantee had been made to implicate Jesse Jr. or whether any *quid pro quo* (the promises made) had been exchanged to produce his confession. Lowe initially denied that any offers or promises were given. Defense counsel was not to be pushed aside so easily. Frank Walsh continued pounding away at a myriad of questions about Lowe's captivity after his arrest, the interrogation by police and detectives and statements made to him by his captors. "Weren't you made promises and offered an award for the confession?" Again Lowe denied the assertion. Neither Detective Harbaugh nor any other detective had offered him a reward for the conviction of the robbers. When Lowe was asked whether Harbaugh had offered to divide the reward money with him, he denied the same.

> Walsh: Didn't they promise you immunity?
> Lowe: No, Sir.
> Walsh: Didn't Chief Hayes advise you to confess?
> Lowe: Yes.
> Walsh: What promises were made to you as an inducement to confess?
> Lowe: He said if I would confess it would go light for me. He said he would use his influence.
> Walsh: Who told you that?
> Lowe: My brother told me first. Chief Hayes told me, too.
> Walsh: Didn't the officers keep asking you before you confessed, if you knew Jesse James?
> Lowe: Yes; they asked me once and I told them I knew him.

Walsh's cross-examination scored points and established many facts: Lowe had participated in the train robbery; Lowe's confession came nearly three weeks after being held captive in hotels, jails, and boarding houses; he did not enjoy benefit of legal counsel; his confession appeared coerced through promises, threats, duress or undue influence; his family members, including his wife and brother, had been manipulated to persuade him to confess; he had difficulty identifying co-conspirators to the crime; and inducements and promises had been made to obtain Lowe's confession.

The hour had reached six p.m. and Walsh had not finished interrogating Lowe. It was clear to the judge that defense counsel's cross-examination of the witness had not concluded. It was a late hour of the day, and the judge interrupted the proceeding and announced he was adjourning the trial until the following morning. The cross-examination of the "confessor" was to be continued.

CHAPTER XVIII
MORE FROM THE STATE

<hr>

Dateline: Friday, February 24, 1899
What's Next for Reed?

Headline:

GIVE YOURSELF AND THE NEEDY
POOR A TREAT BY ATTENDING THE
BENEFIT AT THE GRAND TO-DAY[210]

The general consensus was that the grand opening day for witness testimony in the James trial had been more beneficial to the defense than the prosecution. When Jesse Jr. entered the courtroom on Friday morning, February 24th, he appeared confident and Frank Walsh seemed anxious to finish his assault upon Lowe. An adoring audience of women assembled courtside to witness history unfolding in the city. The *Kansas City Star* accurately reported the true reason for the attention and attraction of the proceedings. "The deep interest in this trial probably comes from the fact that the young man on trial is a son of Jesse James, the rough riding bandit, who kept newspapers of the country well filled with his doings for many years."[211] Day two of the trial was about to begin with the confessor resuming the witness chair.

Frank Walsh began the morning examination by returning to

<hr>

210 *Ibid.*
211 *Kansas City Star*, February 24, 1899.

Lowe's confession. Lowe did not waiver from his previous testimony and continued to deny giving any confession. Walsh returned to the table and picked up two newspapers. This time to impeach Lowe's answers Walsh reviewed the contents of the printed confession as it had appeared in both the *Times* and *Star* back on October 12th. Again, Lowe denied giving the confession and declared he had "told the police and detectives the whole truth, and if they wrote it down that's their business." Lowe further denied any participation in writing it down or seeing the police transcribe it.

Despite the intensity and severity of the questioning, the "confessor" seemed to hold up better than he had on the first day. Lowe appeared unshaken from his original story, and he answered Walsh without hesitation, rarely failing to provide satisfactory answers.[212] Nevertheless, Lowe's overall credibility, as well as that of the police and railroad detectives, appeared tainted by the tenacity of Walsh's two-day inquisition. No further inquiry, your witness Mr. Reed!

Prosecutor Reed, not to be upstaged, went into his redirect examination of the "confessor" with a theatrical flare. Gripping a letter written by Kennedy to Lowe, Reed offered it into evidence as he read it to the jury:

> 8-15-98: K.C. Mo. Mr. Willum lowe dear friend Bil I thought I would write you a few lines once for the first time Say bil when you get this please cum down if you can. Yours as ever
>
> J. F. KENNEDY.

Reed then held aloft the famous "calling card" (*"We, the masked knights of the road, robbed the M.P. at the B. J. tonight . . ."*) left by the robbers the night of the train robbery. Lowe confirmed having seen the card at Andy Ryan's house the night before the crime was committed. Who had the card? "Jesse pulled it out of his pocket" replied Lowe. Reed may have been feeling confident when he asked Lowe if

---

212 *Kansas City Journal*, February 25, 1899.

he had ever seen the defendant's sister, Miss Mary, visiting the jail. No sooner was the question raised did Walsh jump from his seat to strenuously object. Judge Shackleford concurred by ruling the question out of order.[213]

It was not until late morning that Reed ended his redirect of Lowe. Walsh had no further questions. Overall Lowe had been on the witness stand nearly six hours over a two-day period. Despite Reed's valiant effort to rehabilitate Lowe, the overarching sentiment remained unfavorable for Lowe and the State. Had Lowe's testimony been truthful? If not, when, if ever, would Lowe tell the truth? A complete day and a half had been spent on only two witnesses. Could the case go any quicker?

The express messenger for the railroad, Edwin Hills, was sworn as the next witness for the prosecution. His testimony was fairly consistent with the story he had previously recited to the grand jury back in October. Prosecutors considered Hills a valuable witness for several reasons. He was an eyewitness to the crime; he would garner sympathy or empathy from jurors with his description of the terrorizing events he experienced the night of the train robbery; he could provide descriptions of the robbers; and he was qualified to quantify the monetary and physical losses of the railroad company and the cargo.

Hills described the fear and anxiety he felt that night as intense and agonizing. After he discovered the engine, coal and express cars had been uncoupled from the passenger trains, Hills grabbed his "shotgun and put out the lamp and hid" his personal valuables. When the train stopped out by Swope Park, Hills recalled hearing a loud pounding sound against the door and being ordered to, "'Open it or we'll blow the car to,' then somebody said '[g]et the dynamite and we'll blow him up.'" He saw no value in bravado and opened the express messenger's car door and jumped off the train. The bandits searched him and then ordered Hills back into the express car. He nervously and anxiously stood by observing the desperados attach seven sticks of dynamite to the express safe. After their work was done, the felons departed from the

---

213 *Ibid.*

car. Hills promptly started to evacuate the car, but to his horror, he was ordered to remain inside until the dynamite had exploded. Pleading for his life, Hills was finally authorized to abandon the express car. With a gun pointed at the back of his head, Hills was escorted down the track line about fifty yards. There Hills saw the face of one of his abductor's and for his "curiosity" he "was cracked over the head" with the revolver. Hills dreadful experience was not at an end; he was then commanded to cut the engine from the express car. It was during these labors the explosion occurred thrusting Hills to the ground and trapping him under falling debris. Hills could not comprehend how he had survived.

After recounting Hills' nightmare on Belt Line, Reed began questioning him about his ability to identify any of the culprits. Hills responses were more generic than illustrative. One man, he said, wore "a long black mask and black ulster. At one time he had a shotgun, but afterward had two revolvers . . . The man who had on the long mask and ulster seemed to be the leader and did most of the talking." After describing the handguns, Reed asked the witness if he observed any unusual behavior of any of the thieves. Yes, Hills replied. There was one man "constantly" putting his hands to his mouth to prevent the cover from falling off his face. He was asked to describe the mask, and after doing so the witness announced his doubt at being able to identify it. Reed then held up a black mask for Hills to examine and asked him whether the mask compared to the one in his hand. Mr. Walsh objected to this and was sustained by the court.

Reed: What did the man with the long coat and mask say?
Hills: He said: Give me the keys to the local safe. It's unlocked, I said, but you will not find anything there.

Hills' was asked to provide a physical description of the man in the long black mask and black ulster. "The best opportunity that I had to look at the leader was when I was in the rear of the car before the dynamite was exploded. He was about five foot six inches in height and weight 130-145 pounds, had sharp, piercing eyes and a long nose."

Jesse Jr. was then directed by the court to stand so as to allow the witness to take a closer look at him. "He was about the height of defendant." Looking directly and "squarely in the eye" of Jesse Jr., Hills compared the desperado's height to that of the defendant. "He bore a general resemblance to the man who stood-up. He had large piercing eyes as the defendant has," Hills explained. Reed then asked Hills whether the criminals had stolen any money. According to Hills, the train had been carrying $1,000 in silver, $500 in bonds and $560 in currency on the night of the robbery. When the dust had settled and lights restored, the money was taken into the office where they proudly discovered only $30 "remained missing."

Walsh, a skilled lawyer, would have known Hills storytelling of the robbery would have garnered sympathy from the jurors. He limited his cross to the defense theory of the detective conspiracy. Hadn't he been directed by Detective Harbaugh to various places to see the defendant? Hills conceded the point: he had gone to the young man's cigar stand to get a real good look at him prior to the commencement of the trial; he had done the same while Jesse Jr. was in custody in Westport. Neither occasion had helped him identify the man on trial any better than he had during his courtroom testimony. The morning had waned and the judge decreed it was a good stopping point for an afternoon break, and he gaveled a recess until 1:30 p.m.

Reed realized that Hills had failed to live up to the anticipated identification of Jesse Jr. as the culprit wearing the long black mask and black ulster. This probably best explains why he recalled Hills to the stand that afternoon. Reed started slowly asking only minor foundational points until he asked Hills the sensational question: whether he could identify the defendant's voice. To the amazement of everyone, except young Jesse himself, Hills swore he recognized the voice of Jesse Jr. "When did you first hear his voice?" Reed asked. Looking directly towards Jesse Jr., Hills replied it was "on the night of the robbery" and he was confident the defendant had been the "leader of the Leeds gang" as he was the one who had handed to him the "calling card" with the specific instructions to deliver it to the press.[214]

Sticking with eyewitness testimony, the train engineer, Charles A. Slocum, followed Hills to the stand. Reed asked Slocum to identify the gang members. Slocum quickly identified Lowe, the confessor, but was hesitant to identify the director of the band of thieves. "I did not have much of an opportunity to examine him closely. All that I can say is that he was a tall, slender man." Reed wanted another demonstration of Jesse Jr. being pointed out by another witness. Jesse stood, but before Reed could ask a question to his witness, Judge Shackleford quickly interrupted and asked Slocum if he could "recognize that man." Slocum's response was that he "would not say positively" but that he thought he had seen "that man in Mansfield, Missouri." Slocum's editorial of having seen "that man" brought on a heated debate between the attorneys and judge. Walsh protested vehemently that any reference to another person not on trial was totally improper. Judge Shackleford not only agreed with Walsh, but the judge's negative comments compelled the prosecutor to discontinue any further inquiry of Slocum.

Several more railroad employees were called to identify Jesse Jr. as being at the scene of the Leeds robbery. The witnesses included E.L. Weston, the train's fireman D.M. Hissey; the telegraph operator H.M. Carr; the conductor; and S.M. Downer a freight conductor. Weston thought the principal of the gang stood about five foot eight and wore a long coat. Hissey, to the contrary, asserted the same man was shorter, weighing about one hundred and forty pounds, extremely nervous, swearing all the time and "wearing a long-rubber coat, white hat, black mask . . . and armed with a gun, either a rifle or shotgun. The weapon was shaking worse than I was." Reed solemnly asked Hissey if he had "seen anybody since whom you think is that man" who had been the chief of the criminals. Pointing to Jesse Jr., Hissey said he thought that it was "the man right there" but the color of the eyes were different. Hissey would be more certain if he "could see Jesse with that mask on." Walsh comically replied that the witness was "entirely too anxious." Overall the combined testimony of Hissey and Hills was strong "but

---

214 *Ibid.*

failed to come up to the expectations of the state's attorneys."[215]

Neither Carr nor Downer was able to identify Jesse Jr. Carr's testimony however was disconcerting to the defense. Carr announced one of the train passengers had gotten a real good look at the robbers "at close range." Walsh wanted to know all about this mystery person. Carr said that about three weeks earlier he saw Detective Harbaugh at Union Depot with the same unknown man whom Harbaugh introduced as Mr. Smith. Walsh seemed apprehensive and puzzled by the disclosure of this potentially damaging new eyewitness. Why had he not previously heard about Mr. Smith? Who was behind the identification of Mr. Smith? Did he come forward on his own or did railroad detectives locate him? Were the railroads paying him to testify? As Walsh pondered these questions, Jesse Jr. remained, as he had been throughout the entire day, unfettered and untroubled.

The prosecution turned its attention to several witnesses who had allegedly seen Jesse Jr. in the coal and factory town of Leeds prior to the robbery. Residents of the community were the first to testify. T. H. Hutchison, a Leeds grocer and former constable and school director, said Jesse Jr. had been in the district twice the previous summer. The initial visit had been in July when Jesse came to investigate teaching positions for his sister. The next time Hutchison saw the young man was around one p.m. on Sunday, August 28th in the company of a person who was a "stranger to" Hutchison. Albert Myers, another resident of Leeds, testified seeing him in the grocery store out there, but he simply could not remember when this had occurred.

Apparently, Sunday, August 28, 1898 was a big day for bridge painting in Leeds. The prosecution had a number of employees of the Missouri Valley Bridge Company gathered to testify, all of whom had been working on that date. No "blue laws" for painters! First among the crew was William Starkey of Mena, Arkansas. Starkey claimed he had been painting train bridges in Leeds that day and saw young James walking down the Missouri Pacific track line with another person; he did not know the name or identity of the other man. Walsh had one

---

215 *Ibid.*

question: whether the railroad company had given Starkey a pass to travel to Kansas City to testify? Without hesitation Starkey acknowledged having received free passage from Arkansas and free room and board. Starkey was not alone. Three other employees of the same company, and each non-Missouri residents, had been summoned to give the exact same testimony. They were working with Starkey painting bridges in Leeds when they, too, saw the defendant accompanied by an unknown person.

Walsh's cross of each witness was accusatory. He queried how men living in such states as Colorado, New Mexico and Arkansas could identify a man they had never seen before; someone they never knew; and a person they purportedly only saw once and on the same date. Yes, the railroad company had provided each of them remuneration to testify. The defense was puzzled how bridge painters could unanimously recognize Jesse Jr. allegedly walking in Leeds on August 28th with another individual they could not make out and did not know. Walsh was confident that the jury would have the same doubts.

Reed did not want to conclude Friday's evidence with the jury hearing only from employees of a bridge company. He deemed it prudent for his final witnesses to be residents of Leeds—folks who had personally felt and experienced the explosion the night of the robbery. Miss Hunt, a young woman who lived near the site where the express car had been destroyed, described her emotional upheaval and fears when she heard the eruption around 10:45 p.m. Moments later she heard horses galloping rapidly past her window. Her father, William Hunt, gave virtually the same account, except he recalled hearing gunfire before the blast. The final witness of the day was Mrs. Hollenbeck of 45th & Cleveland, the matron of the boarding house. She ratified the time of the detonation and the gait of the horses speeding past her residence.

There certainly had been enough testimony for one day. Judge Shackleford was showing signs of weariness and anxiousness. Did his courtroom demeanor demonstrate distaste for the prosecution's case? His patience was growing thin. The wire story was short but supportive of Reed: *through the testimony of Lowe and of Hills, the express messenger, the state had established that Jesse Jr. had been the Leeds gang leader.*[216] Would the jury agree with the Associated Press? As to the young proprietor, the day's events had been entertaining. He sat during the long day with a smile or a grin on his face despite witnesses bent on his conviction.[217] Uncle Frank sat directly behind his nephew throughout every minute of the hearing. His eyes were affixed on each witness and his ears were attuned to every syllable spoken (*"his eyes had all the seeming of a demon that is dreaming"; "the tintinnabulation tectonic tales they told; and he heard many things in hell"*—or so Edgar A. Poe might have editorialized). He spoke not a word but quietly walked out of the courtroom keeping pace with his dead brother's son.

---

216 *Salt Lake Herald*, February 25, 1899; and *Wichita Daily Eagle*, February 25, 1899.
217 *Ibid.*

CHAPTER XIX
WHY TAKE SATURDAY OFF?

━━►)(◊)(◄━━

Dateline: Saturday, February 25, 1899
Will the State Rest?

Headline:

THE SLAUGHTER OF FILIPINOS
IS DEPLORABLE BUT UNAVOIDABLE.
<u>UNCLE SAM IS NO QUITTER</u>[218]

On Saturday, February 25th, it was unavoidable that the State would resume where it had left off the previous evening—testimony from more Leeds residents and the Hollenbeck household. The first two to take the stand were the young Hollenbeck girls. Miss Cora testified how she and her twelve-year old sister, Nellie, had ridden the following morning to the scene of the train robbery and observed a black workman gathering up a checkered jacket and pair of overhauls. Miss Cora was shown clothes that had been on display in the courtroom the previous day. She verified they appeared to be the same ones she and her sister saw that morning. The prosecution then asked little Nellie the same questions. Her answers corroborated those of her older sister, but she had noticed many buggy tracks as well. The border, William Wotox, next recounted how within fifteen minutes after the detonation he had seen a horse drawn buggy galloping by the house, and had overheard somebody within the vehicle apprehensively yelling

---

218 *Ibid.*

ᴄᴖ 165 ᴖᴄ

out fears that the horse would tumble because of their speed.

The prosecution had lined-up a series of witnesses who had seen carriages hastening through the vicinity of the residence of the James family shortly after the robbery. Richard Hayden, a ten year old, was in an orchard near 35th and Indiana around eleven the night of the train robbery. He recalled seeing two buggies zipping by at a very high rate of speed. William Ackerman and Richard Sexton, neighbors of Jesse Jr., ratified the story of little Richard. Sexton provided more details to the jury. He and his wife had been out driving just south of the James home when they observed two buggies near a clump of trees and several men fixing something about the shaft or the harness. The cross-examination was crisp and precise. It revealed that not one of the three witnesses was able to describe any further details, including the number of men or the identity of those in the carriages.[219]

The State had served subpoenas on the owner and several employees of Warren Self's Livery Stable who had been working the night of the robbery. Proprietor Warren Self was the first to testify. He confirmed leasing two buggies that evening at about 7:30. The lessees appeared to fit descriptions of those involved in the crime. He described one as being a heavy, well-built fellow who had insisted upon a high-spirited horse.[220] Self explained how he had recreated the distance and marked the time from the livery stable to the crime scene. He had ridden the same mare used in the robbery from the scene of the holdup to the vicinity of the James house in twenty minutes, and all the way into the city in twenty-eight minutes.

Frank Walsh on cross-examination continued to pound away at their theory that detectives had conspired to implicate his client in the crime. He went immediately for the jugular. Self admitted Detectives Keshlear and Harbaugh had first arrived at his barn shortly after the robbery and asked him a leading question: hadn't it been Jesse Jr. who had rented the rig? The same detectives later returned to his business after Lowe's confession had been printed in the newspapers. It had been Harbaugh who had suggested to Self the idea of riding the same

219 *Kansas City Times*, February 26, 1899.
220 Self's uncle, William Self, verified the same facts when he was questioned by Prosecutor Reed.

horse and marking the time on how long it took to travel back from the scene of the crime.

The next to testify was the stable employee, L.D. Woods. He had been working at around 11 o'clock p.m. when the horse returned. The animal, Woods remarked, appeared to have been driven very hard and was still attached to the rig. Inside the carriage, Woods discovered a cartridge box. Unlike the cross-examination of Self, the defense's inquiry of Woods was short and uneventful.

The next several witnesses called by Reed did not experience the trial advocacy of Frank Walsh, but rather the lead prosecutor himself had to confront the scorn of Judge Shackleford who clearly was not going to sit back and just rule on objections. Reed asked Albert Shilling, secretary of the Missouri Valley Bridge Company, whether company employees were working on a bridge near Leeds when Jesse Jr. was out there. The judge not waiting for an objection promptly interjected. "That's what you call bolstering up a witness. Don't do it again." Reed may have been convinced he had gone too far and released Shilling without further examination.[221] When Reed recalled the Express Messenger Hills to once again identify the revolver the judge protested and sternly reprimanded the prosecutor for recalling a witness to merely repeat prior testimony. No further questions!

A cavalcade of witnesses followed to testify about known connections Jesse Jr. had with crooks. Each explained having previously seen scoundrels such as Andy Ryan, Jack Kennedy and W.W. Lowe conversing with the defendant at his cigar store. Under cross-examination, not one of the testifiers had any knowledge or information about the nature or content of the alleged conversations. Their testimony had been "far from satisfactory" for the prosecution.[222] County Marshal Murphy chimed in about the young man's association with these same "bad men." He also recounted having seen the accused in the assessor's office examining a map of Jackson County. Reed asked Murphy whether Jesse was "examining the part of the map representing the neighborhood of Leeds." Walsh objected to the question, and the

221 *Kansas City Journal*, February 26, 1899.
222 *Ibid*.

judge promptly sustained the objection. The judge was not finished admonishing Reed. The judge angrily warned Reed about his persistent conduct in the courtroom and severely lectured him on proper criminal procedure, which did not include misleading and suggestive questions. Apparently, Reed had never learned the parental maxim "don't make me tell you again!" Nothing compares to judicial activism in the courtroom.

Walsh, like a prizefighter knowing that his victim is against the ropes, did not let Reed's torment end with Judge Shackleford's blistering commentary. He first landed jabs against the body of Murphy. Didn't everyone know that Jesse Jr. was an avid cyclist? Murphy had to have known that obvious fact. The Marshal admitted knowing of the young man's admiration for the sport; he also conceded his awareness that Jesse Jr. had taken a bicycle trip to Blue Springs about the same time he had seen him examining the map in the assessor's office. Walsh was not through striking blows to the face of both Reed and Murphy. The Marshal acknowledged he had been called to Mr. Reed's office to meet with Detective Harbaugh. This concession was very clear and significant not just to the defense, but for the gallery as it erupted in laughter. Was this the knockout punch for the defense?

The prosecution was clearly on the ropes, but it was not throwing in the towel. Reed then called to the stand his "best card." As the name William J. Smith was announced, it reverberated throughout the room. It was visible to observers that there was "an over abundance of eagerness" and a "craning of necks in a frantic attempt to hear every word" Smith would have to say.[223] Smith's name had been 'Greek' to Walsh until the day before when H.M. Carr, the train conductor, had identified the state's "ace in the hole." Smith, a "middle age" laborer from Stokesville, Missouri, had become the states most heralded witness for obvious reasons. He was not employed by the railroads; he had been a lonely passenger on his way home on the night the Missouri Pacific Train had been robbed; he had seen the suspects up front and personal. The prosecution asserted that Smith would unequivocally

---

223 *Ibid.*

identify Jesse Jr. as the leader of the bandits. With two days to prepare and no opportunity to interview Smith, Walsh would have to focus upon Smith's answers to Reed's direct examination in order to prepare his cross.

Reed, after asking perfunctory foundational questions, asked Smith where he was at the time of the robbery. Smith explained how he had jumped out of the passenger car when the train stopped. He then proceeded to walk up and stand near the bandits. One of the robbers then placed a gun against Smith's breast and ordered him back into the car.

Reed: Did that man have anything over his face?

Smith: He had nothing over his face. He had something black around his neck as if it was a mask slipped down.

Reed: How light was it?

Smith: It was very light. The light streamed out of the mail car door.

Reed: Did you get a good look at that man?

Smith: Yes, Sir.

Reed: Do you see that man in the courtroom?

Without hesitation or reservation, Smith pointed directly to the young man seated at the defense table and insisted vehemently. "That is the man." He was the same person who had difficulties with his mask.

Reed: You mean the defendant, Jesse James.

Smith: Yes, sir; there he sits right over there, I mean Jesse James.[224]

Although the witness had positively identified him, Jesse Jr. responded by merely laughing "out loud." Despite his proclamations and insistence upon his identification, Smith failed to hold up well to Walsh's interrogation. He became "very much confused" and fell victim to the defense's trap. Yes, Detectives Harbough and Furlong had in fact

224 *The Record-Union*, Sacramento, California, February 26, 1899; and *Western News-Democrat*, March 2, 1899 (Valentine, Nebraska).

directed him to the cigar stand "to get a good look at" the defendant before the case started. Yes, seeing him at the business enabled him to better identify Jesse Jr. during the trial. More direct blows against the state! Nonetheless, Smith never wavered from his assertion it was **the** defendant who held up the train back in September.[225] Had Walsh heard reports circulating that Smith had a criminal record? Apparently, the story had escaped the defense's attention as Walsh failed to cross-examine Smith on this point.

There was a procedural and evidentiary problem with which Reed had to contend. How would he get into evidence the items of property, including the clothing, the same clothing seen by Hollenbeck girls that had been unearthed by the black worker? Reed identified the man as Pete White, an employee at the Brush Creek Coal Mines, and since the prosecutor's office had been unable to locate White, Reed attempted to resolve this dilemma by calling Detective John Hayde. After being sworn in by the Deputy Marshal, Hayde explained to the jury that after White found the evidence, he gave it to him. Reed asked Hayde to identify the two pairs of overalls and jumper, but before he could do so, Walsh promptly objected by asserting the prosecutor had failed to lay the proper foundation. Walsh pointed out that the chain-of-custody of the clothing and other evidence had been compromised, as White had not testified to having discovered it. Reed argued there was an exception when as with this man White the witness could not be located. Reed charted the valiant efforts his office had made attempting to get "White upon the stand, but for some reason or other his presence could not be obtained." Having satisfied the exception, Reed insisted Walsh's objection should be overruled. What exception? Attorneys for defendant knew of none. The prosecutor's argument was then followed by the following offer: "Your honor, I introduce this black mask, this hair mask (holding them up for the jury to see), this false hair, this guncase, this laprope, these plyers, and this jumper, in evidence. And now the state rests." It was 4:30 in the afternoon.

No extant accounts or records exist whether the judge sustained or

---

overruled Walsh's lack of foundation objection or whether the judge granted Reed's offer of proof of the physical evidence. From a legal perspective, Walsh had been right; the chain-of-custody had been broken. Presumably, the judge agreed with Walsh as Reed's office continued to diligently search for Peter White over the ensuing weekend. The courtroom audience and defense team was "shocked" when Reed summarily announced the state had rested its case. The abruptness surprised the hearts of all.[226] The tone in the judge's voice seemed relieved and his comment appeared to demonstrate his feelings towards the case. He quickly turned to the jury and remarked. "I am sorry, gentlemen, that I shall be obliged to keep you over Sunday. But such is the case, and the court now stands adjourned until 9 o'clock Monday morning."[227]

The prosecution's case had instantaneously concluded by those magical words articulated by the prosecutor, "Now the state rests." The press pondered whether the combined testimony of Hills and Smith would be enough to convict the owner of the courthouse cigar store. There was no doubt that both men had positively identified Jesse Jr. as one of the train robbers.[228] Did the state play all of their "best cards"? Were there other leading "hands" the state could have played? Was Jesse Jr. guilty beyond a reasonable doubt? Had prosecutors presented their best evidence to attain a conviction? Should there have been additional information provided to the jury? These questions filled the minds of reporters as they pressed detectives and police officers to glean their interpretation of the evidence.

Detective Harbaugh, who Walsh isolated as the leader of the detective band of legal conspirators, spoke on behalf of the law; his response was short and concise.

> I do not think that we will be successful in convicting Jesse James. We did our best and . . . I am glad we made as good a case as we did, for . . . we had reason for accusing Jesse James that we brought this case to trial . . [W]e have been able to

---

226 *Ibid.*
227 *Ibid.*
228 *Arizona Weekly Journal-Miner*, March 1, 1899.

prove that we had a cause to arrest Jesse . . .

Harbaugh held other grave reservations and concerns about the potential outcome of the case. He pinpointed his frustration and irritation at the trial judge. "We have been very much handicapped by the adverse rulings of Judge Shackleford. He has not permitted us to introduce evidence" proving a conspiracy.[229] Reed, strolling out of the courtroom, expressed no recorded parting comments to the press. Perhaps Reed's reluctance to speak was because he shared Harbaugh's criticism of the judge. Would Harbaugh's remarks prove to be prophetic? The defense would have to wait to "have its innings on Monday."[230] Only the Sabbath could interrupt the drama and progress of the trial of the son of the bandit.

229 *Kansas City Journal,* February 26, 1899.
230 *Ibid.*

CHAPTER XX

THE DEFENSE

—➤➤•((◉))•◆—

Dateline: Monday, February 27, 1899
Hearing from Walsh!

Headline:

WHAT THIS WAR CONGRESS
HAS SO FAR ACCOMPLISHED.
IT HAS COVERED A MOST EVENTFUL PERIOD
IN THE COUNTRY'S HISTORY, BUT MUCH NEEDED
LEGISLATION REMAINS TO BE ACTED UPON[231]

Reed had presented the State's case thoroughly and methodically and had scored several accomplishments. His office had fully covered the eventful history of the train's heist, paraded witnesses who identified the defendant as the gang leader or being at Leeds prior to the crime, demonstrated the young man had seedy relationships and "played all the cards" in its arsenal. Would the evidence be enough to achieve the State's singular goal—the conviction of Jesse James, Jr.? The defense team was well prepared to answer this question with an overwhelming no. The day had finally arrived for the defendant's story to be presented.

The press and its adoring public anticipated the defense's trial strategy even before its first witness took the stand. During pretrial interviews with the press, Frank Walsh and his co-counsel did not conceal their legal views or theories. No, their client did not commit the

---

231 *The San Francisco Call*, February 27, 1899.

robbery—he had ironclad alibi witnesses to ratify this point; no, the State's key witnesses had not told credible stories—there was sufficient evidence to show testimony had been tainted or procured by misconduct; no, the charges against poor Jesse were not justified—their allegations were fictional tales, manufactured by railroad detectives and their bosses; no, unlike his guerrilla father, the son had a good reputation—many reputable witnesses would vouch for his character. The attorneys for Jesse Jr. seemed prepared to marshal all their forces in tearing down the prosecution's circumstantial case.

The first action Frank Walsh took that Monday morning created intense excitement. He opened the hearing by making reference to an article reported in the *Journal* the previous day. The story related how the State's principal witness, William J. Smith, had a prior criminal record. Walsh argued that the prosecution had rested its case without disclosing to the defense information that could discredit and impeach Smith. The defense wanted "to have Mr. Smith recalled to the stand." Reed replied that the witness had gone to the Fresco ticket office to return home. Judge Shackleford did not accept the prosecutor's response and immediately issued a body attachment instructing marshals to bring Smith back to the courthouse. Deputy Marshals were then dispatched to the train station.

To avoid any delays while Smith was apprehended, Walsh's encore was to recall Hills, the express messenger. He asked Hills only one question. Hadn't Hills told a deputy marshal on the night of the robbery that the leader was a large man? Hills emphatically denied ever having made such a statement. Walsh, anticipating the denial, had Deputy Marshal Cassimir Welch in the wings. Welch's testimony wholly contradicted Hills' story. Hills had given him the descriptions of two men: "the gang leader, a large man, over six feet tall; and a shorter but heavy-set" fellow. According to Welch when Hills made the statement, Sergeant Caskey was standing nearby Hills and instantly Hills pointed directly toward Sergeant Caskey and insisted that the principal crook compared in size to that of the sergeant. "Have you seen anyone matching Hills' identification of the short, heavy man?" Walsh inquired. Without any hesitation Welch ardently stated the smaller guy looked identical to another person under arrest for the same crime, W.W. Lowe. Walsh had only one more question:

> Walsh: Do you think that Jesse James is anything like either of the men that Hills described?
> Welch: No, I do not!

Former Jackson County Prosecutor Frank M. Lowe was then summoned by the defense. The purpose for calling him was to controvert the prior testimony of W.W. Lowe in which he had asserted, "he had never made a written confession" of the crime.[232] Frank Lowe, an officer of the court and the lead prosecutor until being succeeded by James A. Reed, without reservation maintained the confessor had not only confessed but had told him in his capacity as the former prosecutor the statement was true and complete. He acknowledged giving a copy of the written confession to Mr. R.E. Stout, an editor for the *Star*. There is nothing like a chief prosecutor leaking evidence to the press before trial.

James A. Reed was not pleased with the ethics of the man who had previously held his office. Reed wanted to know how much money the former prosecutor had received from the *Star* in exchange for a copy of the confession. Frank Lowe did not like the tone or implication of the question. He firmly denied ever having received any remuneration or other compensation whatsoever from the *Star* or from any other source. What became of the original statement? Frank Lowe said he had followed standard operating policy by giving it to Mr. Hugh C. Brady, an assistant prosecutor at that time. To verify that no money had been exchanged, the *Star's* editor was called to testify. Stout promptly decreed that no funds whatsoever were involved in the transaction; he only made an exact copy of it at the prosecutor's office in the New York Life Building and left the original with Frank Lowe and his staff.

What did Brady do with Lowe's confession? His response was to an unasked question. "I was assistant prosecuting attorney when W.W.

---

232 *Kansas City Journal*, February 28, 1899.

Lowe made what he said was his confession." Reed promptly objected to the reply as non-responsive and asked the judge to strike Brady's reply. The judge overruled his request. Lowe's statement, Brady said, had been transcribed on a typewriter, and he had personally returned the original to police. What became of it? The former assistant prosecutor had not seen it since that time. With that Walsh asked the judge to allow him to read Lowe's confession to the jury. Reed protested to no avail. If jurors had never read it before, they surely heard it read to them by Walsh. Forcefully and most deliberately, he recited the entire tale and read it straight out of the *Journal* where it had first been published.

A deputy marshal then entered the courtroom and announced the body attachment had been served on Mr. William Smith. Intensity in the courtroom mounted when deputies escorted the fugitive to the judge's bench. Walsh went right to work. He had momentum by having struck a blow against the eyewitness account of Hills so why not take a full swing at the other purported identifier of his client. The gallery was riveted by the inquiry.

> Walsh: Did you testify before the grand jury?
> Smith: No, sir.
> Walsh: Were you in jail two months at Harrisonville charged with larceny?
> Smith: No, sir. I was accused of taking some flour three years ago and I was arrested. I was released on bond about five days later.
> Walsh: Did you pay any of your bond?
> Smith: No. I did not pay any of it myself.
> Walsh: Were you guilty of stealing the flour?

Reed protested and instructed the witness not to answer, but the judge summarily ordered the witness to reply. After some reluctance, Smith uttered the words Walsh had wanted. "I guess that I was guilty of stealing the flour." The inquiry had been short and to the defense point. Smith had admitted being convicted of larceny.[233] It also ap-

---

233 *Salt Lake Herald*, February 28, 1899.

peared he had "jumped bond." The defense was confident that Smith's unlawful conduct would impeach his credibility.

The most sensational feature of the day occurred when Mrs. Samuel, the seventy-four-year old gray haired, paternal grandmother of Jesse Jr., "tottered into the courtroom" to testify. Wearing a plain, black silk dress and black bonnet, the one-armed widow "tremblingly" stepped forward. She was "supported on one side by" her "stern faced, steely eyed" son Frank, and on the opposite side by her young granddaughter Mary, who guided her "with tender care." The aged, escorted woman on her way to the witness stand passed by her grandson. He "arose pressing her hand," and she gave him a "soft smile."[234] This court appearance had marked her first public emergence since her son, Frank, had surrendered to Governor Crittenden at the capitol in Jefferson City on October 5, 1882.

"Hold up your right hand to be sworn," boomed the bailiff to the family matriarch. Did the bailiff give the directive out of habit or was it designed to produce sympathies for the aged woman? Complying with his instruction, Mrs. Samuel raised her right arm, but the hand was missing (she had lost it along with her eight year old son, Archie, to a Pinkerton bomb in January 1875). There was nothing "but an empty sleeve, empty nearly to the elbow." The bailiff asked "Do you hereby swear that everything you say upon this stand shall be the truth, the whole truth and nothing but the truth?" Her response, "I do" was given in a low but firm, determined tone.

Well over "five hundred pairs of eyes were fixed upon her" as attorney Yeager commenced his inquiry. She was in fact Zerelda Samuel of Clay County, the long-suffering mother of her sainted boys, Archie and Jesse. Pointing to his client, Yeager asked if she knew the defendant. "Yes, he is my grandson." The examination elicited that the day before the train robbery she had arrived around noon at her daughter-in-law's house. Mrs. Allen Parmer and two young girls from Wichita Falls, Texas had been in Kansas City visiting the James family, but they were scheduled to return to Texas the following evening. Sarah Parmer

---

234 *Kansas City Journal*, February 28, 1899.

was the second wife of Allen Parmer; Allen had ridden with Frank and Jesse James as a guerilla during the Civil War. Zerelda's only daughter with Reverend James, Susan James Parmer, had been Allen's first wife, but after Susan died in 1889, leaving four small children, Allen married Sarah in 1892 and she helped raise Susan's girls; this made Mrs. Allen Parmer the defendant's step-aunt by marriage.

Yeager directed Mrs. Samuel's attention to the night of the robbery. Sarah Parmer and the girls had tickets to take the 9:05 p.m. "Katy" back to their home in Texas. The elderly witness with a noted tremor of her "aged hand" told how her grandson and daughter-in-law had guided Sarah and the children (her grandchildren) to the cable car around eight o'clock. Jesse Jr. she related did not accompany them to Union Depot.

Yeager: Why did not Jesse go to the depot with his aunt and mother?
Samuel: Because I asked him to stay with me. And I didn't' think there was any use for both of them to go.

Mrs. Samuel could not recall when he returned to the house, but she adamantly professed he and his sister, Mary, were sitting next to her on the front porch when her daughter-in-law Zee returned from the depot. She had no doubt as to the exact time of the explosion because they all had commented about the magnitude of the blast thinking it was from the coalmines. The aged grandmother was excused after spending one hour on the stand; the state agreed to recall her later in the day for cross-examination.

The defendant's mother, Zee James, was the next witness called by the defense. She verified that she and her son, Jesse, had escorted Mrs. Parmer and her two children to catch the northbound trolley. Her son did not continue to Union Depot, and she alone escorted them to the train station to ensure they timely arrived to catch the 9:05 p.m. "Katy." She did not wait for the train to depart the city, but instead returned to her house. Her son, daughter and mother-in-law were all seated on the front porch when she arrived and they visited until about eleven o'clock before retiring for the evening.

(Zee James: Widow of Jesse James & Mother of Jesse Jr.)
(Source: findagrave.com - annonymous)

The widow was turned over to Reed's cross-examination. She admitted not having heard the explosion the night of the robbery. This was explained because of her disabilities, some deafness and long-time illness. She conceded not knowing where her son went after he left the family at the trolley stop. However, she was insistent and positive that young Jesse never left the house after she returned home from Union Depot that evening. Reed's questioning then became subject to protests by the defense. He asked Zee to state the year in which she and Jesse James had been married. Walsh without hesitation jumped from his seat objecting on the grounds that the question was irrelevant. The judge tersely sustained the objection.

Reed: How old is your son?

Zee: He is 23. Will be 24 in August.

Reed: How soon was he born after your marriage?

Walsh shouted out loudly his objection protesting that the prosecuting attorney knew he had no right to ask these questions. The inquiry had nothing to do with the case. The objection was again sustained, and Mrs. James was excused.

Mr. Walsh, looking towards the court deputy, requested: "Call Missy Mary James." The sister of the defendant came in from the witness room and ascended the chair. She was described as "a sweet faced young woman of 19 . . . quietly dressed in black and wore black gloves" who had recently graduated from Central High School.[235] She principally corroborated the stories of her mother and grandmother. Her brother had not been home very long when her mother returned from the train station in the West Bottoms and joined them on the porch. The time was around ten o'clock. "We heard the explosion shortly afterwards, and grandma asked Jesse what it was." She did not recall her brother's answer.

Walsh: Did any man come up and ask where Jesse was that night?

Mary: Why, no.

Walsh: Was any man there at all that night?

Mary: None other than Jesse.

Having completed his examination of the defendant's sister, she underwent Reed's interrogation. Reed first had Mary draw a diagram of her home and then inquired about the layout of the family porch. This was too much for Walsh, and he protested asserting Reed was exploring irrelevant material. The judge concurred thereby terminating this line of inquiry. Reed changed his direction and asked about the date, August 27th, the same day in which her step-aunt, Mrs. Sarah Parmer and her stepchildren had arrived in Kansas City from Texas

235 *Ibid.*

for a visit. No, Jesse did not meet the family at Union Depot that day because he had been playing ball at Exposition Park, but the following morning her brother retrieved their luggage from the depot and then they all went to Troost Park for a family gathering. Reed had prior testimony that Jesse Jr. had been in Leeds that day, not Troost Park. Had Reed established that young Mary had covered for her brother's whereabouts on the 28th? Time would tell.

Reed then questioned her about her brother's whereabouts at the time when the curfew alarm had sounded—the curfew adopted by the city council to ensure children were home by eight-thirty during the school year.

Reed: Did you hear the curfew on the night of the robbery?
Mary: Yes, sir.
Reed: Was Jesse there at that time?
Mary: No, sir. He came in some time afterward."
Reed: Did he leave the house at any time that night after he re-
       turned until you retired, about 11 o'clock?
Mary: No, sir, he did not.

Reed had clearly demonstrated that Mary's brother was not home at the time the curfew had been signaled. With that, Reed released Mary from the witness chair.

Walsh, turning to his twenty-three-year old client, calmly stated, "Jesse, I guess you'd better take the stand." Jesse stood and with a sense of complete confidence quickly walked towards the judge's bench and took the oath. Walsh began his questioning of a chronological history of the financial plight of the family, including the young man's abbreviated education. Walsh reviewed each and every job he had held since age eleven through the opening of the cigar business on January 15, 1898. He fully established that the poor lad had been forced to work at an early age in order to support the family.

(Jesse Edward James—1899 newspaper picture)

Having pulled at the heartstrings of the jury, Walsh went at the main issues of the state's case of guilt by association. He asked his impoverished client about his acquaintances with W. W. Lowe and the other gangsters from Crackerneck, along with his activities on the night of the train robbery.

Walsh: How long have you known Lowe?

Jesse: Since last May. I met him first in Justice Krueger's court-room where both of us testified in John Kennedy's preliminary hearing. After that he came to the courthouse several times and bought tobacco from me.

Walsh: Do you know Andy Ryan?

Jesse: Yes, sir.

Walsh: Has he visited you at the courthouse?

Jesse: Yes, sir. A number of times.

Walsh: Did you ever ask Lowe how to rob a train?

Jesse: I did not.

Walsh: Did you ever plan with him to rob a train?

Jesse: I did not.

Walsh: Where and when did you get shaved on the night of September 23 last?

Jesse: In the barber shop on Thirty-third, near Troost. I went there about 7 and left about 7:30.

Walsh: Where did you go then?

Jesse: I went home, and then, about 8:15, I should judge left with my mother, my aunt, and her two children, to put them upon the cable car. My aunt was going home.

Walsh: And then?

Jesse: I went to Jones' drug store and stood outside for a time listening to some Negroes playing. I went into the store and played the slot machine.

Walsh: How long were you there?

Jesse: Oh, twenty or twenty-five minutes.

Walsh: And then?

Jesse: I went to Hill & Howard's drug store. I had a glass of ice cream soda, talked awhile with some friend, and then went outside. I loafed around there a little while and then went home.

Walsh: Did you see anybody on your way home?

Jesse: Yes, I talked to Mr. and Mrs. Bunch.

Walsh: How did you approach the house?

Jesse: I took the short cut, the way I always go, which cuts off considerable distance. I went around the side of the house, and found grandma and Mary on the porch.

Walsh: Was your mother there?

Jesse: No, she had not returned.

Walsh: When did she come?

Jesse: In about fifteen or twenty minutes.

Walsh: How long afterwards was the explosion?

Jesse: Very shortly.

Walsh: Was there any remark?

Jesse: Yes. Grandma said something; what I don't remember.
Walsh: Had you ever been to Leeds prior to the time of the robbery?
Jesse: Probably 200 times.
Walsh: How did you go there?
Jesse: On my bicycle.
Walsh: Were you there on August 28?
Jesse: I was not.

Jesse explained that on August 27th his step-aunt, Sarah, and two children had traveled from their home in Wichita Falls, Texas and were scheduled to arrive at Union Depot at six p.m. He had initially planned on meeting them but learning the Chicago & Alton Train was delayed, he went to the "baseball game between the courthouse nine and the city hall nine" at Exposition Park. He reaffirmed his sister's story that the next morning he went to the depot and retrieved his aunt's baggage. He vigorously denied being anywhere near Leeds on the 28th, but insisted he had enjoyed the day with his family on an outing at Troost Park.

Walsh then asked Jesse Jr. whether he had been in Leeds at anytime that August.

Walsh: Were you at Leeds on Sunday, August 21?
Jesse: Yes, sir.
Walsh: For what purpose?
Jesse: My sister, Mary, was trying to get a school there and I heard on Saturday that they were going to give it to Miss Howe. I went to see if the report was right?
Walsh: Did you see Mr. Hutchison there?
Jesse: Yes, sir.
Walsh: What was your purpose in going to Leeds?
Jesse: To get a school for my sister.
Walsh: Any other purpose?
Jesse: Only bike rides.
Walsh: When you left, which way did you go?

Jesse: I went south to the rock road and then east.

Walsh: Did you go to Andy Ryan's house on the night of August 21?

Jesse: I did not.

Walsh concluded his examination with a series of questions relating to Hissey, the telegraph operator. Had Jesse Jr. seen Hissey at any time following the robbery? "Yes, about a dozen times." Each time he had seen Hissey was at the courthouse. On one occasion, Hissey had approached and personally spoke to him. What did Hissey tell you? He said, "I could not have been the leader because the man he saw was much larger than me." Jesse gave his height at no more than five feet, eight inches. The defendant had performed well on direct examination, but how would he respond to the aggressive approach of the prosecutor?

Reed went directly at the relationship between Jesse and the confessor.

Reed: You say that you were only acquaintances with W.W. Lowe through meeting him at Krueger's court and at your cigar stand?

Jesse: Yes, sir.

Reed: No other place?

Jesse: No.

Reed: You had no business dealing with him?

Jesse: None other than selling him cigars and tobacco.

Reed: No transactions.

Jesse: No.

Reed, believing he had laid a trap, held up an envelope and presented it to Jesse Jr. Inside was the famous letter dated July 14, 1898, that had been discovered in Lowe's frockcoat at the time of his arrest. As the prosecutor read the correspondence, Jesse intently examined the envelope. Reed renewed the interrogation.

Reed: Isn't the address on this envelope your writing?

Jesse: It looks much like it, but it's not mine.

Reed: Isn't this your signature to this bond given before Justice
        Spitz? Jesse: That is my signature but it's not my writing on
        the envelope.

Reed: Take this piece of paper and a pencil and print—

Before Reed had completed his request for a handwriting sample,
Walsh strenuously shouted another objection, which the judge sustained without hesitation. Reed was not to be derailed. He presented
the witness another written statement.

Reed: Did you ever make this statement to Will Kenny, a reporter
        for the World?

Jesse: No, sir.

Reed: Did you not hand it to him in the courthouse?

Jesse: Yes, sir.

Reed: What do you mean, sir?

Jesse: Well, he wanted a statement and Mr. Milton Oldham
        wrote it for him. I handed it to him, but I didn't write it.

The Defendant's anecdotal response raised a stir in the courtroom
as laughter broke out. The judge was forced to gavel order before proceedings could continue. Handing the letter to Jesse Jr., Reed wanted
to know if he had ever carried it out to the Santa Fe yards. Walsh, either
out of some anxiety over his client's potential answer or a desire to end
this line of questioning altogether, promptly raised an objection. Once
again Judge Shackleford agreed with Walsh. The judge's rulings had
not been going well for the prosecutor.

Throughout Reed's cross-examination, the defendant remained at
ease, giving no outward appearance of buckling under the pressure.
Repeatedly, he disclaimed any intimacy or friendship with Lowe, and
unconditionally denounced ever having introduced the confessor to his
late father's brother, Frank. His uncle would not have approved of any

such introduction—doing so would have produced venom and scorn from Frank James. The "persecuted" son of the outlaw even challenged the veracity of newspaper stories claiming he had given an interview to a reporter after his arrest in October. Reed peppered him with questions over the numerous journeys to Leeds, the visit with Mr. Hutchison, and efforts to get his sister into a school. To each question the young man never flinched. The chief prosecutor was simply unable to elicit any culpable admissions or anything new from the defendant.[236]

Jesse Jr. had been a saint. He worked and supported the family; he intervened for his little sister; he defended an elderly man from an assailant's attack; and he had numerous witnesses willing to defend him. Walsh had assembled a list of the who's who in Jackson County to testify to the good moral reputation of the poor fatherless boy. Each witness was essentially asked the same question. "What is the reputation of the defendant as to veracity, honesty and general good character?" The answers given by Judge John Henry of the circuit court; E.F. Swinney, cashier of the First National Bank; Will P. Hayde, deputy clerk of the circuit court; and William Cargill, assistant superintendent of the Armour Packing Company, were all the same: "Good."

Having established their client was a "good" boy, the defense turned to their alibi defense. Who had seen Jesse Jr. that night? Young Jesse's lawyers had an ensemble of witnesses to answer the question. Mr. & Mrs. H.B. Levens both told Finnis Farr they had seen Jesse Jr. at the Troost cable line around 8:15 p.m. or "it might have been ten minutes either way Jesse got inside the car but did not ride." E.C. Jones, a proprietor of the Hill & Howard Drug Store near the Troost line, gave penny change to the defendant so he could play slots in the store. Jones did not know the time, but Charles Howard, another storeowner, estimated it was shortly before nine. Charles Hovey, an employee of the county clerk's office, claimed he had visited with Jesse around nine near the end of the track line. James S. Rice ratified Hovey's story. Several other patrons of Hill & Howard gave similar accounts and time periods. Neighbors Mr. and Mrs. Samuel Bunch and Joseph Gorsuch had

---

236 *Ibid.*

seen the young man pass by their home that evening after nine. G.W. Daniels, a hack driver, also saw him around the same time. Dr. Thomas Beattle even verified that Jesse Jr. had gotten a haircut at the barbershop around 7:30 that night.

Prosecutor Reed questioned the accuracy of each alibi witness. He compared their answers given on direct examination to previous testimony. Several of the defense witnesses had previously given sworn statements before the grand jury back in October and then again in January. Reed methodically utilized transcripts of those proceedings to reveal contradictory testimony. Mr. Hovey, for one, blamed the inconsistency on the stenographer in the grand jury case having misquoted him; he angrily protested against such mistakes. Some dismissed their differences as having been previously made in error. Others conceded their statements differed, but they had valid explanations; they had spoken to Jesse Jr. either before or after the indictment. He had personally clarified the times in which they had seen him on the night of the robbery; his clarification explained their discrepancies. The prosecution was certainly convinced that young Jesse had coached the witnesses. Would the jury?

The defense was not thrown off by the numerous inconsistencies. Instead, the defendant's attorneys were merely warming up the orchestra. Deputy Marshal Tom Leahy ratified the previous testimony of Deputy Marshal Welch. Leahy specifically recalled Hills, the express messenger, informing him and in the presence of Welch that the gang leader had been someone the size of Officer Caskey. No way did Jesse Jr. resemble Caskey; the latter was a much larger man. Charles K. Bowen, of the Kansas City View Company, under Farr's examination told how he had met the telegraph operator, D.M. Hissey, at the robbery scene in October. During their meeting, Hissey had told him about having gone to the courthouse at the direction of Detective Harbough to see Jesse Jr. What did Hissey tell you after seeing him at his cigar stand? "He was certain it was not Jesse James and that he had not the least idea who the robber was."[237] Reed challenged Bowen by asserting he

---

237 *Ibid.*

had been coached to meet Hissey back in October in order to ask him confusing questions about his previous identification of the defendant. Bowen was not rattled and held firm to his position.

> Bowen: No, I had not been told to ask anything. I asked merely to satisfy my curiosity.
> Reed: That's what killed the cat, I believe.

Despite Reed's efforts, Bowen remained insistent that Hissey had declared to him that the man who had entered the telegraph office and destroyed the instruments was not Jesse Jr.

This was enough for day six of the proceedings.

CHAPTER XXI
THE CLOSINGS & VERDICT

Dateline: Tuesday, February 28, 1899
The Verdict Is?

Headline:

THE BEST ROUTE TO THE PHILIPPINESS
TROOPS WILL BE SENT
HEREAFTER FROM SAN FRANCISCO
PRESIDENT McKINLEY THINKS
AFFAIRS IN THE ISLANDS ARE
PROGRESSING SATISFACTORILY[238]

Taking the most direct route from his office to the courtroom on the morning of February 28th, Walsh possessed a quiet confidence that the courtroom affairs had progressed satisfactorily. He also knew full well this day would mark the conclusion of the case. Reed, too, felt assured that he would be able to stop the defense train and derail it by his closing argument. There was some concluding evidence offered by both sides in the forenoon hours of the seventh day, but in the end, it turned out to be the day of rest.

Before the defense rested, several witnesses were recalled for abbreviated testimony. Among them were Frank Lowe and the James family matriarch. The ex-prosecutor held steadfast; he never said W.W. Lowe had not given a confession. The aged grandmother once again under

---

238   *The Evening Times*, February 28, 1899, Washington City (D.C.).

the guidance of her son, Frank, resumed center-stage. No need for her to re-raise her stub—she remained under oath. Mrs. Samuel's reaffirmed her prior testimony. No, she never said she and her grandson were sitting alone on the porch at the time of the explosion. At nearly 10:30 in the morning the defense wrapped up its case.

Prosecutors were not finished and promptly presented rebuttal evidence. Peter White was the first to be called. Reed's staff had finally located the long missing discoverer. White's testimony was short and to the foundational point. The day after the robbery he had absolutely located the checked jacket and pair of overhauls. Unquestionably, he had given them to Detective John Hayde. The substantive chain-of-custody had been established. Now, Reed could fully display the clothes.

The state was not through attacking the former prosecutor, Frank Lowe. Will Kenny, reporter for the *World*, testified to a conversation he had with Frank after the confessor's confession had been given to the press. Kenny testified that the prior chief law officer of the county had told him he no longer had possession of the written instrument. This scored no points for the prosecution as it failed to contradict Frank Lowe's own testimony.

Reed had not finished with his efforts to provide a comparison of the penmanship and cursive style of the defendant. The prosecution had served subpoena duces tecum (bring the documents) upon two managers of Armour. They were ordered to deliver to court the employment records of the company's former employee, Jesse Jr. The defendant had purportedly signed the documents. Little, if anything, developed from these business instruments, as neither man was qualified in the field of handwriting analysis. Harry Crane, a bank representative of National Bank of Commerce, took the stand. His employer was the depository of the defendant's business accounts. Without objection from defense counsel, Crane expressed the opinion that the writing on the Armour papers compared with the signature on the letter allegedly sent by Jesse Jr. to W.W. Lowe. The judge did not allow Crane to express an opinion as to the identity of the author of either the correspondence or the Armour records.

Prosecutors had more evidence to present to further bolster the state's case. They wanted another shot at the defendant. Reed quickly announced the state was recalling the defendant. Frank Walsh would not passively sit back and allow this prosecutorial maneuver to materialize. He vociferously objected, and the judge agreed; Jesse Jr. did not have to answer any more questions. While other rebuttal witnesses testified, including investigators and railroad detectives, nothing new was disclosed or established. The trial evidence concluded around 11:50 on the morning of February 28th.

The judge advised the jury that under the law they were to be governed by certain instructions, which he then read. They had to find the defendant guilty beyond a reasonable doubt, and if not they were to dismiss the indictment against him. All witnesses were competent to testify, including Jesse Jr. and W.W. Lowe. If they believed Lowe, they had to convict James. The judge instructed them on this defense of alibi as it compared to the defendant's community reputation. "The question of the alibi should be carefully considered. If you find the defendant guilty his good character neither excuses or extenuates his crime." With that, it was time for lunch and then closing arguments.

The lawyers provided the judge the order in which the closing arguments would be presented. Mr. Frank G. Johnson would open for the prosecution; the defense's presentation was arranged with R.L. Yeager going first, to be followed by Finnis Farr and concluding with Frank Walsh's final remarks. The Jackson County Prosecutor James A. Reed would go last and provide the State's summation.

Assistant Prosecutor Frank Johnson began by directing the jury's attention to the close relationship the defendant had with men of dubious character. He likewise challenged the alibi defense. It was undisputed that Jesse Jr. was well acquainted with W.W. Lowe.

The testimony of Lowe has been confirmed by an unwilling witness, Mr. Smith. We have shown that Jesse conversed with Lowe many times; that he was near the scene of the robbery August 28. The defense denies the latter, but has made no attempt to show where he was. Lowe's story has been corroborated in every detail. . . . The principal point advanced by the defense is the effort to prove an alibi for Jesse. We have only the statements of his mother, sister and grandmother to prove his alibi.

Next, Assistant Prosecutor Johnson clarified the State's position as to where Jesse Jr. had been on the night of the Leeds robbery. He explained that they did not question or discount the fact the defendant had been at Hill & Howard Drug Store around 9:00 on the evening of the crime. Johnson insisted that even if he had played slots in the drugstore, he and his compatriots had "ample time to reach the scene of the robbery" by the horses they had leased from Self's Livery Stable. The prosecution's evidence had fully demonstrated that the roundtrip to Leeds could have been made during the periods of time in which the defense had provided absolutely no account of the defendant's actual whereabouts. "I say to you gentlemen, that the alibi is shattered."

Johnson had more to say about the character of the grandson. "His grandmother said that Jesse did not go to the depot with his mother because she asked him to remain at home. If his grandmother had asked him to remain with her, why didn't he do as he was asked instead of loafing around the drug store?" If he truly had such "good character" he would not have loafed about but would have gone home to care for the elderly woman. Johnson further insisted the boy's so-called good reputation was not persuasive and should be ignored. The first shot by the State had been delivered, and the defense had to respond.

School Board President Yeager and Finnis C. Farr followed Johnson. Yeager promptly reminded the jury his client had never concealed his movements on the night of the robbery. He underscored how Detective Harbaugh had made Jesse Jr. "omnipresent" that evening. Maybe he was a saint possessing powers of bilocation. Yeager fully outlined each discrepancy in Lowe's confession and testimony. He concluded by ridiculing the story of the state's key witness, W.J. Smith.

Finnis Farr at around 3:00 that afternoon addressed the jury. He emphatically declared it was not incumbent upon the defendant to prove his innocence. It was the state's burden to prove his guilt beyond a reasonable doubt. Farr pounded upon the defense theory that the charges against their client had been the scheme of railroad hounds. The proper caption of the criminal case should have been "Del Harbaugh versus Jesse James." Farr strenuously argued this point. Harbaugh, he said, was a hired detective who had followed "the case from beginning to end with blood money as his goal. If the statement of Lowe is eliminated, the state" had "no grounds for a case." This, Farr declared, explained why Harbaugh and other detectives had secreted and held Lowe in captivity like an animal until he told them want they wanted to hear about Jesse Jr.

Would Frank Walsh prove the old wives tale: "*the third time is the charm?*" He began with a simple but compassionate remark:

> "A man who has led the life that young James has, death is preferable to imprisonment . . . Mr. Johnson has told you that character means nothing, but the law tells you that a man with such a character and such a reputation as has the defendant cannot be guilty of the crime with which he has been charged."

Walsh renewed the defense assault against William W. Lowe. He rhetorically raised several points about the confessor's testimony and confession. Would a man commit a robbery that carries the penalty of death not knowing two of the co-conspirators? Hadn't his confession completely exonerated "Jack Kennedy from all blame?" Walsh directly challenged the State's asseretion of the veracity of Lowe. Why did Kennedy remain locked up for duplicity in the same crime? If Lowe told the truth, the "Quail Hunter" would have been released and charges against him should have been dropped. The jury knew that Kennedy and Bill Ryan remained in custody, but jurors did not know they were held in the county jail in Springfield, Missouri accused of another train robbery. Reed had failed to explain the reason for their captivity and Walsh exploited this point to his benefit.

Walsh, not letting go of Lowe's moral turpitude, reviewed the state's story of the infamous date of August 28th, a date Walsh described as the "Rock of Gibraltar upon which the state" had rested its case. Hadn't Lowe proclaimed he and Jesse Jr. had travelled by train to Leeds on that day for reconizance purposes? Didn't the state parade a paint crew of witnesses from all over the country to corroborate this story? Lowe testified that the name of the brakeman on the freight train on the 28th was Mr. Downer. Yet, the evidence established it had not been Downer, but rather it was H.P. Vallee, a former classmate of Jesse. Walsh insisted that if anyone would have been able to identify his client as being on the freight train that day it would have been Vallee. So where was Vallee? Why had the State not served a subpoena on him or paid his transportation to Kansas City? Walsh raised these puzzeling queries to further illustrate to the jury the depth of the railroad conspiracy.

The most significant defense strategy, accusing detectives of conspiring to convict his client, became Walsh's final 'swan song.' He reminded the jurors about the plot of the railroads:

> The Missouri Pacific Railway Company had removed Vallee so that he could not be brought here to testify. I ask you not to convict this boy for the Missouri Pacific Railway, for I believe in giving even a dog a square deal . . . If this is the one bit of evidence that holds the young man's life in the balance, we should be permitted to have Vallee as a witness, but they won't let us have him.

Walsh, obviously excercised, reminded the jury that the raillines had no problem returning the painting crew from all over the country to testify, but they could not bring back Vallee. If Vallee had come forward to testify that Jesse Jr. had not been on that train, the "Rock of Gilbrator" would have been destroyed by a volcano. This, according to Walsh, explained why the railroad captains did not bring Vallee back to Kansas City.

Walsh's closing editorial remarks had been borrowed from Major

John N. Edwards commentary over the slaying of the young defendant's father back on April 3, 1882.

> Gentleman of the jury, this trial is over as far as my small part is concerned, and I leave it all to you and will state that this case means something more than the vindication of this boy. It means that those old bears on the seal of state should be taken down and in their place the picture of Del Harbaugh should be substituted. Surely, if you should return with a verdict of guilty, the gods would weep upon this court house.[239]

Reed knew full well that he would have to trump Walsh's flowering prose when he summed-up the state's case.

James A. Reed slowly but deliberately walked to the bar separating him from the jury. In a self-depricating commencment speech, he proclaimed, "A skilled orator can weave a web of fancy out of very thin material. The defendant has had all that skilled lawyers and eloquence can do for him." Their abilities do not make Mr. James innocent. He wanted to assuage any concerns jurors may have had about the motives his office had in pursuing the charges and seeking a conviction. "What object could we have in weaving a web of circumstantial evidence against an innocent man?" Prosecutors had received nothing from the Missouri Pacific Railway, no monetary compensation and no reward. The only service the State had received was from Detective Harbaugh who had only performed his duties as an officer of the law, nothing more. Reed asked what his motive would have been to punish the defendant if he thought he was innocent. He had nothing to gain by it. Reed told jurors he had prayed Lowe's testimony would have been "shaken" so "the young man could go free." This did not come to fruition, as Lowe had not been rocked from the truth. He even hoped the "charges against the defendant would be proved to be unfounded, but there is no escaping the fact that he is guilty of this crime." The defendant had been the leader of the Leeds gang.

---

239 *Kansas City Journal*, March 1, 1899.

Reed became visibly troubled by the defense tactic of harrasing William J. Smith. He pointedly contended Smith had nothing to gain by his testimony—no reward. He reminded jurors that both Hills, the express messenger, and Lowe had testified the defendant had trouble with his mask. Smith's story had been consistent as he, too, had seen it repeatedly fall off the leader's face. "Was not a mask found . . . the next day?" This for Reed proved Smith had testified honestly. "Gentleman, I am certain that Smith was on the train and told . . . the truth."

The prosecutor next attacked the character and alibis of the defendant. No one denied Jesse Jr. knew Lowe or Kennedy. The defense had admitted the truth of these facts from the outset of the case. "If the defendant was the model young man that he has been pictured to you, what link bound him to a train robber? It was the link of crime." As to the alibi stories, Reed held firm to the proposition these witnesses had actually hurt the boy and corroborated Lowe's confession. There is no question Jesse had been at the drug store, but there was likewise no account of his whereabouts during the period in question. Reed accused the defendant of having coached his exculpatory witnesses following his indictment. "Jesse James persuaded them to change the times" in which they had seen him that evening.

> I believe that Jesse was home a part of the evening of the robbery, but what mother or grandmother is there that would not stretch the imagination in order to keep off a great shadow from the home, and there is the grandmother who defended this boy's father.

For Judge Shackleford, Reed's last remark had crossed the line. The judge quickly interrupted the prosecuting attorney and demanded he refrain from referring to matters that had not come up in the evidence. Perhaps his honor having resided in another part of Missouri had been under the misguided belief that no one on the jury knew the history of the James boys or their mother.

James A. Reed had finally reached the closing moments of his argument. He was not the prosecutor who had filed the charges; he had no involvement in presenting evidence to the first grand jury; he became an unwilling participant only after his election to office; as the new prosecutor, he began reviewing and preparing for trial; he became convinced of the integrity of the State's case; and the evidence warranted a conviction. His intentions were pure; he had no desire to convict an innocent man; and he bore no malice towards the defendant.

> I would rather lose my right arm to be instrumental in convicting an innocent man. I ask you to show the world that crime can be punished in the State of Missouri, and I ask you to return a verdict that will say that the prisoner is guilty.

As Reed began to walk away, he asked the jury to "do its duty without being influenced by sympathy." With those concluding remarks, the evidence and arguments in <u>State of Missouri v. Jesse E. James</u>, was turned over to the twelve men on the jury to consider.

Judge Shackleford following six hours of closing arguments delivered the case to the jury at 6:30 that evening. The jurors were immediately taken to supper before being returned at 8:00 to begin their deliberation. While the jury dined and then pondered the evidence, Jesse Jr. sat in the crowded courtroom and quietly awaited their final decision. He had demonstrated no outward signs of nervousness or anxiety. The young defendant visited and talked nonchalantly with many friends about such topics as "sporting events and matters of interest peculiar to the average young man who does not have to face a trial for his life."[240]

While his nephew seemed unmoved, Frank James remained pensive and calculated. He sat glued next to his nephew as if in a trance. Was Frank recalling memories of his own legal plight when he had awaited the verdicts in the Winston Train Robbery in Gallatin, Davies County, Missouri in September 1883, or the federal trial for stagecoach robbery in Muscle Shoals, Alabama in April 1884? Throughout the

---

240 *Ibid.*

final day of the trial, Frank had exhibited much more interest in the case than his late brother's son. He closely observed and monitored every word spoken and sat transfixed during the closing arguments, uttering not a syllable. His demeanor remained unchanged throughout the three hours in which the jury considered the evidence. Frank may have been wondering if his nephew would be acquitted, just as he had the two occasions he faced a jury.

Around a quarter after nine, a loud knock emitted from the jury room. Instantly, the uncertain droning of conversations in the courtroom ceased. Several deputies rushed towards the door to inquire if a decision had been reached. Soon reverberations bellowed throughout the corridors that the jury had an announcement to deliver. Everyone was anxious to receive the answer to the usual questions: Had the jury reached a decision? What would be their judgment? Was Jesse Jr. guilty or not guilty? Would the jurors be able to agree on a verdict?

After the twelve men had resumed their seats in the jury box, excitement mounted when Judge Shackleford asked foreman, Harry Clark, a former resident of Guthrie, Oklahoma,[241] whether a verdict had been reached. Clark's response was short and succinct. "Yes." With that one word reply, the courtroom became as silent as a tomb, or as Charles Dickens in the *Christmas Carol* would have said, 'as dead as a doornail.' Judge Shackleford asked Clark to read their conclusion. Hearts pounded, palms sweated, tenseness mounted, eyes swelled as the foreman announced:

We the jury fine the defendant, Jesse James, not guilty as charged in the indictment.

With these words, intense pandemonium broke out from the great multitude of spectators. There was a "wild outburst of applause which the serene-looking judge and the deputy marshal made no attempt to curb."[242] Hats were waving, hands were clapping and yells were deafening. Many people rushed to the young defendant grasping his hand and extending their warm and heart-felt congratulations to his team of

241 *Guthrie Daily Leader*, March 1, 1899.
242 *Ibid.*

defense attorneys. Walsh turning to his young client remarked, "Now my boy, go home, and don't let yourself ever be called upon to make an explanation" for doing so could become "embarrassing and expensive."

The jury had deliberated for less than one hour and had taken only one vote before reaching its not guilty verdict. The jurors had given no credit to the theories tendered by detectives, police or any portion of the confession of W.W. Lowe. Several members of the panel reported that police had simply "located James in too many places in a very brief time, and were unable to show that he was away from his home in Kansas City a full hour on the night of the robbery."[243] The judge following the verdict described the jurors as an "intelligent looking body of men" and congratulated them on their hard work ethics.

As the gathering of spectators and idol worshipers dwindled out of the courtroom, Jesse Jr. for the first time since the trial had opened lost his composure and became quite emotional. With eyes watering, he bowed to the men who had befriended and defended him throughout the ordeal. He politely expressed his most sincere gratitude and appreciation for their friendship and noble work. After he made these remarks, the nephew and uncle began to exit the courtroom arm in arm. Upon reaching the door leading to the hallway, Jesse Jr. turned to those who had remained and said, "I'll be at the cigar stand tomorrow. Come over, everybody."[244] With that, he and Uncle Frank disappeared through the door and out of sight.

The courtroom commotion and excitement over the acquittal was equally celebrated on the city streets. It was like the festivities and light parade of the Priests of Pallas had returned for an encore performance. Everyone wanted to toast the young cigar vendor and his noted guerilla uncle. Before going home, Jesse Jr. and his late father's brother made a stop at the tavern inside the Midland Hotel located at the southeast corner of 7th and Walnut. The accumulated crowd gathered around the two men with congratulatory, heartfelt toasts and laudatory hand shacks and backslapping. The heroes, Frank and Jesse James (at least the Jr.), had made another appearance in Kansas City.

243 *Saint Paul Globe*, March 1, 1899.
244 *Kansas City Journal*, March 1, 1899.

CHAPTER XXII
HEARING FROM THE PRESS

―――――》(()《―――――

Dateline: Wednesday, March 1, 1899
The Press of K.C. & U.S.

Headline:

IS ACQUITTED
JESSE JAMES JURY
REQUIRED BUT ONE BALLOT[245]

The bold printed headline of the Jesse James jury verdict was heralded across most newspapers in the United States following his acquittal. News stories and editorials filled columns and even volumes of pulp with diversity of opinions and commentaries. Press attitudes, feelings and viewpoints praised, lauded, criticized, questioned, ridiculed and celebrated the verdict. Each storyline felt a certain compulsion to draw the parallel between father and son.

The *Wichita Daily Eagle* sarcastically proclaimed:

Another train robbery case has been concluded in the courts of Kansas City, Missouri, with the usual result. The defendant was a scion of the notorious James gang of robbers of whose exploits and history in Missouri is so proud. The robbing was denied, and witnesses testified to the presence of young James on the ground at the time, but the jury of twelve good and true

245 *Ibid.*

Missourians cleared him on the first ballot, at which the court house rang with cheers and the judge looked serene. It is a safe thing to belong to the gang and live in Missouri.[246]

Likewise, the *Princeton Union*, in Princeton, Minnesota (the same state in which the famous James-Younger gang had met their Waterloo in the Northfield bank robbery raid on September 7, 1876) analogized the father-son tale in its lead story.

JESSE JAMES ACQUITED

Young Jesse James "son of the notorious bandit" whose name he bears, was adjudged not guilty of complicity in the robbery of a Missouri Pacific express train at Leeds in the outskirts of Kansas City, last September.[247]

The *Omaha Bee* followed the familiar press theme of compare and contrast:

Son of Notorious Bandit is Found Innocent of Leading Attack on a Train.[248]

The overlapping stories between the saga of Jesse James and his son would never become too old. The boy knew it as well. This explains, in part, his motivation later in the year of his acquittal for writing the first family book entitled, My Father, Jesse James. It was a mixture of a biography of the life of his late father and a partial autobiography of his own experiences as a defendant. He insisted his poor dead father had been wrongfully maligned and he, himself, had been maliciously prosecuted for no other reason than his name was James.

For Prosecutor James A. Reed, the case had worn on him. He had departed the courtroom embittered and angry. The following day

---

246 *Wichita Daily Eagle*, March 2, 1899.
247 *Princeton Union*, March 1, 1899.
248 *Omaha Bee*, March 1, 1899.

disgusted over the verdict he dismissed the cases against the other eight men who remained under indictments for the same crime as the acquitted man. The Leeds gang consisting of W.W. Lowe, Andy Ryan and older brother, Bill, John F. Kennedy, Charles Polk, Caleb Stone, James Flynn and George Bowlin, were all free—that is with the exception of the Quail Hunter and the long-time train robber, Bill Ryan (the sole hold-out from the old James' Gang). The two continued to be held in the Springfield, Missouri jail suspected of what else, train robbery! In discussing these dismissals, Prosecutor Reed explained he could not hope to convict any of the other defendants after the James' verdict, inasmuch as he considered his strongest case was having been the one against Jesse Jr.[249]

Jesse Edwards James, the son of the noted bandit was free. As Reed dismissed the cases against the Leeds gang members, the young proprietor returned to his cigar stand to resume his trade. All day long a bevy of women bearing flowers flocked to him, and he did not shy away from their attentiveness. One of the ladies that day was Stella McGowan. Handing him a bouquet of flowers, she told him that she never doubted his innocence. He cordially accepted her gift, and in return he extended to her an invitation to attend a football game with him.[250] Perhaps it would be the beginning of a special courtship for the young bachelor.

In the days following his acquittal, editorials and stories focused upon many issues and questions. Examples included: whether Jesse Jr. had really been innocent; whether he had been "railroaded" by the railroad detectives or Pinkerton's; whether he had just been lucky; whether he would continue to be the mainstay of the family; or whether he was a desperado like his bandit father. What lay ahead for the not-guilty, so-called leader of the Leeds gang and courthouse cigar salesman, Jesse Edwards James, would continue to be of central interest to reporters and to a public captivated by anything "James."

---

249 *Wichita Daily Eagle*, March 2, 1899.
250 *St. Louis Republic*, March 4, 1900.

EPILOGUE
WHAT HAPPENED NEXT?

—————◦((◦))◦—————

"Character Lives Inside A Man, A Reputation is Outside Him"[251]

The tender gender always seemed to gravitate towards the youthful James. Their caring may have been to his calling, cuteness, character, charisma, charm, community or Christianity or they may have been allured to him by an attraction and affection arising out of his ambiguous ancestral heritage. Whatever the reasons, this fascination intensified during his ordeal in the courtroom as a medley of girls "brought him flowers and lingered over the counter to try to make him talk."[252]

Among the attentive ladies pouring out their interests was the pretty eighteen-year-old Stella Frances McGowan. She and the cigar storeowner had coincidentally met on Valentine's Day just two days before the jury selection process had commenced. She had not "become seriously interested in him until she saw him fighting" for his life during the trial. Like many of the young man's adoring gallery of beauties, she, too, sat through many portions of the circumstantial case. After his acquittal, the couple began courting. Her parents openly opposed their daughter's relationship with the son of a bandit, a man accused of train robbery. Despite their protestations, the relationship of Stella

---

251 A quote from the opening line in the silent film, *Jesse James Under the Black Flag*. The movie was dedicated to the four daughters of Jesse Jr. and Stella.
252 Yeatman, Ted, P. <u>Frank and Jesse James</u> at p. 296.

and Jesse became serious, and within the year, he was seeking her hand in marriage.

On January 24, 1900, Stella and Jesse Jr. were married in her parents' home located at 415 Landis Court in Kansas City. Reverend Dr. S.H. Werlein of Kansas City Methodist South performed the ceremony. The new bride was described as having a slight figure, a girlish pretty face and shy of manner. Those attending the wedding were restricted to close friends and family members. Nuptial guests included the groom's Uncle Frank, cousin Robert, County Court Clerk Thomas Crittenden Jr., his former employer and benefactor; and R. L. Yeager, his defense attorney. His mother, Zee, was too ill to attend. She had continued to suffer physically and emotionally throughout her son's courtroom ordeal.

(The Newlyweds: Jesse James & Stella James)
(Courtesty Jackson County Historical Society)

After the ceremony, the newlyweds left the city for a holiday. They traveled to the James Farm in Kearney. It was there that they spent their honeymoon (while the groom's father laid buried in the yard). After their sojourn, the married couple returned to Kansas City. They took up residence at the James house on Tracy, and the young bride became a member of the household alongside her husband, mother-in-law and sister-in-law. Life returned to normalcy as Stella settled into her new home and her new spouse resumed his work in his courthouse cigar shop with an eye towards expansion.

The popularity of the newly married man began to take on dimensions that were not of his design, but were not the unexpected consequences of the notoriety of his family name. In 1901, a man identifying himself as Jesse A. James came to Kansas City claiming he was the son of Frank James, cousin to Jesse Jr. He further declared having possession of a revolver his "uncle Jesse James" owned at the time he was killed. Jesse Jr. called the man a liar and said he had grown sick and tired of people making money off his father's name.[253] In August 1903, Jesse had two men arrested for attempting to swindle him and his good name. On another occasion in 1908, a man claimed to be the son of the famous bandit after his arrest for larceny in Carthage, Jasper County, Missouri. Police, along with the local newspapers, were convinced that the jailbird was in fact the real Jesse Edwards James. The truth was not unveiled until after the "bogus James" had been released from the county jail. Discovering the thief was a fraud, the *Jasper News* acknowledged their mistake (or it "ate crow") and promptly apologized by affirming "Jesse James is a solid and reputable business man in Kansas City and can be reached any time by phone. He would be in poor business leaving a profitable business to engage in petty thieving."[254] Such are the realities of notoriety or popularity—the James name had it all.

Zee's health had been compromised, and she suffered from "grip" throughout her son's trial.[255] Most agreed that she had never fully re-

---

253 *St. Louis Republic*, February 28, 1901.
254 *Jasper News*, February 13, 1908.
255 *The Oak Grove Banner*, Saturday, November 17, 1900. In a letter to the editor of the *New York Times* dated March 24, 1900, a doctor provided to the columns' readers the following definition of grip: "the inability of the doctor to specifically diagnosticate his patient's diverse and confluent symptoms . . ." and it is "a germ disease" and the "bug" or "germ" preys upon a body's weakened organs, and is often fatal for the elderly and long-term sick as it destroys their lungs, which will result in fluid build-up and pneumonia, eventually causing death. Although Zee was not old, she had been ill for

covered from her husband's murder. Tragically, later in the year of her only surviving son's marriage the poor widow lapsed into a coma. She finally passed away in her home in Kansas City on November 13th. Nearby her deathbed stood the crayon portrait of her late husband, fully displayed on an easel in the family parlor (the same picture James A. Reed had unsuccessfully attempted to have described during the trial).[256] After her death, it was undecided whether she should be buried next to her husband on the family farm or in a cemetery. Until a final decision could be made, Jesse Jr. had his mother's body deposited in a holding vault at Elmwood Cemetery in Kansas City. There the corpse of the poor widow languished over eighteen months until her son was in a position to make final arrangements to have her reunited in death with her notorious husband.

While Zee's body remained within the vault at Elmwood, her only surviving son's business continued to flourish and he became active in political issues. In 1901, a soda fountain was added to his cigar business, and in March of the same year, he traveled to Jefferson City to meet Governor Alexander M. Dockery. The purpose of the meeting was to protest the new law that made possession of slot machines in business establishments a felony offense. Slots had been one of his passions, a gaming device he played the night of the robbery. Having such a strong admiration for the gaming device, he was undoubtedly disappointed when the governor did not veto the bill. Good-bye legal slot machines!

By the end of that summer, Jesse Jr. elected to enter into a new business venture, a pawnshop. From his small tobacco stand in the courthouse corridor, he had saved $5,000, which was quite a fortune in 1901. These profits enabled him to lease a "whole store in the very heart of Kansas City" (located at 1215 ½ Grand) for his new business. "I am out for the money," said young Jesse, "and there is more money in the pawn broking business. I guess the gang will come around to see me."[257] Was he referring to the Leeds gang or those who

---

years. Hence the cause of her death was listed as "grip."

256 St. Louis Republic, November 14, 1900.

257 St. Louis Republic, August 6, 1901.

had befriended him at the courthouse?

On June 29, 1902, some twenty years after his burial in the family yard, the body of Jesse James was exhumed on a very gloomy day with temperatures in the fifties. A family decision had been made for his remains to be re-interred at Mount Olivet Cemetery in Clay County alongside his recently departed and long-suffering widow, Zee James. Before the relocation, Mrs. Samuel wanted to ensure that her son's body had not been stolen. This required the reopening of the casket at the gravesite, the same spot where Jesse Jr. (or little Tim—even as an adult, his friends often referred to him as "Tim") had stood back on that mournful day in April of 1882. He was no longer a child; he had become a husband and father, too. Did his mind wonder back to that fateful day a score of years gone by? As the metallic coffin lid was opened, the long-suffering mother insisted upon seeing her poor Jesse. Her son, Frank, and grandson, Jesse, restrained her from doing so.

With rain beating upon his face, Jesse Jr. looked down at the corpse of his father. The casket had fared poorly over the test of time; the glass cover was broken; the wood had decayed into "moldering bits."[258] Why had his father's expensive coffin become so worn? After the lid was pulled off, the embalming was discovered compromised even though they had paid for his body to be preserved in that fashion. The boy saw gold teeth in the mouth of the skull. This prompted him to recall his grandmother's words; he had gold in his teeth. He then brushed aside his father's dark brown hair and located the quarter size hole under the left ear of the back of the skull—the hole made by Bob Ford's bullet. After making these observations Jesse Jr. confidently proclaimed, "We can be sure it is my father."[259]

The bandit's bones were transferred to a new black coffin with a silver nameplate on top and transported into the house, the same dwelling in which Pinkerton Agents had thrown the turpentine bottle back in January 1875. Among those serving as pallbearers were the decedent's only son and several former Quantrill guerillas. After a quiet family service, the long deceased Jesse James was removed, and in

258 *St. Louis Republic*, June 30, 1902.
259 *St. Louis Republic*, July 6, 1902.

a persistent driving thunderstorm he was taken to the new cemetery where it was buried next to his wife and other family members. Several hundred people observed the reburial. Frank James held an umbrella over his mother while grandson Jesse supported her. After the mound was made and the boards driven in, Frank James turned to the pallbearers and said, "Boys this is all we can do!" The group of spectators who had stood by silently and respectfully slowly dispersed.[260] The one-armed mother walking towards an awaiting buggy commented that her saintly son was now "at rest with his wife and his little brother." The long-suffering mother no longer felt an "uneasiness over" his body as she knew her son's soul rested safely in eternal peace, reunited with his wife and by Jehovah.

After "all the tragedy" she had experienced, the mother of the James boys prayed she would spend the remaining years of her life "in peace." She hoped her son, Frank, and his wife, Ann, would move into the James farm and assist her with the chores (and marketing) around the homestead; they eventually moved to the house but not until the family matriarch herself had passed from this life. Zerelda Cole James Simms Samuel died in March 1911 at the age of 86. At the time of her death, she was on a train near Oklahoma City, Oklahoma, returning home from a long visit with her son Frank who was at the time living near Fletcher, Oklahoma. There must have been a certain sense of poetic irony in the minds and souls of the James family survivors when it was learned she had died on a train. She was buried near her last husband, Dr. Reuben Samuel, her sons, Jesse and Archie, and Jesse's widow. Her grandson, Jesse, had served as one of her pallbearers.[261]

After the mother of the James boys passed away, her son Frank took over running the James farm. He, too, knew there was revenue to be

---

260 *St. Louis Republic*, June 30, 1902.
261 At the time of her death Frank James was the only surviving child of the union of Rev. James and Zerelda. Of their four children, Robert, lived about one month and died on August 21, 1845; Jesse had been killed on April 3, 1882, and the only daughter, Susan Lavenia James Parmer, died in childbirth on March 3, 1889. She married Allen Parmer in 1870. Susan's husband had served as a guerilla with her brothers during the Civil War). When she died in 1889 at the age of thirty-nine, the couple had four surviving children: Flora, age 13, Zelma, age 10, Susan, age 4, and Feta, age 1 (three other children had died). Her husband had her buried in Wichita Falls, Texas. In December 1892, Allen Parmer married his second wife, Sarah Kathleen Ogden.

made at the house. Frank followed his late mother's course by charging an admission price, twenty-five cents (or 2 bits) where he barred Kodak cameras. Four years later, Uncle Frank went to his glory. A train took his body to St. Louis, where he was cremated. Frank had left specific directions for his body to be cremated. He did not want to be "dug-up" like his young brother, Dingus (a nick-name of Jesse James).

(Frank James: By Gate to the James Farm: Circa 1914)
(Courtesy Jackson County Historical Society)

After Frank's ashes were returned to Kansas City, a funeral service was held for the elder James boy at the Kearney residence. Former Federal Judge John Phillips, the hero of Byron's Ford in the Battle of Westport in October 1864, and Frank's lead defense counsel in the Winston Train Robbery Case in 1883, gave the eulogy for his former client and friend.[262] Stella, Jesse and their four girls attended the service, but their daughters became gravely ill with diphtheria following

---

262 *Kansas City Journal*, February 21, 1915.

the ceremony and were forced to remain on the farm for several days.[263] The remains of Frank James were stored in a bank vault in Kansas City where they remained until his wife, Ann, joined him in the grave. Upon her death in 1944, she was also cremated, not in St. Louis as her husband, but at Elmwood Cemetery. Their ashes were buried at Hill Park in Independence on property once owned by the family of Ann Ralston James mother and near Ann's childhood home (the home still stands today as does their grave).

Jesse Jr., during his early years of marriage, pursued an education in law while working full time. He attended the Kansas City School of Law by night and operated his pawn and jewelry store by day.[264] In 1906, at the age of thirty-one, he graduated with distinction with a law degree and received his diploma on the stage of the Shubert Theatre. Within a year, he opened a law office in the Scarritt Building downtown. He said he had chosen not to pursue a practice in criminal law because he felt that there was not "enough money in that class of work. The money is in corporation law and in will cases." He was described as a "book" lawyer who never lost a case in an appellate court because of an improperly prepared petition. His specialty area grew into a civil law practice.[265]

By 1908, he, Stella and their four daughters, Lucielle Martha, Josephine Frances, Jessie Estell, and Ethel Rose, were living at 809 Elmwood Avenue in Kansas City. Their marriage was proving not to be the story of those who lived 'Happily Ever After.' They even separated on one occasion for about three months before reconciling. This proved not to be their only separation. The addition of each child coupled with the added pressures of his law practice (or his staying out late) brought on marital problems. On November 5, 1909, the *Kansas City Post* headline was demonstrative of their struggles:

---

263 *Kansas City Journal*, February 23, 1915.
264 *Kansas City Times*, March 27, 1951. The pawn store was located at 207 East 12th Street, Kansas City, Missouri.
265 *Ibid.*

Jesse James, Son of Famous Bandit, Sued for Divorce

Stella's divorce pleadings filed the preceding day asserted her husband had frequently quarreled with her, failed to return home until late hours and refused to disclose his whereabouts. Hadn't his late father been away for long periods of time? Apparently, on one of the many evenings her husband had been out, a burglar entered the front door of the family home and ascended the stairway. Stella, unable to reach her husband on the telephone, fled into her bedroom, grabbed a revolver and fired at the man. The prowler apparently escaped the house uninjured.[266] The couple remained separated for about six months before Stella dismissed her divorce papers and Jesse returned to the home on January 1, 1910. It proved to be just a short term Happy New Years.

The third separation was not charming. On July 8, 1910, Jesse Jr. moved out of the family residence and rented an apartment in the Victoria Hotel. By September 20th of that year, their marital troubles found the columns of local newspapers. On that day, the *Post* reported that Jesse had sued Stella for divorce alleging she had tried to shoot him one night while he was in his room at the Victoria Hotel.[267] Stella denied the allegations and filed a counter petition for divorce. Their case was bitter, hotly contested and focused primarily over custody of their four daughters. Their domestic struggles were so contentious that Jesse removed two of the girls, Jessie and Ethel, from Missouri to avoid a writ of habeas corpus.[268] The third separation resulted in a divorce. Stella was granted custody of the children and awarded $100 per month in alimony. Jesse Jr. was granted the right to visit the kids at all reasonable times.

After the divorce, Stella grew very ill and was hospitalized in 1911. During her long illness the children resided with their father, and he regularly took them to see their mother. The many visits he and the girls had with Stella seemed to unbind their marital discord. When she

---

266 *The Montgomery Tribune*, May 1, 1909, Montgomery City, Missouri.
267 *Kansas City Post*, September 22, 1910.
268 *Kansas City Post*, September 20, 1910.

recovered, Jesse began taking his former wife on long rides in his auto, and the couple soon discussed reconciliation and remarriage. Friends of Jesse and Stella asserted it was out of love for their children that their relationship was rekindled. They were remarried on September 15, 1911.[269] It marked the end of any future headline news stories of separation or divorce.

In between the domestic squabbles of Stella and Jesse, some comforting intelligence came from St. Louis in 1910. The ole' confessor, William W. Lowe, reappeared in the news. His reputation as a train robber had never ended, and he faced new charges after being identified as the leader of the Glencoe train heist. While thievery had remained Lowe's professional calling, his post-arrest statement to police was unique. His latest "confession" became front-page news fodder across the country.[270]

CLEARS JESSE JAMES JR.
PRISONER CONFESSES HE FALSELY ACCUSED BANDIT'S SON OF TRAIN ROBBERY

Lowe declared he lied about Jesse Jr. in the Leeds case. He hauntingly announced his perjury had been the source of all the serious misfortunes he had experienced since the James trial. Lowe attributed the history of his grave problems on his perjured testimony against the bandit's son. Had the dead brigand cursed the traitor for lying about his poor little boy in the same way many felt the fallen soldier had haunted the cowards who had murdered him in April 1882? No one would ever forget that Charlie Ford committed suicide on May 6, 1884. Was it guilt or the ghost of Jesse James? Bob Ford, the coward, too was dead. He had been blown away by a shotgun blast by Edward O'Kelley in Creede, Colorado on June 8, 1892. Was it revenge or the specter of "Mr. Howard?" Lowe recanted his 1898 confession and his 1899 trial testimony and gave the following chilling statement about his arrest that year:

269 *Kansas City Post*, September 16, 1911.
270 *New York Times*, February 20, 1910; Pence, Samuel, A., at p. 401.

I was arrested two days after the robbery. I was living at the time in Kansas City, I was married had a young wife and a son about 4 years of age. Thomas Furlong was then chief of what was known as the 'potters' of the Missouri Pacific Railroad. He caused my arrest. While I was living in Kansas City, I met the acquaintance of young Jesse James. James was not in that robbery. After my arrest, Furlong found in my pocket a letter from James, written some months before. Furlong then and there tried to get me to say that James was in the robbery. I refused to do anything of the kind as the boy was innocent and had no knowledge of the robbery. When I was on the verge of insanity I said that James was in the robbery. James was at once arrested, and what followed is history. He was found not guilty. In fear of my life I swore that James was in that robbery. After he was acquitted, the case was dismissed and I was turned loose.[271]

So, why nearly twelve years later did Lowe tell another story? Was it to make an act of contrition or a desire to end the terror that the elder James had been inflicting upon him for his former lies? There were those who believed so. Which "confession" was the truth? No one would really ever know, but for the James jury it proved to be no revelation as back on February 28, 1899, they had previously reached the same conclusion—Lowe had lied about young Jesse.

The entertainment and theatrical community had a long-standing fascination in profiteering on the notoriety and celebrity of all things "James." The name would certainly generate ticket sales. It had been part of the dime novel and pulp fiction nostalgia for years. After his acquittal, Jesse Jr. received letters and wires offering him leading roles in productions with theatrical companies or invitations to appear at fairs and other similar events. The majority of these proposals he rejected or left unanswered proclaiming his satisfaction with his tobacco business. His unwillingness was predicated more upon the sentiments expressed by his mother and grandmother, not his own disinterest. They had

---

271 *St. Louis Post Dispatch*, February 19, 1910.

disapproved of the money, lore and "blood and thunder" depicted in the stage shows. It had been a tenant of the family never to discuss the days before Frank's final acquittal in April 1884 or the period prior to his own exoneration in February 1899.

Jesse Jr. did not fully share the viewpoints of his mother or grand-mother to avoid exploitation of their family name in public performances. The entrepreneur knew there was potential for generating handsome re-turns by profiteering upon the fame and notoriety of the name, Jesse James. He had an interest in seeking profits from his identity or that of his bandit father, but it was not until his late father's brother gave his blessing did he pursue such activities. In fact, Frank James and Jesse Jr. both began making personal appearances at venues throughout the city, countryside and neighboring states. At a fair in Richmond, Ray County, Missouri in 1899, Jesse Jr. received ten dollars to play ball and fifteen cents of the gate receipts. He was considered an accomplished ball player.[272] Later in October of the same year, he and Uncle Frank were featured at the fair in Guthrie, Oklahoma.[273] Had they traveled there out of appreciation and gratitude because the jury foreman Harry Clark in young Jesse's trial had once resided in the town?

Uncle Frank, a strong supporter of the "Rough Rider," Teddy Roosevelt, realized America was a capitalist society. He became the fam-ily's catalyst in profiting on their name in the field of entertainment. In November 1901, he took up acting (despite his protestations he was not an actor) and appeared on the stage in St. Louis in a play entitled, *Across the Desert*. Why not? Hadn't he served as a doorkeeper in a theatre in St. Louis? His name meant money, and he was well versed in every-thing Shakespeare. When Frank's long-time friend, Thomas Coleman "Cole" Younger, was paroled from prison in Stillwater, Minnesota, in July 1901, they chose to unite their reputations and pasts for capitalistic endeavors. Frank and his "ole pard," Cole, began touring the country with their show, "The Great Cole Younger-Frank James Historical Wild West." Would Jesse pursue a similar career or would he always adhere to

---

272 *Kansas City, Journal*, June 28, 1899; and *Kansas City Journal*, September 26, 1899; and *Kansas City Journal*, July 14, 1899.

273 Hale, Donald, R., <u>Jesse and Frank James Scrapbook Volume One</u>.

the dictates of his late mother and avoid the stage?

At the dawn of the 'Roaring Twenties,' the law practice of the former cigar purveyor and pawn-jeweler had proven so successful that he and his young family were living in a plush, stately home at 4117 St. John in Kansas City. The house was located just minutes east of R. A. Long, the lumber baron's, seventy-two-room, French Renaissance mansion on Gladstone Boulevard.[274] In 1920, Jesse Jr. made the decision to expand his prosperity. He elected to tell his ancestral story in films; he chose to wind-down his legal career and go into acting.[275] In the spring of that year, he entered into a three-year contract with the Kansas City-based, Mesco Pictures Corporation to star in silent films.

The terms of the agreement with Mesco appeared favorable to Jesse Jr. and his family. Under the contract, he was to receive a lucrative salary; he also retained the authority to object to any scene that would "outrage unjustly" his father's memory. Any dispute or interpretation of the ambiguous term "outrage unjustly" would be submitted to arbitration. Judge Ralph Latshaw was selected as arbitrator in the event controversy arose during the production (Latshaw was the same judge who had presided over the trial of Dr. Hyde for the murder of Col. Swope in 1910—the same one in which James A. Reed prosecuted and Frank Walsh defended).[276] Jesse and other family members even invested generously in the productions.

What reaction would his late mother and grandmother have had in seeing their family name and story on the screen? Didn't Grandma Zerelda sell admission tickets and rocks from the grave of his late father while she was alive? Perhaps, he rationalized that soundless movies, which had just come into existence at the time of his acquittal, were different from theatrical performances.

In the 1920 and 1921 productions, Jesse Jr. portrayed his father in two movies, *Jesse James Under the Black Flag* and *Jesse James the Outlaw*. Both movies were intended to be historical studies of the life and

---

274 The Jesse James Jr. family previously resided at 809 Elmwood, in the Lykins Neighborhood, of Kansas City. The Lykins Neighborhood Guidebook, p. 62.

275 *Independence Examiner*, October 9, 1920.

276 *Kansas City Post*, July 24, 1920; and Monaco, Ralph A., II, The Strange Story of Col. Swope and Dr. Hyde.

adventures of his namesake's life. Jesse Jr. described the movies as being "authentic photoplays" of Jesse James. Cast in the leading role, the young son of the bandit was not the only James family member in the pictures, as many relatives, including Stella, were integrated in both films.[277] Curiously, one of the managers and actors in the *"Black Flag"* was Harvey "Harry" Hoffman who portrayed Cole Younger (several scenes were shot on Hoffman's property). Hoffman had been Jackson County Marshal from 1917-1921 and Grand Kleagle of the Ku Klux Klan. He also had a long-standing relationship with the James family. He helped identify Jesse James after his death in 1882 and he had served as pallbearer for Frank James in 1915 and for Cole Younger in 1916.[278]

(Jesse Jr. in Under the Black Flag)

---

277 *St. Joseph Observer*, August 7, 1920.
278 *Kansas City Post*, July 24, 1920.

In the first movie, "*Black Flag*," written and directed by Franklin B. Coates, Jesse Jr. portrays the part in which his "father took with the Quantrill gang during and after the Civil war." The *Black Flag* is a depiction of a young Jesse James joining William Quantrill's raiders and taking up their banner, the 'Black Flag.' The guerrillas, or "partisan rangers" as they were said to be "legally" defined, consisted of a band of combatants who fought Union soldiers during the Civil War, primarily along the Missouri-Kansas border. According to the picture's theme, the young hero had been forced into the woods by the actions of Federal troops both during and after the War; it even includes his meeting and falling in love with Zerelda "Zee" Mimms. The bandit's son proclaimed that *Jesse James the Outlaw* was designed to be a study that depicted and explained why his father had been "driven into a life of crime and banditry."[279] The films proved to be economic failures and created financial hardships for Jesse Jr. as he had invested most of the family's savings in the ventures. Following these debacles, it seemed that the health of Jesse Jr. began to suffer.

The economic disasters resulting from the motion pictures were followed by other tragedies. On Saturday, May 10, 1924, Jesse was involved in a head-on car wreck. The following day the *Excelsior Springs Daily Herald* ran the bold storyline:

"Jesse James Wrecked—Armed to Teeth."

Neither James' knee injury nor the wounds suffered by the two boys in the other vehicle was as significant as the weapons found in Jesse's car, a shotgun and two revolvers.[280] The pistols discovered in the car had unique histories. One had belonged to Jesse James until his death. Uncle Frank had retained possession of the revolvers but they reverted

---

279 *St. Joseph Observer*, August 7, 1920.

280 Truewest. "Ugly Duckings, No More." November/December 2011, at p. 40. This had not been the first time Jesse Jr. had a run-in with the law after his acquittal in 1899. On August 28, 2005, he was in a "brawl" with a man at Thirty First and Campbell. Jesse was some thirty pounds heavier than the victim whom he "knocked down three times." It was further claimed that Jesse possessed a pistol, but he adamantly denied the allegation. It was quite fortunate for the barrister that the "victim" would not prosecute him, and he was not charged. Was it intimidation or the loser's own culpability? Source: Kansas City Times, August 29, 1905.

to the son of Jesse James when Frank died in 1915. Jesse Jr. claimed that one of the pistols had killed his father. The handguns had even been previously displayed at the Farmer's Fair in Columbia, Missouri on Friday, May 5, 1916.[281] After the police arrived at the scene of the collision, the father of four was arrested, but he defended his action claiming to have been on patrol for the State Highway Commission. Some maintained it was for the Klu Klux Klan (KKK). The diagnosis rendered by his physician, Dr. J.F. Lowrey of Excelsior Springs, was he had suffered a nervous breakdown and had him institutionalized in a sanitarium for a month. There is no question that the car wreck raised concerns for the family and plenty of eyebrows around the community.

Two months before the auto accident, Jesse Jr. had been representing a beautiful woman with an unusual checkered past. She was the well-known and well-traveled Zeo Zoe Wilkins, a pioneering female in the field of osteopathic medicine. Dr. Wilkins would also be his last high-profiled client in Kansas City. Zoe was said to have been loaded with money. She had a successful career, not in medicine, but in manipulating and marrying wealthy men and fleecing them of their fortunes. By the age of seventeen, Zoe, the "ruthless" beauty, was in medical school where she met and married a promising classmate, but they divorced within a couple of years. He would not be the last victim that the greedy vampire would weave around her beauty and catch in her web. On the morning of March 16, 1924, Zoe's brutally stabbed body was found lying on the floor in a house she rented at 2425 Park Avenue in Kansas City, a victim of murder from the preceding night. She was only thirty-eight. The maze of evidence assembled by police, including the arrest of her brother, failed to trap her slayer or slayers. In a recent book entitled *The Love Pirate and the Bandit's Son* the author, Laura James (no kinship to Jesse James), reaches a startling verdict. She offers the supposition that Zoe's killer may very well have been Jesse Jr., whom she describes as the "twisted son of America's most legendary outlaw."[282] Readers and students must decide the answer for themselves. Good luck in trying!

281 *University Missourian*, May 7, 1916, Columbia, Missouri.
282 James, Laura, The Love Pirate and the Bandit's Son, The London Press, 2009.

Following his financial collapse after the failed movie ventures, the highway crash and the shocking murder of Zoe Wilkins, Jesse's health grew worse. He became melancholy and suffered from mental illness. A decision was made that it would in his and the girls' best interests to move to another city and state, just about as far away from his adopted home of some forty-five years.[283] They relocated to the west coast in October 1926. Why did they shuffle off to California? Was it sparked by his poor health, his youngest having finished high school, a desire to return to acting, to avoid prosecution or something sinister?

In Los Angeles, Jesse's health improved sufficiently enough that he resumed the law practice and dabbled once again in motion pictures. In 1927, he provided technical assistance in the Paramount production of *Jesse James* that starred cowboy actor, Fred Thomson and his horse, Silver King. Unlike the movies produced in the early 20's, this one about the life and time of his late father proved to be a box office success.

Sadly, for poor Jesse and his family the California air did not revitalize his condition, and he never recaptured his youthful health. For the next twenty years, his vitality, especially his mental health, was compromised. In 1931, two of his daughters, including the youngest Ethel Rose, went into business as owners of a roadside café near Culver City, California. The sister proprietors proudly displayed a number of their grandfather's personal effects, including his spurs and Winchester rifle.[284] The family name sparked interests in California as it did in Missouri; it still does everywhere.

Despite his poor health, Jesse Jr., his wife, Stella, and two daughters, Jo Frances and Ethyl Rose, made a pilgrimage back to his adopted home in 1937. He was described as "an old man, broken in health and unable for several years past to practice his profession of the law."[285] Jesse perhaps thinking his days were numbered desired to return to the house in which his father had once laid buried in the yard. Jo Frances

---

283 *Kansas City Star*, October 11, 1927. The *Star* article reports Josephine living at 105 N. Gladstone Blvd, Kansas City, Missouri in 1927.
284 *Missouri Historical Review*, Vol. 25, Issue 2, January 1931, at p. 337.
285 *Kansas City Star*, May 16, 1937.

drove the family out in her folks' "motor car." Jesse noted little changes along the way and even commented about the "same old honey locust tree in the yard . . . the same old log house with its narrow-paned windows . . . and same old coffee bean tree in the shadow of which Jesse James was buried so long ago."[286] They stayed at the "ole place" for several hours visiting Cousin Bob, his wife, and his aging, nearly blind mother, Ann Ralston James, the widow of Frank. Their conversation had included memories of bygone times, family secrets unknown to the world and dreams for the future. Young Jo surely raised questions to consider or answer as she and her three sisters were determined to write the "true" story of their grandfather's life "not as it has been written by novelists, but as it was lived." Jo had "a deep admiration and love" for her grandfather, and described him as "a brave knight" and spoke proudly "that his blood" ran through her veins.[287] His blood runs through many veins even veins of those unrelated to him.

There are no reported accounts of Jesse Jr. ever returning to Kansas City following the trip in May of 1937. His health continued to decline, and on March 26, 1951, he died at his home in Los Angeles following a long illness; he was seventy-five. He was buried at Forest Lawn Memorial Park in Glendale, California.[288] As exemplified by the bold column in the *Kansas City Times* following his death, even in death he was subordinate to his infamous father:

JESSE JAMES, JR. DIES:
Son of Missouri Outlaw Had A Varied Career.

At the time of his death, Uncle Frank's son, Jesse's first cousin, Robert Franklin James, the cousin he once thought was named Mary, was living at the James farm in Kearney. After his father, Frank, had died in 1915, Robert had taken over the family tradition by residing

---

286 *Ibid.*

287 *Ibid.* Jo passed away unexpectedly on March 31, 1964 at the age of fifty-eight, and she was buried in Forest Lawn Memorial Park in Los Angeles.

288 On March 16, 1901, Jesse's sister, Mary Susan, married Henry Lafayette Barr (1867-1935). The couple had four children. Mary preceded her older brother in death and died at Research Hospital on October 11, 1935; she was fifty-six. See, headline in the *Kansas City Times*, March 27, 1951.

on the farm, taking care of his aged mother, Ann (which he did until she died in 1944), giving tours of the homestead and marketing the name 'James.' In the year the bandit's son passed from this life, Bob was charging fifty cents (or 4 bits) to anyone who wanted a tour of the site during summer months.[289] Today the home is owned by Clay County and for an admission fee it is open to the public. The tradition continues!

The widow of Jesse Jr. did return to Kansas City to visit her former home in October 1965. One place Stella toured was the former Jackson County Jail in Independence, the same detention center her deceased husband's Uncle Frank James had been held from October 4, 1882 through February 5, 1883 while awaiting trial.[290] Mrs. James Jr., during her jail stopover, recalled an incident when she had been a guest at a club meeting for one of her daughters. Each girl in the organization had been assigned the lecture topic: "My Most Interesting Ancestor." Her daughter had chosen as her theme, Daniel Boone. This is because Stella through her mother's bloodline had descended from the trailblazer. Another young lady who spoke immediately prior to her daughter had dedicated her remarks to the storyline, "My grandfather rode with Jesse James." After the girl's presentation, Mrs. James' daughter rose to talk about her ancestor, Daniel Boone. Before giving her speech, but not wishing to detract or take-away from the preceding speaker, she wanted the audience to know something about her grandpa. While the previous presenter's grandfather may have ridden with Jesse James, she told those assembled that "my grandpa was in fact the Jesse James."[291] It is easy to imagine what a great stir this created.

One of those historical oddities of the James family pertains to the employment path followed by a few descendants of Jesse James, in

---

289 *Missouri Historical Review, Vol. 46, Issue 1, October 1951, at p. 15.* The last surviving child of an issue of Frank and Jesse to die was Frank's son, Robert. He and his second wife, Mae A. Sanboth James, moved from the James residence in the mid 1950's and relocated to Excelsior Springs, Clay County. On November 18, 1959 Bob died at the I.O.O.F. Hospital in Excelsior Springs. Bob never had any children. He first wife was May Sullivan. His second wife, Mae, died at the Excelsior Springs Hospital in April 1974 at the age of eighty-nine.

290 The Jackson County Historical Society has owned the historic site since 1958, and the Society operates it as a living history home, jail and museum. Today the landmark is on the National Registry of Historic Places.

291 *Jackson County Historical Society Journal,* Vol. VI, No. 18, December 1965, p. 6.

particular, two granddaughters and one great grandson. The youngest girl of Jesse and Stella, Ethyl Rose, was employed as a secretary at the Federal Reserve Bank in California. Another daughter, Josephine, was employed as a teller and escrow agent for Bank of America in Culver City, California. How strange for the bank robber's granddaughters to have been hired by banks. Wasn't the first crime laid at the feet of their grandfather the daytime bank robbery in Liberty on February 13, 1866? It is simply one of those ironies.

In 1925, Josephine married Robert Ross and the couple had a son named James R. Ross who was born in Independence, Missouri. When the elder Ross fell victim to the "demon rum," Jo and her little boy moved to California to live with her mother and father. Jesse and Stella became like surrogate parents to Jo's son, their grandson, James Ross.[292] The young boy spent twenty-five years residing with his grandparents and he affectionately referred to his grandpa as "daddy." Eventually, James Ross followed the career path of his grandfather, Jesse Jr., and became a lawyer. Later, he served many years on the bench as a superior judge in California; he died at the age of eighty in Fullerton, California on March 5, 2007. During his lifetime, Judge Ross, like his ancestors had an economic, historical and academic interest in his genealogy. He authored in 1988 a book about the life and times of his great grandfather entitled I, Jesse James. Much of the information contained within the book came from taped interviews with his grandfather, the bandit's son. In 1995, the judge played an instrumental role in orchestrating the DNA exhumation of his namesake. He, like his relatives before him, had grown tired of all the imposters. Ironically, Judge Ross in 1997 made his own headline news when he was accused of four counts of judicial misconduct, one complaint included attempting to sell his book while on the bench. The California Judicial Commission offered to dismiss three of the charges if he would admit to one count of exhibiting an angry demeanor towards attorneys in a personal injury case. The judge refused and tersely wrote, "I will not back down. As a direct descendant of Jesse James, no one in our family backs down." The

292

Commission composed of three judges censored Judge Ross and prohibited him from further service on the bench.[293]

Jesse James had a lawyer for a son (an acquitted train robber); banks employed two of his granddaughters; a great grandson became a judge (impeached from the bench). He would have chuckled knowing the career paths of his issues.

Stella died in 1971 and was buried next to her husband of some fifty years. The book she wrote, In the Shadows of Jesse James, was not published until after her death. Strangely, Stella never mentions in her manuscript one word about the marital discord between she and her late husband, Jesse. It was like it never happened.

The last of the children of Jesse and Stella, and the last of Jesse James' grandchildren to die, was Ethel Rose James Owens. She passed away of natural causes on December 21, 1991 at the age of 83. She was living in a retirement home in Huntington Beach, California at the time of her death. She was buried next to her husband, Calvin, in Inglewood Park Cemetery, Inglewood, California; the couple had no children. Ethel's childhood memories had included sitting on the lap of Cole Younger, her Uncle Frank's friend, and playing the piano for him. After she graduated from Northeast High School in 1926, she moved with her parents to California. She enjoyed frequent trips back to her home state because she claimed her heart always remained in Missouri.[294]

The name of the bandit, Jesse James (such a poetic rhythmical name), has produced some endless yarns, plethora of stories, books, novels (dime and otherwise), movies, films, songs (such as "The Ballad of Jesse James"), plays, documentaries, articles, exposés, historical analysis, editorials, comedies, comparative studies, treatises and tales—even tall tales. Some are mythical, mythological, historical, fictional, credible, incredible, awful, delightful, sensational, unbelievable, comical, wonderful, or legendary. How many children, grandchildren, etc. have been named after him? How many others have cried at the sound of his name? It is unquestioned that the former outlaw has become iconic.

293 *Los Angeles Times*, March 9, 2007.
294 *Kansas City Star*, December 30, 1991.

(Jesse Woodson James, Age 32)
(Courtesy of Jackson County Historical Society)

There is no doubt that opinions of the man, Jesse James, have been varied, dependent and predicated upon a person's perspective. To Pinkerton Agents, he committed every crime in America during those post-war years. For Governor Crittenden and other law officials, he pinned the name "Outlaw State" upon Missouri. To editor and fellow rebel, John N. Edwards, dime novelists and other apologists, he was a martyr for the "cause." For many widows and orphans, he was their "Robin Hood" or "night in shining armor." As for his victims or their survivors, he was a cold-blooded, ruthless murderer and a wanted, evil desperado. To 'doubting Thomas' and disbelievers, no way did a kid in St. Joe kill him. Many have proclaimed, professed, pronounced, proffered and pontificated themselves to be *the* Jesse James. Are they all dead yet?

The scope of the exploits of Jesse James and the James-Younger gang has thrilled, fascinated, intrigued, mesmerized, captivated, and

(Courtesies of Michael and Carrie Englert, Sibley, Mo.)

enthralled a clamoring public through the ages. Generations of families have claimed and continue to claim being his direct lineal descendants. Some are, some are not. Court hearings have been held and arguments made to exhume or not to exhume his body; archeological excavation sites have been dug in search of his buried treasure; scientific genetic DNA testing has been conducted on his heirs and non-heirs (findings conclude he died in St. Joseph; findings conclude scientists cannot agree on their findings); hundreds, if not thousands, of books, including comic, fictional and historical, magazines, essays, journals, articles and stories have been written on his life and time; stage plays, living history programs, shootouts and robberies (trains and banks) and theatrical shows have been performed (including Bob and Charlie Ford's encore presentations reenacting their assassination of Jesse James); countless novelty items, board games, toy guns, whiskey bottles, knives, figurines (even a coffin) and dolls have been created, marketed and sold under his name; innumerable television programs and movies have been aired and viewed by the millions, tens of millions. From 1908 through 2010 there have been well over eighty movies and documentaries—silent, full-length and shorts—directly or indirectly about his life and starring such legendary names as Jesse Jr., Fred Thomson, Tyrone Power, Roy Rogers, Audie Murphy, Robert Wagner, James Keach, Peter Fonda, Kris Kristofferson, Colin Farrel, Rob Lowe, Brad Pitt and even Bob Hope. Yes, Jesse James was a comedian, too. These have all produced stories and accounts that never grow too old.

In the end, one thing is undisputed. Jesse James loved his family. He had a true affection for his wife and children. Too many folks attested to that fact. Even his surviving spouse declared it to be true, and she had a strong influence over him.[295] Another truism, and tragically despite his dedication to his family, he could not escape the path of his chosen criminal career. This eventually caused his death leaving behind a widow and orphaned children to mourn for him. To those who claim Jesse James was not killed in St. Joseph on the morning of April 3, 1882, or to those who have claimed down through the years as being "the man himself," there are some difficult questions to answer or at least ponder:

> Did Jesse James fake his death and thereby abandon his wife, Zee, his son, Jesse Jr., and his daughter, Mary?

> Hadn't they been on the run living under assumed names for years—at least six years for his son?

> Why would he walk out on a family he loved and leave them virtually penniless and homeless?

> How could he allow his beleaguered mother never to see him again?

> Why would he never have had an interest in seeing his mother?

> Would a man who so loved his family disappear never to see them again?

---

295 *The Oak Grove Banner*, Saturday, November 17, 1900, Oak Grove, Mo.

Isn't it a fact Zee never did cast away her black attire?

Could he really have allowed his wife to mourn for him for the rest of her life?

How could he have permitted his only surviving son to toil for his mother, Zee, and sister, Mary Susan?

For all the good, bad and ugly that may be said about Jesse James, it is difficult to reach any conclusion but one: his life came to an abrupt end in St. Joseph, Missouri, on Monday morning, April 3, 1882, at the hands of that coward, Bob Ford, while he stood on a chair in that one-story, white painted framed cottage with green shutters. He had no intention of abandoning his family. They were left without any financial support, and this he would not have permitted. His mother, wife and children never saw him again. For Jesse James, this would have been unconscionable. He truly loved his family. The conclusion is simplistic; the ramifications are not. Jesse Woodson James was shot and killed by a young assassin without making any provisions for his family. This left poor little Tim, the kid who did not know his true identity until after his father's death, the man of the family and subjected him to living out the rest of his life, the son of a bandit.

THE END?
THE STORY OF JESSE JAMES
& HIS FAMILY WILL NEVER END!

BIBLIOGRAPHY

__Archival__:
__A Legacy of Design, An Historical Survey of the Kansas City, Missouri,__
__Parks and Boulevards System, 1893-1940__, 1955, Kansas City Center
for Design Education and Research in cooperation with the Western
Historical Manuscript Collection—Kansas City, Mo. Public Library.

Chicago Historical Society Northwestern University Wet With Blood,
www.chicagohistory.org/wetwithblood/bloody/libby/index.html.

Civil War St. Louis:
http://www.civilwarstlouis.com/history/jamesgangoutlaws.html.

Discover St. Joseph, Missouri:
http://www.stjomo.com/see-do/experience-history/jesse-james.cfm.

Discover St. Joseph, Missouri:
http://www.stjomo.com/see-do/experience-history/pateehouse.cfm.

Ehrlic, Nancy, M., Samuel Raltson Family Group Chart, Jackson
County Historical Society, No. A 144/352.

Giessel, Jess, *Black, White and Yellow*, The Spanish American War
Centennial, website. http://www.spanamwar.com/press.html.

BIBLIOGRAPHY

Jackson County Historical Society Journal, Vol. VI, No. 18, December 1965, p. 6, Mo. Valley Room, Kansas City, Mo. Public Library.

James Family History, Old West Kansas Families, Kansas Family History. www.kansasheritage.org/families/james.html.

Library of Congress, *Chroniclingamerica.loc.gov.*

Missouri Secretary of State. "Missouri Digital Heritage Collections", the Newspapers Collections. Located at: http://cdm.sos.mo.gov.

Missouri Secretary of State. "Missouri Digital Heritage Collections", the Browse Collections. Located at: www.cdm.sos.mo.gov/mdh/browse.

Mays, William, A., 2007, *National Police Gazette*, New York; www.policegazette.us/FromTheMorgue.

Old West Legends, "Zee James—Jesse's Poor Wife" www.legendsofamerica.com/we-zeejames.html.

Mo. Rev. St. 1899 §1955 (1895).

Snyder, Joe, <u>County Seat Paper a Glimpse into the Life and Times of One Small Town, Gallatan, Missouri</u>, Missouri State Archives R-93-49.

State of Missouri Historical Society. http://www.statehistoricalsocietyofmissouri.org.

<u>State v. Stubblefield</u>, 157 Mo. 360, 58 S.W. 337 (Mo. 1900).

<u>Territory v. Ketchum</u>, 65 P. 169 (N.M. Terr., Feb. 1901).

<u>The School Journal</u>, Vol. 60 at p. 554 (1900) at google.books.

The Truth, The American Weekly. Vol. 17, Number 605, November 23, 1898, pp 20-22. Western Missouri Valley Room, Special Collections 73.

Unitah County Western Heritage Museum: http://www.westernheritagemuseum-uc-ut.org/jesse-james.html. Where These Rocky Bluffs Meet, The Chamber of Commerce of Kansas City, Missouri, 1938. Western Missouri Valley Room, Western Historical Manuscript Collections, Kansas City, Mo. Public Library.

Whitney, Carrie Westlake, Kansas City Missouri, Its History & Its People 1808-1908, Vol. I, The S.J. Clark Publishing Co., 1908. Western Missouri Valley Room, Western Historical Manuscript Collections, Kansas City, Mo. Public Library.

Whitney, Carrie Westlake, Kansas City Missouri, Its History & Its People 1808-1908, Vol. II, The S.J. Clark Publishing Co., 1908. Western Missouri Valley Room, Western Historical Manuscript Collections, Kansas City, Mo. Public Library.

Whitney, Carrie Westlake, Kansas City Missouri, Its History & Its People 1808-1908, Vol. III, The S.J. Clark Publishing Co., 1908. Western Missouri Valley Room, Western Historical Manuscript Collections, Kansas City, Mo. Public Library.

Books & Other Sources:
Brant, Marley, Jesse James The Man And The Myth, Berkley Books, New York, 1998.

Breihan, Carl, W., The Day Jesse James Was Killed, Frederick Fell, Inc. Publishers, 1961.

Brown, Theodore, A. and Lyle W. Dorsett, K.C. A History of Kansas City, Missouri, Pruett Publishing Company, 1978.

BIBLIOGRAPHY

Crittenden, H. H., The Crittenden Memoirs, G. P. Puntam's Sons, New York, 1936.

Croy, Homer, Jesse James Was My Neighbor, University of Nebraska Press, Lincoln, Nebraska, first published, 1949, the Bison Book Edition, 1997.

Garwood, Darrell, The Crossroads of Kansas City, the Story of Kansas City, W.W. Norton & Co., Inc., New York, 1949.

Good Bye, Jesse James, Six Major News Stories Concerning the Life, Death, and Funeral of America's Greatest Outlaw, First printed in 1882, The Jesse James Bank Museum, Liberty, Missouri, 1967.

Green, George, F., A Condensed History of the Kansas City Area, Its Mayors and Some V.I.P.s, The Lowell Press, Kansas City, Missouri 1968.

Hale, Donald, R, Jesse and Frank James Scrapbook Volume One.

Hale, Donald, R, Jesse and Frank James Scrapbook Volume Two.

Hansen, Ron, The Assassination Of Jesse James By The Coward Robert Ford, Harper Perennial, 1983.

Haskell, Harry, Jr. and Fowler, Richard B., City of the Future-A Narrative History of Kansas City, 1850-1950, Kansas City Star & Frank Glen Publishing Co., Inc. Kansas City, Missouri 1950.

Haskell, Harry, Boss-Busters & Sin Hounds, Kansas City and Its Star, The Curators of the University of Missouri Press, Columbia, Missouri, 2007.

Hoffhaus, Charles E., Chez Les Cansas, Three Centuries At Kawsmouth,

The French Foundations of Metropolitan Kansas City, The Lowell Press, Kansas City, Missouri, 1984.

Isaacson, Darlene, and Elizabeth Wallace, Kansas City in Vintage Postcards, Arcadia Publishing, Charleston, South Carolina, 2003.

James, Stella Frances, In the Shadow of Jesse James, The Revolver Press, 1989.

James, Jesse E., Jesse James My Father, The Sentinel Printing Co., 1899.

James, Laura, The Love Pirate and the Bandit's Son: Murder, Sin, and Scandal in the Shadow of Jesse James, London Square Press, 2009.

Jesse James, The Best Writings of the Notorious Outlaw Jesse James, edited by Harold Dellinger, Morris Book Publishing, L.L.C., The Globe Pequot Press, Guilford, Connecticut, 2007.

Kansas City Then & Now, The Kansas City Star Books, Kansas City, Missouri, 2000.

Larsen, Lawrence, H. Federal Justice in Western Missouri the Judges, the Case, the Times, University Missouri Press, Columbia, Missouri, 1994.

Larson, Erik, Devil in the White City, Vintage Books, a Division of Random House, Inc., New York, 2004.

Little, L. A., Vintage Kansas City Stories, Early 20th Century Americana as Immortalized in the Kansas City Journal 1907-1909, at p. 38, Vintage Antique Classics Publishing Co., 2009.

Lives, Adventures, Exploits Frank and Jesse James With An Account of the Tragic Death of Jesse James, reprinted by Nifty Nut Novelty

BIBLIOGRAPHY

Co., Excelsior Springs, Missouri, 1947.

Mayer, Catherine, *Tabloid Bites Man*, Time Magazine, July 25, 2011, p. 29.

McClure, Alexander, K. and Charles Morris, <u>The Authentic Life of William McKinley</u>, Memorial Edition, Library of Congress, 1901.

Meriwether, Lee, <u>Jim Reed Senatorial Immortal</u>, Mound City Press, St. Louis, Missouri, 1948.

Missouri Historical Review, Vol. 46, Issue 1, October 1951, at p. 15.

Missouri Historical Review, Vol. 25, Issue 2, January 1931, at p. 337.

Monaco, Ralph A. II, <u>The Strange Story of Col. Swope & Dr. Hyde</u>, Two Trails Publishing, Independence, Missouri, 2010.

Missouri Secretary of State. "County Officers." Official Manual of the State of Missouri, 1896-1898 at p. 192.

Missouri Secretary of State. "County Officers." Official Manual of the State of Missouri, 1899-1900 at p. 211.

Missouri Secretary of State. "Judicial Department: Other Courts." Official Manual of the State of Missouri, 1899-1900 at p. 187.

Missouri Secretary of State. Winn, Kenneth, H. "IT ALL ADDS UP: Reform and the Erosion of Representative Government in Missouri 1900-2000." Official Manual of the State of Missouri, 1999-2000 at p. 28.

Montgomery, Rick and Shirl Kasper, <u>Kansas City An American Story</u>, Kansas City Books, Kansas City, Missouri, 1999.

Muehlberger, James P., *Wallace Electrifies the Court During the Blue Cut Trial*, James Family Journal, p. 4, Volume 22, No. 1, January, 2010.

Pence, Samuel, A., I Knew Frank I Wish I Had Known Jesse, Two Trails Publishing, Independence, Missouri, 2007.

Political History of Jackson County: Biographical Sketches of Men Who Have Helped to Make It, Marshall & Morrison, 1902.

Pomerantz, Gary, M, The Devil's Tickets, Crown Publishers, New York, 2009.

Rabas, Chuck, Jack "Quail Hunter" Kennedy, Independence, Missouri, Joann Eakin, 1996.

Reddig, William M., Tom's Town: Kansas City and the Pendergast Legend, J. B. Lippincott Co., 1947.

Ross, James, R., I Jesse James, Dragon Publishing Corp., 1989.

Scull, W.E., The Authentic Life of William McKinley, Library of Congress, 1901.

Settle, William A., Jr., Jesse James Was His Name, The Curators of the University of Missouri, 1966.

Spalding, C.C., Annals of the City of Kansas and the Great Western Plains, Van Horn & Abeel's Printing House, 1858, & republished by Frank Glenn Publishing, 1950.

Spencer, Thomas, M., *"Priests of Pallas: Kansas City's Forgotten Fall Festival,"* Jackson County Historical Society Journal, Autumn 2003, at p. 11.

BIBLIOGRAPHY

The Lykins Neighborhood Guidebook, edited by Harold Dillinger, Lykins Neighborhood Association, Kansas City, Missouri, 2000.

Thomas, Evan, The War Lovers: Roosevelt, Lodge, Hearst and the Rush to Empire, 1898, Little, Brown & Company, New York, 2010.

Thruston, Ethylene, Ballard, Echoes of the Past, The Lowell Press, Kansas City, Missouri, 1973.

Traxel, David, Crusader Nation, The United States in Peace and the Great War 1898 to 1920, Alfred A. Knopf, New York, 2007.

Traxel, David, 1898 The Birth of the American Century, Alfred A. Knopf, New York, 1998.

Triplett, Frank, The Life, Times & Treacherous Death of Jesse James, The Swallow Press, Inc. 1970, and said to be the Authentic Reprint of the Long Suppressed, 1882 Edition, Barnes & Noble Books, New York.

"Ugly Duckings, No More", Truewest. November/December 2011.

Ventimigilia, Jack, M., Jesse James in the County of Clay, The Friends of the James Farm, 2001.

Wallace, William H., Speeches and Writings of William H. Wallace and Autobiography, The Western Baptist Publishing Co., Kansas City, Missouri, 1914.

We Never Sleep: The First Fifty Years of the Pinkertons, Smithsonian Institute, Washington, D.C., 1981.

Worley, William, Kansas City Rise of a Regional Metropolis, Heritage Media Corp., 2002.

Yeatman, Ted P., <u>Frank And Jesse James—the Story Behind the Legend</u>, Cumberland House Publishing Co., Nashville, Tennessee, 2000.

Yeatman, Ted, P., *Jesse James' Assassination and the Ford Boys*, <u>Wildwest</u>, December, 2006.

Younger, Cole, <u>The Story of Cole Younger By Himself</u>, first published in 1903, and reprinted by Oak Hills Publishing, Springfield, Missouri 1996.

<u>Newspapers--Periodicals:</u>
Arizona Weekly Journal-Miner, Prescott, Arizona
Daily Advocate, Newark, Ohio
Evening Bulletin, Oahu, Republic of Hawaii
Excelsior Springs Daily Herald, Excelsior Springs, Missouri
Guthrie Daily Leader, Guthrie, Oklahoma
Jasper News, Joplin, Missouri
Kansas City Daily Times
Kansas City Evening Star
Kansas City Journal
Kansas City Journal-Post
Kansas City Post
Kansas City Star
Kansas City Times
Kansas City World
Liberty Tribune
Los Angeles Times
Milwaukee Republican
Montgomery Tribune, Montgomery City, Missouri
National Republican, Washington City (D.C.)
New York Times
New York Tribune
Paducah Daily Sun, Paducah, Kentucky
Record-Union, Sacramento, California

BIBLIOGRAPHY

Richmond Democrat, Richmond, Ray County, Missouri

Rolla New Era, Rolla, Missouri

St. Joseph Observer, St. Joseph, Missouri

St. Louis Daily Globe-Democrat

St. Louis Dispatch

St. Louis Post-Dispatch

Saint Paul Globe, St. Paul, Minnesota

Saline Republic, Marshall, Missouri

Salt Lake Herald, Salt Lake City, Utah

San Francisco Call, San Francisco, California

Sedalia Democrat, Sedalia, Missouri

Sedalia Weekly Bazoo, Sedalia, Missouri

The Anderson Intelligencer, Anderson Court House, S.C

The County Paper, Oregon, Missouri

The Courier, Lincoln, Nebraska

The Daily Gazette, St. Joseph, Missouri

The Evening Times, Washington City (D.C.)

The Holt County Sentinel

The New York Times

The Oak Grove Banner, Oak Grove, Missouri

The Princeton Union, Princeton, Minnesota

The Richmond Dispatch, Richmond, Virginia

The Sun, New York

The Times, Washington City (D.C.)

The Tombstone Epitaph, Tombstone, Pima County, Arizona Territory

The Yakima Herald, North Yakima, Washington

University Missourian, Columbia, Missouri

Weekly Graphic

Weekly Missouri Republican, St. Louis, Missouri

Western News-Democrat, Valentine, Nebraska

Wichita Daily Eagle, Wichita, Kansas

INDEX

Name	Page
Ackerman, William:	166
Anderson, Bill:	69
Armour Meat Packing Company:	40, 49, 94, 142, 187, 191
Atwood, John:	112, 133
Baker, Ray Stannard:	43
Ball, David:	97
Barr, Henry Lafayette:	Footnote 288
Barr, Mary Susan (James):	
Alibis of brother:	98
As sister of:	147, 157, 178
As daughter of:	29, 41, 43, 57, 228, 229
At father's funeral:	26-28
At brother's trial:	177
At Palm Sunday Services;	6
Death of:	Footnote 288
Photo of:	21
Trial testimony about:	178, 183, 184
Trial testimony of:	180, 181
Bates, Charles Austin:	52
Beattle, Thomas, Dr.:	188
Beckett, Elizabeth:	Footnote 40, footnote 45

INDEX

Bond, William:	27
Boone, Daniel:	223
Bowen, Charles K.:	188, 189
Bowlin, George:	62, 106, 136, 203
Boyle, Detective:	93, 142
Brady, Huge C. (Assistant Prosecutor):	102, 103, 175, 176
Broder (Police Chief St. Joseph):	76
Broughal, Joseph E.:	142
Brown, John J.:	148, 149
Brown, Sam:	69
Bryant, Detective:	93, 136
Bugler, Henry:	Footnote 15
Bugler, John:	Footnote 15
Bunch, Samuel (Mr. & Mrs.):	85, 86, 183, 187
Cargill, William:	187
Carr, H.M. (telegraph operator):	161, 162, 168
Caskey, Sergeant:	174, 188
Central High School:	38, 180
Chicago Cubs:	40, footnote 76
Chiles, Samuel H. (County Marshall):	73, 75, 106, 111-113, 122
Chouning, W.H.:	15
Chouteau, Francois:	43
Clark, Harry G.:	142, 199, 216
Cleveland, S. Grover (President):	Footnote 90, footnote 166
Clinton, Bill (President):	Footnote 167
Coates, Franklin B.:	219
Columbus, Christopher:	40, footnote 88
Comingo, Abram (Congressman):	24, footnote 35
Craig, Enos (City Marshall):	12, 17
Craig, Henry (Police Commissioner):	11, 16, 19, 25
Crane, Harry:	191
Crittenden & Phister Real Estate Company:	39

Crittenden Family: 133

Crittenden, Thomas (Governor):   8, 11, 13, 14, footnote 15, 16, 20, 23-
                                                25, 32, 39, 94, 99, 133, 177, 226

Crittenden, Thomas, Jr.:

   As Benefactor of Jesse Jr. & Family: 41, 57, 58, 121, 130, 133

   As Employer of Jesse Jr.:   39-41

   At wedding of Jesse Jr.:   206

   Photograph of: 39

   Relected County Court Clerk: 121, 122, 132

   Elected Mayor of Kansas City: Footnote 169

Daniels, G.W.:   188

Davidson, Bernard: 136, 137

Delong, John (Detective):   74, 93

Denton, Albert Hamilton: 68

Dickens, Charles: 199

Downer, S.M. (train brakeman):   147, 148, 161, 195

Durrett, John J.:   141, 142

Edwards, Jonathan Newman (Major):   23, 29, 196, 226

Ehrlich, Nancy: Footnote 6

Eliot, Charles William: 55

Elmwood Cemetery: 208, 212

Evans (unknown defendant):   89, 100, 103, 104, 106, 126, 150, 151,
                                                153

Ewing, Thomas (General):   Footnote 35

Ewing, William: 141

Farr, Finnis C.:

   As attorney before trial: 94, 96, 112-115, 127, 133

   As Bondsman for Jesse Jr.:   96, 106

   As defense counsel at trial: 187, 188

   As Governor's Press Secretary: 32

   Closing argument of: 192-194

Farrel, Colin: 228

Finch, Thomas (Deputy Sheriff):   12

Finley, Charles: 59

Fisk, John: 56

Flanders, Benjamin: 27

Flynn, James: 62, 106, 136, 203

Fonda, Peter: 228

Ford Brothers: 16, 17, 19, 21, 23, 27, 32, 39, 214,
                                          227

Ford, Charlie:

   At Coroner's Inquest: 15-17

   Death of: 214

   Mentioned: 21, 32, 227

Ford, J.D.:   27

Ford, Robert:

   As Shooter of Jesse James: 3, 15-17, 20, footnote 193, 209, 229

   At Coroner's Inquest: 16-19

   Death of: 214

   Mentioned: 32, 227

   Photograph of: 17

Fox, Richard, K.:   7, 8

Frink, Daniel A. (Mayor of K.C.):   20

Furlong Secret Service Agency: 74

Furlong, Thomas (Detective):   74, 75, 80, 81, 89, 93, 103, 136, 169,
                                          215

Gates Edward P. (Judge):   135

George, William H.:   15

Germania Life Insurance Company: 40

Gibson, James (Judge):   135

Gillham, Robert: 47

Gillis Opera House: 50, 108

Gorsuch, Joseph: 187

Graham, J.W.:   12, footnote 14

Green, Robert W.:   69

Guy, Christian D.:   137

Haire, Mr. (attorney): 33

Halphin (Detective): 76, 95, 111, 126, 136

Hannibal Bridge: 43, 44

Harbaugh, Dell (Detective):
  As investigator: 74, 75, 87, 89, 93, 126, 128
  At Union Depot: 162
  Statements to press: 171, 172
  Trial testimony about: 136, 148, 149, 154, 160, 162 166, 168, 169, 188, 193, 194, 196

Hayde, John (Detective): 170, 191

Hayde, Will P. (Deputy court clerk): 187

Hayden, Richard: 166

Hayes, John (K.C. Police Chief):
  Arrest of Jesse Jr.: 59, 93, 95
  Investigates Leeds robbery: 75-79, 88, 89, 95, 125, 126
  Mentioned by Jesse Jr.: 85
  Mentioned at trial: 136, 154
  Photograph of: 59

Hearst, William Randolph: 1, 52, 55, footnote 96

Heddens, James, W. (Coroner): 12, 15, 19

Henderson, James: 27

Henry, John W. (Judge):
  As Circuit Judge: 95, 96, 135
  Trial testimony of: 187

Hill, Adam: Footnote 6

Hill & Howard Drug Store: 85, 183, 187. 193

Hill, Mary Catherine: Footnote 6

Hill, Mr.: 85, 86

Hill, William: Footnote 6

Hills, Edwin N. (express messenger):
  As victim of train robbery: 67-70
  Mentioned: 175, 176, 188, 197
  Trial testimony of: 158-161, 163, 167, 171, 174

INDEX

Hissey, D.M. (telegraph operator):

    As victim of train robbery: 66, 67

    Mentioned: 185, 188, 189

    Trial testimony of: 161

Hoffman, Harvey "Harry":   218

Hollenbeck, Cora: 165

Hollenbeck Family (Residence):   69, 70, 75, 165

Hollenbeck Sisters: 170

Hollenbeck, Mr.:   69

Hollenbeck, Mrs.:   69, 163

Hollenbeck, Nellie: 165

Hope, Bob: 228

Hotel Savoy:

    As Marquee hotel: 46

    As headquarters of detectives: 75, 77, 79, 87, 152

    Photograph of: 74

Hovey, Charles:

    As alibi of Jesse Jr.:   85, 86

    Trial testimony of: 187, 188

Howard, Charles: 187

Howell, Strother (Ass. Prosecuting Attorney):   134

Hunt, Miss: 163

Hunt, William: 163

Hutchinson Reformatory: 125-128

Hutchison, T.H.:   162, 184, 187

Hyde, B. Clark (Dr.):   Footnote 171, 217

James, Anne (Ralston):   Footnote 6, 60, 210, 212, 222

James, Ethel Rose (Owens):

    Daughter of: 212, 213, 221

    Death of: 225

    Employment of: 221, 224

James Family: 7, 19, 28, 29, 32, 39, 46, 58, 63, 76,
                                           93, 97, 99, 105, 124, 136, 137, 166,
                                           177, 190, 200, 218, 223

James, Frank:
  Aliases of: 4, 5
  As actor: 216
  As criminal suspect: 8, footnote 15, footnote 35, footnote
                                           105, 92, 94, 99, 134, footnote 193,
                                           223
  At court proceedings: 99, 109, 110, 114-116, 136-138, 143,
                                           164, 177, 191, 198-200
  At reburial of brother: 209, 210
  Attends marriage of Jesse Jr.:   206
  Death of: 211, 212, 218, 220, 222
  Father of: 5, footnote 6, 207
  Husband of: Footnote 6, 60, 212, 222
  Legends about: 12, 23, 33,136, 200, 203, 207
  Mentioned: 108, 150, 178, 219, 225
  Operates James Farm: 210, 211
  Photographs of: 110, 211
  Siblings of: 28, 29, footnote 261
  Son-in-law to: 124
  Trial testimony about: 186, 187
  Whereabouts of after brother's   31, 32, 36, 50
  death:
James Gang: 14, 19, 59-61, 92, 105, 136, 201, 203
James, Gould: 29
James, Jesse E. Jr.:
  Alibi statements of: 85-87
  Arraignments of: 96, 129
  Arrest of: 83, 91-101
  As acquaintance of criminals: 59, 63, 64, 147, 148, 150, 151, 182,
                                           186
  As a father: 251, Footnote 212, 213, 225

As a grandfather: 224

As a lawyer: 224

As an actor: 108, 215-219, 228

As an athlete: 40, 168, 216

As an author: 202

As entrepreneur—tobacco store: 57-59, 91, 124, 127, 203, 205

As entrepreneur—pawnshop: 208, 209, 212, footnote 264

As Defendant in February: 122, 131-134, 137, 140, 142-146, 149, 152-154, 156, 157, 162, 164, 166, 167, 171, 173, 174, 178, 180, 188, 189

As Defendant in October: 111-117

As Little Tim: 4, 5, 14, 17, 18, footnote 25, 29, footnote 46, footnote 47, 30, 37, 228, 229

As student: 38, 41, 147, 212

As suspect: 76, 80-82, 84, 89, 90, 120, 220

At father's auction: 33-35

At father's funeral: 26-28, 31

At Frank's funeral: 211

At Palm Sunday Services: 6

At reburial of father: 209, 210

Auto accident of: 219, 220

Being identified at trial: 160-162, 169, 170

Closing arguments about: 192-198

Death of: 222

Employment history of: 39-41, 147, 181, 191

Friend of T. Crittenden, Jr. 39, 41, 58, 121

Gift from father: 6, 34, photo of gift 35

Greets grandmother during trial: 177

Health problems of: 219-221

Indictments of: 106-109, 113, 123-126, 128-130

Imposters of: 207

Lowe recants confession of: 214-215

Marital problems of:	212-214
Marriage of:	205-207, 214
Mother's death:	206-209
Photographs of:	21, 182, 206, 218
Relocates to California:	221
Residences of:	30, 31, 36, 37, 41-43, 56-58, 212, footnote 274
Revisits city:	221, 222
Poem about:	9
Subject of Grand Jury Hearing:	102-105
Trial testimony of:	181-187, 192
Verdict of:	199-203

James, Jesse Woodson:

Alaises:	4, 6, 7, 12, 15, 21, 211
As criminal suspect:	6, 8, 9, 11, footnote 15, 16, 20, footnote 105, 68, 81, 90, 94, footnote 193, 136
As Father:	5, 6, 13, 15, 18, 29, 30, 81, 82, 133, 228
As Husband:	13, 15, 16, 36, 179, 228
At Palm Sunday Services;	6
Autopsy of:	12, 13
Coroner's inquest of:	15-20, 30
Death of:	3, 6-8, footnote 14-17, 19, 23, footnote 35, footnote 45, 32, 33, 39, 50, 92, 94, 133, 177, 218, 222, 228, 229
Descendants of:	223-225
Funeral of:	26-28, 218
Guns of:	207, 219-221, footnote 280
Impact to family on death of:	12, 21, 35-38, 228, 229
Legends of:	12, 23, 25, 32-35, 58, 60, 83, 90, 92, 93, 106, 134, 136, 156, 200-203, 213, 214, 216, 218, 223-229
Letters to press:	7, 8

Photographs of:	13 (postmortem), 226
Press Reports of after coroner's verdict:	22-25
Reburial of:	209, 210
Siblings of:	28, 29, 177, 178, 200
James, Jessie Estell:	
Daughter of:	212, 213
James, Josephine Francis:	
Daughter of:	212, 221, 222
Death of:	Footnote 287
Employment of:	224
James, Laura:	220
James, Lucielle Martha:	212
James, Mae A. Sanborth:	Footnote 289
James, May Sullivan:	Footnote 289
James, Montgomery:	29
James, Robert:	Footnote 261
James, Robert Franklin:	
Alias of:	5
As caretaker of James Farm:	222, 223
At marriage of Jesse Jr.:	206
Death of:	Footnote 289
Son of:	Footnote 6, footnote 289
James, Robert, Rev.:	29, footnote 261
James, Stella, McGowan:	
As author:	225
Attends Frank James funeral:	211
Attracted to Jesse Jr.:	203, 205
Death of:	225
Marital problems of:	212, 213
Marriage of:	206, 207, 214
Mother of:	212, 221, 224
Photograph of:	206

Revisits city: 221-223

James, Zerelda, Mimms:

    Aliases: 4, 5, 12, 15, 17

    As Mother: 15, 29, 41, 43, 57, 228, 229

    As Widow/Wife: 3, 16, 18, 37, 38, 219, 228, 229

    At husband's auction: 33-35

    At husband's funeral: 26-28

    At Palm Sunday Services: 6

    Coroner's testimony of: 15-17

    Death of: 208, 209

    Final illness of: 206, 207, footnote 255, 207

    Interviewed by press: 15, 16, 36

    Photographs of: 21, 179

    Residences of: 30, 31, 36, 37, 41, 57

    Trial testimony of: 178-180

James-Younger Gang: 2, 29, 60, 61, 68, 89, 105, 126, 202, 226

James, William: 55

Johnson, Frank G. (Ass. Prosecutor):

    As assistant prosecutor: 132, 134, 194

    Closing argument of: 192, 193

Jones, E.C.: 187

Jordan, Sarah: Footnote 6

Kansas City Methodist South: 206

Kansas City School of Law: 47, 212

Kansas City View Company: 188

Keach, James: 228

Kennedy, Bridget: 60

Kennedy, John: 60

Kennedy, John "Jack" ("Quail Hunter"):

    Aliases—how obtained: 63

As acquaintance of Jesse Jr.:   59, 84, 90, 104, 148, 151, 167, 182, 197

As admirer of James-Younger: 60, 92, 105

As criminal suspect: 61-64, 72, 73, 75, 76, 78-80, 88, 89, 103, 107, 108, 194

As railroad employee: 61, 78

Indictment of: 106, 129, 130

Indictment dismissed: 203

Letters of: 69, 80, 157

Meets Bill Ryan: 61

Trial testimony about: 136, 148, 150, 151, 167, 182, 194, 197

Kennedy, Mike (Acting Lieutenant):   93

Kenny, Will: 186, 191

Keshlear, Joseph (Detective):   93, 96, 136, 166

Kessler, George E.:   49

Kristofferson, Chris: 228

Krueger, (Judge):   151, 182, 185

Latshaw, Ralph (Judge):   217

Leahy, Tom (Deputy Marshal):   188

Leak, George: 63

Levens, H.B. (Mr.& Mrs.):   85, 86, 187

Libby Prison: Footnote 76

Libby Prison Museum: 40

Liddle, Dick: 19, 30

Lodge, Henry "Cabot" (Senator):   55

Long, R.A.:   48, 217

Lowe, Frank M.:

As prosecutor: 62, 75, 95, 96, 111, 114- 117

Losses re-nomination: 120

Trial testimony of: 175, 190, 191

Lowe, Mrs. (wife of W.W. Lowe):   79, footnote 122, 80, 88, 103

Lowe, Rob: 228

Lowe, William W.:

    As acquaintance of Jesse Jr.:   59, 147, 182, 185, 186, 191, 192, 197

    As criminal suspect: 62, 76, 93, 107

    Confession of: 87, 89-91, 93, 94, 99-101, 112

    Cross-examination testimony of: 151-157

    Grand Jury testimony: 102-104, 107

    Indictment of: 106, 111, 113, 129

    Indictment dismissed: 203

    Photograph of: 78

    Recants confession: 214, 215

    Trial testimony about: 136, 146-148, 158, 161, 163, 166, 167, 175, 176, 182, 185, 186, 190-197, 200

    Trial Testimony of: 149-151, 157, 158

Lowrey, J.F., Dr.:   220

Martin, J.M.P. (Pastor):   27, 31

McAlear, James: 76

McBride, Charles: 30

McBride, Charles, Mrs.:   36

McEntee, Eugene: 137, 141

McKinley, William (President):   54, 55, 73 (headline), 95 (headline), 120, 190 (headline)

McNiney, Frank: 114

Mesco Pictures Corporation: 217

Meyer, August R.:   49

Miller, Albert: 141

Miller, George, Rev.:   6, footnote 6, 22

Milton, Charles, Harry: 87, 88, 136

Mimms, Tom: 37

Missouri Valley Bridge Company: 162, 163, 167

Moberly, William E. (Colonel):   24

Moore, J.W.:   15

Morgan, James: 76

Mount Olivet Cemetery:	209
Mullins, William E.:	142
Murdock, Robert:	Footnote 96
Murphy, Audie:	228
Murphy, Deputy County Marshal:	167, 168
Myers, Albert:	162
Neal, George A.:	120
Nelson, William Rockhill:	49, 51, 53, 121
New York Life Building:	
As law school:	47
As prosecutor's office:	46, 123, 175
Photograph of:	48
Norris, Thomas:	15
O'Connell, Joseph M.:	142
O'Kelley, Edward:	214
Oldham, Milton J. (Ass. Defense Attorney):	133, 186
O'Malley, Emmet:	38
Parmer, Allen:	178, footnote 261
Parmer, Feta:	Footnote 261
Parmer, Flora:	Footnote 261
Parmer, Sarah Ogden (Mrs. Allen Parmer):	85, 177, 178, 180, footnote 261
Parmer, Susan James:	29, 178, footnote 261
Parmer, Zelma:	Footnote 261
Peacock, Charles H. (attorney):	114
Pendergast Goats:	52, 53, 120, 136
Pendergast, James:	52, 53, 120
Phillips, John F. (Federal Judge):	Footnote 35, 94, 211
Pike's Peak:	46
Pinkerton's (Pinkerton Agency):	8, 16, 28, 63, 74, 77, 83, 98, 134, 176, 203, 209, 226
Pitt, Brad:	228

Poe, Edgar A.: 164

Polk, Charles, Jr. (Governor of 111
Delaware):

Polk, Charles:

    As suspect: 76, 89, 99, 100, 103, 104

    Indictment dismissed: 203

    Letters of: 112, 113

    Trial testimony about: 136, 150, 151

Polk, James, K. (President): 111

Porch, James, W.: Footnote 14

Powell, King R.: 141

Power, Tyrone: 228

Priest of Pallas: 50, footnote 90, 88, 89, 200

Prudhomme, Gabriel: 43

Pulitzer, Joseph: 1, 52

Quantrill, William (and guerillas): Footnote 35, 209, 219

Ralston, John: Footnote 6

Ralston, Margaret: 60, footnote 105

Ralston, Rowena: Footnote 6

Ralston, Sam: Footnote 6, 124, footnote 174

Ralston, Sarah: Footnote 6

Richie, T. H. (Marshal): Footnote 25

Redmond, Jim: 69

Reed, James, A.:

    As Pendergast Goat: 53

    As prosecutor: Footnote 171, 125, 127, 128, 134, 143, 144, 171-173, 192, 194, 217

    Closing argument of: 196-198

    Continuance request: 130, 131

    Convenes new grand jury: 123, 124, 129

    Cross of alibi witnesses: 188, 189

    Cross of Defendant's grandmother: 190, 191

    Cross of Defendant's mother: 179, 180, 208

INDEX

Cross of Defendant's sister:	180, 181
Cross of Defendant:	185-187
Cross of previous prosecutors:	175, 176
Elected as Prosecutor:	120, 122
Examination of Bridge Co. employees:	162, 167, 168
Examination of Brown (first witness):	148
Examination of Detective Hayde:	170
Examination of Edwin Hills:	158-160
Examination of James' neighbors:	166
Examination of Leeds Residents:	163, 165
Examination of livery stable employees:	166, 167
Examination of Mo. Pacific employees:	160, 161
Examination of Smith:	168, 169
Examination of W.W. Lowe:	149-151, 157, 158
Objects to recalling Smith:	174, 176
Opening Statement of:	145-147
Photograph of:	121
Picking a Jury:	135-137, 140, 142
Reaction to verdict:	202, 203
Reed, J.E. (Deputy Marshal):	27
Reed, Thomas (Speaker of U.S. House):	55
Rice, James S.:	187
Rodgers, William S.:	141
Rogers, Roy:	228
Roosevelt, Theodore (President):	55, 72 (headline), 118 (headline), 120, 216
Rose, Emma Younger:	60
Rose, Rett:	60

Rosebrook, Seth: 125, 126

Ross, James R. (Judge): 224, 225

Ross, Robert: 224

Ruggles, D.L.: 80

Ryan, Andy:

    Acquaintance of Jesse Jr.: 59

    Arrest of: 93

    As criminal suspect: 62, 73, 76, 89, 100, 103, 104

    Brother of Bill Ryan: 59, footnote 100, 61, 73, 92, 106, 136

    Indictment of: 106, 129, footnote 184, 130

    Indictment dismissed: 203

    Mentioned at trial: 136, 150, 151, 153, 157, 167, 182, 185

Ryan, Bill:

    As criminal defendant: Footnote 100, 92

    As criminal suspect: 61, 62, 69, 75, 131, 194

    Aliases: 61, 62, 130

    Brother of Andy Ryan: 59, 61, 73, 92, 106, 136, 203

    Indictment of: 106

    Indictment dismissed: 203

    Mentioned at trial: 136

Ryan, John: 76

Samuel, Archie: 28, 98, 177, 210

Samuel, Zerelda (James):

    As caretaker of James Farm: 28, 217

    At Coroner's hearing: 18, 19

    At Jesse's funeral: 28, 29, footnote 46

    At reburial of Jesse James: 209, 210

    Comments after arrest of Jesse Jr.: 97, 98

    Comments after coroner's hearing: 21

    Death of: 210, footnote 261

    Photograph of: 98

    Trial testimony of: 177, 178, 190, 191

Visits the "Quail Hunter":	63
Samuel, Reuben, Dr.:	210
Samuels, Warren:	15
Sanderson, Detective:	87
Schumacher, Emma:	63
Schumacher, J.H.:	74
Scott, Charles:	27
Self's Livery Stable:	78, 99, 166, 193
Self, Warren:	88, 102, 149, 166
Sexton, Richard:	166
Shackleford, Dorsey W. (Judge):	
Criticism of Reed:	168, 174, 197
Elected to Congress:	Footnote 194
Instructs the jury:	192, 198
Photograph of:	140
Presiding over trial:	129, 134, 135, 139, 140, 143-145, 148, 163, 199
Re-elected judge:	117, 121, 135
Requested to preside over trial:	114, 116
Ruling on objections:	151, 158, 161, 167, 172, 174, 176, 179, 180, 186, 192
Shakespeare, William:	Footnote 84, 216
Shannon, Joseph:	52, 53
Shannon Rabbits:	52, 53, 136
Shelby, Jo, General:	23
Shepard, George:	7
Shilling, Albert:	167
Sidenfaden's Funeral Parlor:	12
Sindenfanden, William:	12
Slocum, Charles (train engineer):	67, 151
Slover, James (Judge):	135
Smith, R.C.:	Footnote 14

Smith, William J.:

    Arrest of: 174, 176

    At Union Depot: 162

    Trial comments about: 192, 193, 196, 197

    Trial testimony of: 168-171, 176, 177

Sousa, John Phillips: 50

Spence, Samuel E.: 142

Spencer, Jake: 12

Spencer, O.M. (Prosecutor): 32

Spitz, Judge: 96, 104-106, 186

Stephens, Lawrence (Governor): 73

Starkey, William: 162, 163

Stone, Caleb: 89, 100, 103, 104, 129, 136, 151-153, 203

Stone, Robert S. (Sheriff): 122

Stout, R.E.: 175

Stowell, Chad: 125, 126

Straus, Topeka Police Chief: 125-127

Sweeney, E.F.: 96, 106, 130, 187

Swope, Thomas H. (Colonel): 48, 49, 68, footnote 171, 217

Thompson (Court clerk): 106

Thomson, Fred: 228

Tillotson, Detective: 136

Timberlake, James, Sheriff: 11, 16, 25, 27

Tinker, Joe: 40, footnote 75

Traxel, David: 1

Turner, William: 15

Vallee, Harry P.: 148, 195

Van Brunt, Henry: 49, footnote 88

Veugelen, Leonard: 141

Volker, William: 48

Wagner, Robert: 228

Wain, William: 69, 70, 75

Wallace, William H.:

As prosecutor: 14, footnote 15, footnote 100, 92

At arrest of Jesse Jr.: 91, 92, footnote 137

Photograph of: 91

Walsh, Frank W.:

As bondsman: 106

As defense attorney: 122, footnote 171, 127, 130, 133, 134, 150, 173, 187, 190, 200, 217

As Shannon Rabbit: 53

Closing argument of: 194-196

Cross of bridge workers: 162, 163

Cross of Brown: 149

Cross of Deputy Murphy: 168

Cross of Edwin Hills: 160, 174

Cross of Leeds residents: 163

Cross of livery stable employees: 166, 167

Cross of other Mo. Pacific employees: 161, 162

Cross of Smith: 169, 170, 176

Cross of W.W. Lowe: 151-156, 158

Direct of Frank Lowe: 175

Direct of Defendant's sister: 180

Direct of Deputy Welch: 174, 175

Direct of Jesse Jr.: 181-185

Making trial objections: 151, 157, 159, 161, 167, 170, 171, 179, 180, 186, 192

Opening Statement of: 146-148

Photograph of: 133

Picking a jury: 136-138, 143

Warner, Charles Dudley: 48

Washington, George (President): 143-145

Welch, Cassimir (Deputy Marshal): 174, 188,

Werlein, S.H. Rev.: 206

Weston, E.L. (train fireman):   67, 161
Westport, Battle of: 211
White, Peter: 170, 171, 191
Wilde, Oscar: 33, 34
Wilkins, Zeo Z., Dr.:   220, 221
William Jewell College: 29
Withers, Constable of Mayview: 76, 77
Wofford, John W. (Judge):
    As trial judge: 106, 107, 113-116
    Disqualification of: 114, 115, 117, 135
    Reelected judge: 121
    Photograph of: 107
Woods, L.D.:   167
Woods, Whitfield: 137
World Columbian Exposition: 40, footnote 76
World Hotel (Patee Hotel):   17, footnote 19
Wotox, William: 70, 75, 165
Yeager, R.L.:
    As defense attorney: 106, 112, 114, 115, 133
    As school board president: 94, 96, 97, 133
    At marriage of Jesse Jr.:   206
    Closing argument of: 192, 193
    Examination of Mrs. Samuel: 177, 178
    Photograph of: 94
    Press criticism of: 97
Yonge, H.A.:   80
Yonge, H.A. (Mrs.):   81
Yost, Charles C.:   118
Young, Alice Emily: 68
Younger, Jim: 60
Younger, Robert: 61
Younger, Thomas "Cole":   60, 216, 218, 225

ILLUSTRATIONS

The James House: St. Joseph, Missouri   10

Postmortem image of Jesse Woodson James   13

Robert "Bob" Ford   17

Zee & Jesse Jr. & Mary Susan   21

The Auction: "Selling Little Timmy's Puppy"   35

Thomas T. Crittenden, Jr.   39

West Bottoms (Electric Car & Depot)   45

New York Life Building   48

The City Junction   56

Jackson County Courthouse at Kansas City   58

Kansas City Police Chief John Hayes   59

Missouri Pacific Railroad train: circa 1890's   66

Hotel Savoy: circa 1898   74

William W. Lowe   78

William H. Wallace   91

R. L. Yeager   94

Zeralda James Samuel   98

Judge John Wofford   107

Alexander "Frank" James   110

James A. Reed   121

Frank Walsh   133

Judge Dorsey W. Shackleford   140

Kansas City Convention Hall 1899   146

Zeralda "Zee" James   179

Jesse Edward James, Jr.   182

Newlyweds: Jesse & Stella James   206

Frank James at James Farm: circa 1914   211

Jesse Jr. in Under the Black Flag   218

Jesse Woodson James   226

Drive-in Movie: Jesse James v. Daltons: circa 1954   227

ACKNOWLEDGEMENTS

———⟫◦⟪———

It is simply impossible to write a book without support, input and guidance from others. No writer could ever produce a publishable work unless assistance is provided from various contributors. Without the help of several unique individuals and organizations the history of the son of a bandit would never have come to life. To them, I wish to express my gratitude.

Jackson County, Missouri is so rich in history that notable historian and Pulitzer Prize winner David McCollough describes it as a place in which there is no greater historical significance in the United States. Named for General Andrew Jackson (he was not President when the county acquired his name in 1826) and the home of the 33rd President of the Untied States Harry S. Truman, the Jackson County Historical Society's mission is the "dedication to the future of its past." Without the Historical Society this book would not have been possible. Several individuals within the Society deserve specific recognition; to David Jackson, the Society's Archivist, who read and reviewed the manuscript, I am grateful for his significant insight and true friendship; to Steve Noll, the Society's Executive Director, I express my appreciation for his full support and leadership—JCHS is fortunate to have him at the helm; to Board Member Shirley Wurth who reviewed the book so many times that she probably memorized many of its lines, I am profoundly appreciative for her technical guidance and stewardship; and finally to past-President and current Board Member Ben Mann much thanks is extended for his thorough assistance in coordinating and organizing the presentation of the Re-trial of Jesse Edward James.

In today's age, a writer is unable to effectively publish or market a book without assistance from those who possess Internet, website and modern, marketing knowledge and skill. Gina Sifers of Liberty, Missouri, tirelessly spearheaded the creation and design of the book's official website: www.SonOfaBandit.com, and Gina's daughter, Jodi, played the pivotal role as graphic design artist. Their mother-daughter combination was like a new "dynamic duo." As to the book's publicity campaign, I was most fortunate to have Stephen Monaco of Overland Park, Kansas as the marketing genius. Steve has a national marketing reputation and his abilities are unparalleled. He constructed the strategy and social media campaign to promote the book. To them, I am sincerely grateful for their combined guidance, kindness, direction and contribution. They put the letter "T" in the word "Team." Honorable mention must also be extended to Mr. Tim Camper of Independence, who provided valuable technical assistance in the layout of the website.

I would also like to thank my friends in the Clay County Historical Society and the Friends of the James Farm in Kearney, Clay County, Missouri. Specifically, I extend my appreciation to Elizabeth Beckett, the Clay County Historic Sites Director, for her review of the manuscript and her insightful directions and corrections. Likewise, I want to thank Ms. Nancy Ehrlich of Independence, Missouri, a cousin of the Ralston Family, who provided historical details and insights into the James-Ralston families. To Ms. Sharon Snyder of Independence, I thank her for showing an interest in the book and directing me to knowledgeable resources within the community.

Finally, I would like to express my appreciation to the Director of Continuing Legal Education, Daniel McCarrol of U.M.K.C. Law School in Kansas City, Missouri, the City of Independence and William Jewell College for hosting the retrials of State v. James. Their commitment to education and living history ensures the lofty goal of preserving the future of our past. I also extend my thanks to the cast members of <u>State v. James</u> who gave of their time and talents to recreate the 1899 trial at the law school and at the Memorial Building (the same hallowed hall in which President Truman and his wife, Bess, once voted). Each of the members of the cast and the roles in which they portrayed are listed below—and to them I give my personal thanks.

CAST OF CHARACTERS

———— ⟫(⦾)⟪ ————

State v James

HISTORICAL CHARACTER:	PERFORMER
Jesse E. James—the Defendant:	Paul D. Anderson, Esq.
Judge Dorsey Shackleford—Judge	Judge John Torrence
Deputy Marshal—Bailiff:	Dr. Michael E. Monaco
James A. Reed—Lead Prosecutor:	Judge Michael D. Manners
Frank Johnson—Prosecutor:	Judge Jack Grate
Strother Howell—Prosecutor:	Judge J.D. Williamson
Frank Walsh—Defense Counsel:	Benjamin F. Mann, Esq.
R. L. Yeager—Defense Counsel:	Honorable W. Stephen Nixon
W.W. Lowe—Pros. Witness:	Joe Hudgens, Esq.
Edwin Hills—Pros. Witness:	Mr. David Bears
Mrs. Hollenbeck—Pros. Witness:	Ms. Gloria Smith
William Smith—Pros. Witness:	Aaron J. Racine, Esq.
E.C. Jones—Alibi Witness:	Dennis J. Bonner, Esq.
Judge Henry—Character Witness:	Dan C. Sanders, Esq.
Zerelda Samuel—The Matriarch:	Ms. Shirley Wurth
Frank James—The Uncle:	Mr. Gregg Higginbotham
Caleb Stone—Co-defendant:	Police Chief Jim Lynch
Del Harbaugh—Detective	Mr. Keith Fangman
Jesse Jr.—The Narrator:	Ralph A. Monaco, II, Esq.

ABOUT THE AUTHOR

Ralph A. Monaco, II is a lifelong resident of Raytown, Missouri with a passion for living history and historical presentations. He is known for his first person portrayals of such Nineteenth Century historical notables as George Caleb Bingham (painter), Col. Thomas H. Swope (philanthropist), Manuel de Lisa (Spanish fur trader), Edgar Allen Poe (author and poet), James Slover (defense attorney for Frank James and circuit judge) and Abram Comingo (U.S. Provost Marshal and U.S. Congressman). Ralph is also a Civil War living historian and has been reenacting for over twenty years. He graduated from Rockhurst College in 1978, *summa cum laude*, with a degree in history and political science, and he earned his juris doctorate degree from U.M.K.C. School of Law in 1981. He is a practicing attorney and member of the Kansas City law firm of Monaco, Sanders, Gotfredson, Racine & Barber, L.C. Mr. Monaco is a former member of the Missouri House of Representatives, where he served as Chairman of the House Judiciary Committee. He has a long-standing record of public service, including President of the Raytown School Board, Board of Director of the Keith Worthington Chapter of ALS, Board of Trustees of Elmwood Cemetery, Board of Director of the Rice-Tremonti House, Board of Director of Stepping Stones,

Acorn Life Member of PTA, and Board of Director of the Jackson County Historical Society where he currently serves as Board President. Mr. Monaco, a well-known living historian and public speaker, has been recognized for his historical presentations with such awards as the Outstanding Service Award from the Jackson County Heritage Programs & Museums, Making History Come Alive Award from the Jackson County Historical Society, Kentucky Colonel, recipient of the Pioneer of Harrodsburg of Kentucky, Lifetime Membership Award in the Raytown Historical Society, and the Outstanding Service Award from Jackson County Parks & Recreation. Mr. Monaco was attracted to the story of Jesse Jr. based upon overlapping tales discovered in his research on his first book, <u>The Strange Story of Col. Swope & Dr. Hyde</u>. He and his wife, Karen, live in Raytown, and they have two daughters, Lindsay and Lisa.

Visit the book's website: www.SonOfaBandit.

CPSIA information can be obtained at www.ICGtesting.com
Printed in the USA
LVOW061947300512

284020LV00002B/3/P